Andreas Wiebe and Nils Dietrich (Eds.)

Open Data Protection

Andreas Wiebe
and
Nils Dietrich (Eds.)

Open Data Protection

Study on legal barriers to open data sharing – Data Protection and PSI

With contributions by

Nils Dietrich, Lucie Guibault, Olivia Salamanca, Krzysztof Siewicz, Gerald Spindler, Andreas Wiebe and Svetlana Yakovleva

Bibliographische Information der Deutschen Nationalbibliothek

Die Deutsche Nationalbibliothek verzeichnet diese Publikation in der Deutschen Nationalbibliographie; detaillierte bibliographische Daten sind im Internet über <http://dnb.dnb.de> abrufbar.

The OpenAIRE2020 project has received funding by the European Commission under grant agreement no. 643410

Contact
Andreas Wiebe, Faculty of Law, University of Goettingen
e-mail: andreas.wiebe@jura.uni-goettingen.de

Set and Layout: Nils Dietrich
Language Editing: Carolyn Fox

Reviewers: Prodromos Tsiavos and Fruzsina Molnár-Gábor

DOI: https://doi.org/10.17875/gup2017-1061

Table of Contents

List of Abbreviations

AEPD	Agencia Española de Protección de Datos (Spanish Data Protection Authority)
AHESR	Act on Higher Education and Scientific Research (Netherlands)
AHRC	Arts and Humanities Research Council
API	Application programming interface
BCR	Binding corporate rules
BDSG	Bundesdatenschutzgesetz (German Federal Data Protection Act)
BGH	Bundesgerichtshof (German Federal Court of Justice)
BNE	Spanish National Library
BVerfG	Bundesverfassungsgericht (German Federal Constitutional Court)
CNIL	Commission Nationale de l'Information et des Libertés (French Data Protection Authority)
DDPA	Wet bescherming persoonsgegevens (Dutch Data Protection Act)
DMP	Data management plan
DOI	Digital object identifier
DPA	Data protection authority
DPA 1998	Data Protection Act 1998 (UK)
EC	European Community
ECHR	European Convention on Human Rights
ECJ	European Court of Justice
EDPS	European Data Protection Supervisor
EEA	European Economic Area
EFTA	European Free Trade Area
EU	European Union
FDPA	French Data Protection Act
GDPR	General Data Protection Regulation (2016/679/EU)
GIODO	Generalny Inspektor Ochrony Danych Osobowych (General Inspector for the Protection of Personal Data in Poland)

ICO	Information Commissioner's Office
IP	Internet Protocol or Intellectual Property
IPR	Intellectual property rights
IT	Information Technology
IWG	German Federal Act on the Re-use of Public Sector Information
KB	Royal Library of the Netherlands
KNAW	Royal Netherlands Academy of Arts and Sciences
LOPD	Spanish Data Protection Act
NA	National Archives
NDSG	Data Protection Act of Lower Saxony
NERC	Natural Environment Research Council
NSF	The US National Science Foundation
OECD	Organisation for Economic Co-operation and Development
OGL	Open Government Licence
OPSI	Office for Public Sector Information
PET	Privacy-enhancing technologies
PSB	Public sector body
PSI	Public sector information
RCUK	Research Councils UK
REBIUN	Spanish Association of University Libraries
RLUK	Research Libraries UK
ROI	Return on investment
SGB X	German Social Code X
SSL	Secure sockets layer
TEU	Treaty on European Union
TFEU	Treaty on the Functioning of the European Union
UK	United Kingdom
US	United States

Summary

This study analyses legal barriers to data sharing in the context of the Open Research Data Pilot, which the European Commission is running within its research framework programme Horizon2020.

In the first part of the study, data protection issues are analysed. After a brief overview of the international basis for data protection, the European legal framework is described in detail. The main focus is thus on the Data Protection Directive (95/46/EC), which has been in force since 1995. Not only is the Data Protection Directive itself described, but also its implementation in selected EU Member States. Additionally, the upcoming General Data Protection Regulation (2016/679/EU) and relevant changes are described. Special focus is placed on leading data protection principles.

Next, the study describes the use of research data in the Open Research Data Pilot and how data protection principles influence such use. The experiences of the European Commission in running the Open Research Data Pilot so far, as well as basic examples of repository use forms, are considered.

The second part of the study analyses the extent to which legislation on public sector information (PSI) influences access to and re-use of research data. The Public Sector Information Directive (2003/98/EC) and the impact of its revision in 2013 (2013/37/EU) are described. There is a special focus on the application of PSI legislation to public libraries, including university and research libraries, and its practical implications.

In the final part of the study the results are critically evaluated and core recommendations are made to improve the legal situation in relation to research data.

Introduction

OpenAIRE aims to establish an integrated research information space that links research results, including publications and research data. As an open and participatory infrastructure it encourages authors and contributors to share their publications and research data with other users.

The European Commission supports open access. Within its 7th Framework programme (FP7) it has been running the open access Pilot. The Commission defines open access as the practice of providing online access to scientific information that is free of charge to the end-user[1]. The Commission expects that in today's "information economy", where knowledge is a source of competitive advantage, open access can potentially realise a variety of benefits. Hence all projects receiving Horizon 2020 funding are required to make sure that any peer-reviewed journal article they publish is openly accessible free of charge (Art. 29.2 Model Grant Agreement). A novelty in Horizon 2020 is the Open Research Data Pilot, which aims to improve and maximise access to, and re-use of, research data generated by projects. Originally covering only a few programme areas, the Open Research Data Pilot has recently been extended to cover all new Horizon 2020 projects from the beginning of 2017 onwards[2].

Projects taking part in the Open Research Data Pilot are obliged to deposit the research data that support findings in peer-reviewed publications, as well as other data they define, preferably in a research data repository (online research data archive) and take measures to enable third parties to access, mine, exploit, reproduce and disseminate (free of charge for any user) these research data[3].

OpenAIRE provides researcher support and services for the Open Research Data Pilot and investigates its legal ramifications. Within this study, legal barriers to data sharing in the context of the Open Research Data Pilot are analysed. The study focuses on two legal issues which are of relevance for the implementation of the Pilot, namely data protection law and public sector information (PSI). For the first issue, European data protection legislation is analysed in detail. The main focus is on the Data Protection Directive (95/46/EC), which has been in force since 1995. Not only is the Data Protection Directive itself described, but also its implementation in selected EU Member States. Differences are highlighted to show that the situation under the directive, which was supposed to achieve

---

[1] European Commission, Fact sheet: Open Access in Horizon 2020, available at: https://ec.europa.eu/programmes/horizon2020/sites/horizon2020/files/FactSheet_Open_Access.pdf.

[2] See https://www.openaire.eu/opendatapilot.

[3] See European Commission, Guidelines on Open Access to Scientific Publications and Research Data in Horizon 2020, Version 2.1, 15 February 2016, pp. 9 et seq. available at: http://ec.europa.eu/research/participants/data/ref/h2020/grants_manual/hi/oa_pilot/h2020-hi-oa-pilot-guide_en.pdf.

harmonisation, still differs between the Member States. Additionally, the upcoming General Data Protection Regulation (2016/679/EU) (GDPR) and relevant changes to the legal system are described. Special focus is placed on leading data protection principles and the open access online sharing of research data as intended under the Open Research Data Pilot.

This study was conducted between January 2015 and December 2016. When we started working on the study, the GDPR was far from being adopted. Therefore we had to analyse the legal situation under the regime of the Data Protection Directive. Moreover, the specific aim of our task was to analyse legal barriers to data sharing in the context of the Open Research Data Pilot and the Pilot for its part has been running under the regime of the directive. This will not change before the new regulation enters into force in May 2018.

However, for the sake of completeness and given the potential influence of the new legal rules of the GDPR for running the Pilot, we include a chapter on the regulation and the changes it brings. As it happens, the basic rules of the directive and the regulation are in line with each other. The leading data protection principles of the directive relevant for the running of the Pilot will continue to be in force under the new GDPR. Hence the legislative changes will not affect the main findings of the study.

The outcomes of the descriptive part of the study, where the legal situation is described on a general level, serve as a basis for the next part of the study. This section is dedicated to the use of research data as intended under the Open Research Data Pilot. We analyse to what extent data protection law applies to such use and how the respective laws, especially the leading data protection principles, affect the use of data as it is intended in the Open Research Data Pilot. In order to complete the study with some practical background, the experiences of the European Commission in conducting the Open Research Data Pilot so far, as well as basic examples of repository use forms, are considered.

The second issue that is analysed within this study is that of PSI. We describe the extent to which legislation on PSI influences access to and re-use of research data. There is a special focus on the extent to which public libraries, including university and research libraries, fall under obligations specified by EU and Member States for public sector bodies (PSBs) on PSI with regard to access and re-use of this information, and what the exact consequences of those obligations are.

The PSI Directive and in particular the impact of its revision in 2013 (2013/37/EU) are considered. The findings of this second sub-task show to what extent access and re-use of PSI are harmonised within the EU and how the regime of PSI influences the Open Research Data Pilot.

In the final part of the study the results are critically evaluated and some recommendations are given on improving the legal situation in relation to research data.

1 Data Protection Issues

Research results often contain information traceable to individuals that can potentially qualify as personal data. This makes data protection law relevant in the context of making research results available to other researchers or a broader public.

If research involves personal data it is necessary that the entire research process, starting from collection of the data, should comply with the relevant data protection law. This study focuses on the legal barriers that EU and Member States' data protection laws create for data sharing in the context of the Open Research Data Pilot.

This study does not aim to provide a comprehensive overview of all EU Member States' data protection rules. It rather aims at a more general level. It briefly describes the international data protection landscape, then going on to focus on the European level, with the current Data Protection Directive and the upcoming GDPR taken into account. Specific case studies of particular EU nations are then analysed. The countries analysed were chosen to show how the Data Protection Directive is implemented in different areas of the EU, central/west (Germany, the Netherlands, France), south (Spain), east (Poland) and under different legal systems (UK).

After this more general description of the legal situation, the use of research data within the Open Research Data Pilot is analysed. We determine the extent to which data protection laws apply to the intended use and what the consequences of the application of leading data protection principles are. Additionally we describe methods to legitimise the use of personal data within the Pilot.

1.1 International development of data protection

Data protection law emerged at the beginning of the 1970s[4]. The world's first privacy Act was the Data Protection Act of the federal state of Hessen in Germany. It came into force in 1970[5]. In the following years further laws on data protection were passed in other European states[6] and the issue of data protection began to appear on the agenda of international institutions.

---

[4] Bygrave, *Data Privacy Law*, Oxford, Oxford University Press, 2014, p. 99.

[5] See Kühling/Seidel/Sivridis, *Datenschutzrecht*, 2nd edition, Heidelberg, C.F. Müller, 2011, p. 5.

[6] For example the Swedish Data Protection Act in 1973 or the German Bundesdatenschutzgesetz (BDSG) in 1977. See Mehde, in Heselhaus/Nowak, *Handbuch der Europäischen Grundrechte*, Munich, C.H. Beck, 2006, § 21 para. 7.

1.1.1 Guidelines of the United Nations and the OECD

In 1980, the Ministerial Council of the Organisation for Economic Co-operation and Development (OECD) adopted Guidelines on the Protection of Privacy and Transborder Flows of Personal Data[7]. Ten years later, in 1990, the General Assembly of the United Nations adopted a resolution on guidelines on the use of computerised personal data flow[8]. However, these guidelines were not legally binding under international law, but rather recommendatory in character[9]. Nevertheless, these guidelines helped to place the issue of data protection on the agendas of national and international legislators.

1.1.2 Council of Europe Convention for the Protection of Human Rights and Fundamental Freedoms

The Council of Europe is a human rights organisation in Europe. It was one of the first international bodies to begin developing normative responses to the threats posed by computer technology to privacy-related interests[10]. Some important instruments relating to data protection can be found in the law of the Council of Europe. The most important basic instrument on the protection of human rights is the Convention for the Protection of Human Rights and Fundamental Freedoms (European Convention on Human Rights –ECHR) of 1950[11].

Art. 8 ECHR states:

> *(1) Everyone has the right to respect for his private and family life, his home and his correspondence.*
>
> *(2) There shall be no interference by a public authority with the exercise of this right except such as is in accordance with the law and is necessary in a democratic society in the interests of national security, public safety or the economic well-being of the country, for the prevention of disorder or crime, for the protection of health or morals, or for the protection of the rights and freedoms of others.*

Unlike the United Nations' and OECD Guidelines, the ECHR is binding on all its signatories. Member States' compliance with the rules of the convention is ensured by the European Court of Human Rights. Currently, the Council of Europe includes 47 Member States. All of them have signed the ECHR[12]. All

---

[7] OECD document C (80) 58 (final).

[8] Resolution of the General Assembly 44/132, 14 December 1990.

[9] Taeger, *Einführung in das Datenschutzrecht*, Frankfurt am Main, Deutscher Fachverlag, 2014, chapter I paras 18 and 24.

[10] Bygrave, *Data Privacy Law*, Oxford, Oxford University Press, 2014, p. 31.

[11] The text of the convention is available at: http://conventions.coe.int/treaty/en/Treaties/Html/005.htm.

[12] See http://www.coe.int/en/web/about-us/who-we-are.

Member States of the EU are also members of the Council of Europe. Moreover, the EU itself is supposed to become a signatory of the ECHR. Art. 6 sections 2 and 3 of the Treaty on European Union (TEU) states:

> *The Union shall accede to the European Convention for the Protection of Human Rights and Fundamental Freedoms. Such accession shall not affect the Union's competences as defined in the Treaties. Fundamental rights, as guaranteed by the European Convention for the Protection of Human Rights and Fundamental Freedoms and as they result from the constitutional traditions common to the Member States, shall constitute general principles of the Union's law.*

However, due to some problems of legal competence, the EU has not yet joined the Council of Europe[13].

Art. 8 of the ECHR lays down a human right to privacy protection, covering data that relate to the private and family life of a person, their home and their correspondence. The duty to comply with the right according to Art. 8 of the convention leads to two duties of the Member States of the Council of Europe. First, the state itself, particularly its public administration, shall not be allowed to interfere with the privacy of its citizens unless an exception in Art. 8(2) ECHR is applicable. Exceptions exist for national security, public safety or the economic well-being of the country, for the prevention of disorder or crime, for the protection of health or morals, or for the protection of the rights and freedoms of others. But this is not enough to comply with Art. 8 ECHR. Additionally the state must institute safeguard measures to prevent misuse of personal data by others[14]. This means that the state has to introduce legal rules which ensure that privacy protection is also respected between private persons.

According to the European Court of Human Rights, every act of collecting, storing, disclosing or otherwise processing personal data leads to an interference with the right in Art. 8 ECHR and must be justified[15]. Thus the Court takes into account the circumstances of the collection and storage of data, the kinds of data, the way in which the data are used and processed, and the consequences of all these factors[16].

---

13 See Bengt/Beutler, in Groeben/Schwarze/Hatje, *Europäisches Unionsrecht*, 7th edition, Baden-Baden, Nomos, 2015, EUV Art. 6 paras 20 et seq.

14 See Meyer-Ladewig, *Europäische Menschenrechtskonvention Handkommentar*, 3rd edition, Munich, Nomos, 2011, Art. 8 paras 2 et seqq.

15 See the cases of *Kruslin v France*, Application no. 11801/85 (24.04.1990), http://hudoc.echr.coe.int/sites/eng/pages/search.aspx?i=001-57626; *Kopp v Switzerland*, Application no. 13/1997/797/1000 (28.03.1998), http://hudoc.echr.coe.int/sites/eng/pages/search.aspx?i=001-58144; *Amann v Switzerland*, Application no. 27798/95 (16.2.2000), http://hudoc.echr.coe.int/sites/eng/pages/search.aspx?i=001-58497.

16 See the cases of *Peck v The United Kingdom*, Application no. 44647/98 (28.01.2003), http://hudoc.echr.coe.int/sites/eng/pages/search.aspx?i=001-60898; *S. and Marper v The United Kingdom*, Application nos. 30562/04 and 30566/04 (04.12.2008), http://hudoc.echr.coe.int/sites/eng/pages/search.aspx?i=001-90051.

1.1.3 Council of Europe Convention for the Protection of Individuals with regard to Automatic Processing of Personal Data

In 1981 the Member States of the Council of Europe adopted the Convention for the Protection of Individuals with regard to Automatic Processing of Personal Data[17]. According to Art. 1:

> *The purpose of this convention is to secure in the territory of each Party for every individual, whatever his nationality or residence, respect for his rights and fundamental freedoms, and in particular his right to privacy, with regard to automatic processing of personal data relating to him ("data protection").*

Pursuant to Art. 3, the requirements of the convention need to be applied to automated personal data files and automatic processing of personal data in the public and private sectors.

The convention formulates a number of basic principles of data protection law. According to Art. 5:

> *Personal data undergoing automatic processing shall be: (a) obtained and processed fairly and lawfully; (b) stored for specified and legitimate purposes and not used in a way incompatible with those purposes; (c) adequate, relevant and not excessive in relation to the purposes for which they are stored; (d) accurate and, where necessary, kept up to date; (e) preserved in a form which permits identification of the data subjects for no longer than is required for the purpose for which those data are stored.*

Additionally the convention sets regulations regarding data security (Art. 7), sensitive data (Art. 6) and additional safeguards for the data subject (Art. 8).

Like the ECHR, the guidelines of the Convention for the Protection of Individuals with regard to Automatic Processing of Personal Data are binding and must be followed by all the Member States of the Council of Europe. The convention is thus the first binding international law instrument on data protection.

The Council of Europe has additionally issued some recommendations dealing specifically with data processing in particular sectors. Those are not legally binding but have strong persuasive force[18].

1.1.4 Summary

In the 1970s the legislative process of introducing data protection regulations started on a national level. In the 1980s the guidelines of the OECD and the United Nations placed the issue of data protection on the agenda of European and international legislators. However, it was the Council of Europe that made history by adopting the Convention for the Protection of Individuals with regard

---

[17] The text of the convention is available at: http://www.conventions.coe.int/Treaty/en/Treaties/Html/108.htm.

[18] See Bygrave, *Data Privacy Law*, Oxford, Oxford University Press, 2014, pp. 41 et seq.

to Automatic Processing of Personal Data as a binding European framework on data protection[19]. Much later, the EU introduced binding rules on privacy protection.

1.2 The EU legal framework on data protection

It took a little longer for the EU to adopt binding rules on data protection. The EU instruments that were eventually adopted have nonetheless been the most ambitious, comprehensive and complex in the field[20]. Today, the right to data protection is recognised in the Union's secondary as well as in its primary law.

1.2.1 Charter of Fundamental Rights of the European Union

On 7 December 2000 the Charter of Fundamental Rights of the European Union was proclaimed by the EU. However, the legal status of the Charter was uncertain and it did not have full legal effect[21]. This changed with the entry into force of the Treaty of Lisbon in December 2009[22]. Art. 6(1) TEU now states that:

> *The Union recognises the rights, freedoms and principles set out in the Charter of Fundamental Rights of the European Union … which shall have the same legal value as the Treaties.*

This means that the Charter of Fundamental Rights has the same status as the TEU and the Treaty on the Functioning of the European Union (TFEU) and is part of the Union's primary law.

Art. 7 of the Charter of Fundamental Rights provides that:

> *Everyone has the right to respect for his or her private and family life, home and communications.*

And according to Art. 8 of the EU Charter:

> *(1) Everyone has the right to the protection of personal data concerning him or her.*
>
> *(2) Such data must be processed fairly for specified purposes and on the basis of the consent of the person concerned or some other legitimate basis laid down by law. Everyone has the right of access to data which has been collected concerning him or her, and the right to have it rectified.*

---

19 Kühling/Seidel/Sivridis, *Datenschutzrecht*, 2nd edition, Heidelberg, C.F. Müller, 2011, p. 11.

20 Bygrave, *Data Privacy Law*, Oxford, Oxford University Press, 2014, p. 53.

21 Craig, in Craig/De Burca, *EU Law: Text, Cases and Materials*, 4th edition, Oxford, Oxford University Press, 2008, chapter 11 "Human rights in the EU", p. 15.

22 See Tinnefeld/Buchner/Petri, *Einführung in das Datenschutzrecht*, 5th edition, Munich, Oldenbourg Verlag, 2012, p. 10.

Art. 7 of the EU Charter guarantees the protection of private and family life and communication. It is formulated in a similar way to Art. 8 ECHR. Moreover, according to Art. 52(3) of the EU Charter, the meaning and scope of this right shall be the same as that of the ECHR.

Art. 8 of the EU Charter includes data protection and strengthens it as a fundamental right[23]. According to the European Court of Justice (ECJ), Art. 8 EU Charter is closely connected with the right to respect for private life expressed in Art. 7 of the Charter[24]. The right to respect for private life with regard to the processing of personal data, recognised by Arts 7 and 8 of the Charter, concerns any information relating to an identified or identifiable individual[25].

However, Art. 8(2) of the Charter authorises the processing of personal data if certain conditions are satisfied. Moreover, Art. 52(1) of the Charter accepts that limitations may be imposed on the exercise of rights such as those set forth in Arts 7 and 8 of the Charter as long as the limitations are provided for by law, respect the essence of those rights and freedoms, and, subject to the principle of proportionality, are necessary and genuinely meet objectives of general interest recognised by the EU or the need to protect the rights and freedoms of others[26].

According to Art. 51(1) of the Charter:

> *The provisions of the Charter are addressed to the institutions, bodies, offices and agencies of the Union with due regard for the principle of subsidiarity and to the Member States only when they are implementing Union law.*

In the area of privacy law, the Data Protection Directive[27] is of particular relevance and needs to be implemented by the EU Member States.

It is worth noting that in addition to the EU Charter, Art. 16(1) TFEU lays down a fundamental right of data protection too. However, besides the data protection right in Art. 8 EU Charter, the right mentioned in Art. 16 TFEU has no independent meaning[28].

---

[23] Bernsdorff, in Meyer, *Charta der Grundrechte der Europäischen Union*, 4th edition, Baden-Baden, Nomos, 2014, Art. 8 para. 1.

[24] ECJ Joined Cases C-92/09 and C-93/09 (9.11.2010), *Schencke and Eifert v Hessen*, para. 47.

[25] Ibid., para. 52.

[26] See ibid., paras 49 et seq.

[27] Directive 95/46/EC on the protection of individuals with regard to the processing of personal data and on the free movement of such data.

[28] Kühling/Seidel/Sivridis, *Datenschutzrecht*, 2nd edition, Heidelberg, C.F. Müller, 2011, p. 19; see also Bernsdorff, in Meyer, *Charta der Grundrechte der Europäischen Union*, 4th edition, Baden-Baden, Nomos, 2014, Art. 8 para. 17.

1.2.2 The Data Protection Directive

Although the Council of Europe adopted the Convention for the Protection of Individuals with regard to Automatic Processing of Personal Data, there was some reluctance to ratify. This lack of ratification, in particular, led to the work of the EU on its own data protection framework.

The EU's drafting and adoption of a directive on the protection of personal data took over five years and was subject to heated debate and frenetic lobbying[29]. Nevertheless, in 1995 the European Parliament and the Council reached agreement on the Data Protection Directive[30]. The Data Protection Directive introduced for the first time binding rules on data protection with which the Member States of the EU must comply[31]. However, it is important to note that the directive introduces minimum standards of data protection[32] and so it is possible that in individual cases the national rules differ from Member State to Member State.

1.2.2.1 Aim of the directive

According to Art. 1 Data Protection Directive:

> *(1) Member States shall protect the fundamental rights and freedoms of natural persons, and in particular their right to privacy with respect to the processing of personal data.*
>
> *(2) Member States shall neither restrict nor prohibit the free flow of personal data between Member States for reasons connected with the protection afforded under paragraph 1.*

As can be seen from even this first article, the directive has two objectives. First, the fundamental rights and freedoms in the field of data protection must be guaranteed and secondly, the free movement of personal data within the EU must not be hampered[33].

1.2.2.2 Scope of application

The rules set out by the Data Protection Directive are only applicable to data concerning natural persons. According to Recital 24 of the directive, the legislation concerning the protection of legal persons with regard to the processing data which concerns them is not affected by the directive.

---

[29] Bygrave, *Data Privacy Law*, Oxford, Oxford University Press, 2014, pp. 6 et seq.

[30] OJ L 281, 23/11/1995 P. 0031 – 0050.

[31] See Johlen, in Tettinger/Stern, *Kölner Gemeinschaftskommentar zur Europäischen Grundrechte-Charta*, Munich, C.H. Beck, 2006, Art. 8 para. 14.

[32] Hatt, *Konfliktfeld Datenschutz und Forschung*, Baden-Baden, Nomos, 2012, p. 134.

[33] See Dammann/Simitis, *EG-Datenschutzrichtlinie Kommentar*, Baden-Baden, Nomos, 1997, Art. 2 para. 1.

Art. 3(1) Data Protection Directive defines the scope of its application.

> *The Directive shall apply to the processing of personal data wholly or partly by automatic means, and to the processing otherwise than by automatic means of personal data which form part of a filing system or are intended to form part of a filing system.*

Data protection rules apply only to that information which qualifies as personal data. Therefore, the first and the most crucial question in the assessment of compliance with the personal data framework is whether relevant data qualify as personal data and whether data protection rules are applicable to the handling of the relevant data.

The directive is applicable in every case of automatic processing of personal data. Automatic processing means the analysis of data by using data processing systems[34]. It is sufficient for only part of the processing to be carried out by automatic means. In addition, the directive shall apply when personal data are processed by non-automatic means but the data are stored or are intended to be stored in a filing system.

Art. 3(2) Data Protection Directive clarifies that the directive shall not apply to the processing of personal data in the course of an activity which falls outside the scope of Community law or the processing by a natural person in the course of a purely personal or household activity.

Territorially, Art. 4 of the Data Protection Directive stipulates that the national law of a Member State is applicable where the data processing is carried out in the context of the activities of an establishment of the controller on the territory of the Member State (domicile principle).

1.2.3 Fundamental legal terms

Art. 2 Data Protection Directive contains some important definitions for the understanding of the directive. The most important legal terms will be described below.

1.2.3.1 Personal Data

Art. 2(a) Data Protection Directive defines "personal data" as:

> *Any information relating to an identified or identifiable natural person ("data subject"); an identifiable person is one who can be identified, directly or indirectly, in particular by reference to an identification number or to one or more factors specific to his physical, physiological, mental, economic, cultural or social identity.*

The term personal data consists of the key elements "any information", "relating to", "identified or identifiable" and "natural person".

---

[34] Kühling/Seidel/Sivridis, *Datenschutzrecht*, 2nd edition, Heidelberg, C.F. Müller, 2011, p. 24.

The term "personal data" is thus a broad concept, which includes "any kind of information" (both subjective and objective) about a person, in any form. It is not limited to traditional kinds of personal data, such as name and address of a person, but means any kind of information about a natural person[35]. As can be seen from Recitals 14 to 17 of the Data Protection Directive, images and sound files are also included.

A peculiar type of personal data is biometric data, defined by the Article 29 Working Party[36] as "biological properties, physiological characteristics, living traits, or repeatable actions where those features and/or actions are both unique to that individual and measurable, even if the patterns used in practice to technically measure them involve a certain degree of probability"[37]. Biometric data not only contain information about a person, but can also be a means to identify a person.

According to the Article 29 Working Party, information is "relating to" a natural person, when the following are present:

- a "content" element, i.e. when information is about the person; or
- a "purpose" element, i.e. when the data are used or likely to be used with the purpose of evaluating, treating in a certain way or influencing the status or behaviour of a person; or
- a "result" element, i.e. when data relate to a person because their use is likely to have an impact on a person's rights and interests[38].

The meaning of "identified" natural person is straightforward. It refers to a person who can be distinguished from all other members of the group[39].

The characteristic "identifiable" is less clear cut and provides more room for interpretation. In general, it implies the possibility of identifying the person[40]. The Article 29 Working Party points out that the most common identifier is the name of the person, or the name combined with other information.

At the same time, the concept "directly or indirectly identifiable" is very context specific. Data that may enable the identification of a person in certain circumstances may not be able to do so in another setting.

---

35 See Dammann/Simitis, *EG-Datenschutzrichtlinie Kommentar*, Baden-Baden, Nomos, 1997, Art. 2 para. 2.

36 Regarding the legal nature of the Article 29 Data Protection Working Party see below Section 1.2.4.12.

37 Article 29 Data Protection Working Party, *Opinion 4/2007 on the concept of personal data*, adopted on 20 June 2007, available at: http://ec.europa.eu/justice/policies/privacy/docs/wpdocs/2007/wp136_en.pdf, p. 8.

38 Ibid., pp. 10 et seq.

39 Ibid., p. 12.

40 Ibid., p. 12.

The criterion of "indirectly identified or identifiable persons" typically relates to the phenomenon of 'unique combinations', whether small or large in size", which allow one to "single out" a particular person. Thus, "identifiable" does not necessarily mean the ability to discover someone's name[41]. This is especially important to keep in mind in the context of research data, which often do not contain identifying data, but may still, alone or in combination with other available data, allow a particular person to be singled out.

Recital 26 of the Data Protection Directive clarifies that "to determine whether a person is identifiable, account should be taken of all the means likely reasonably to be used either by the controller or by any other person to identify the said person". This means that a mere hypothetical possibility of singling out the individual is not enough to consider the person as "identifiable"[42].

When considering "all the means likely reasonably to be used" the following factors should be taken into account: the cost of conducting identification, the intended purpose, the way the processing is structured, the advantage expected by the controller, the interests at stake for the individuals, the risk of organisational dysfunctions (e.g. breaches of confidentiality duties) and technical failures. At the same time this test is dynamic. It is sensible to apply it in the light of the state of the art and technology at the time of processing and during the period of data processing[43].

The latter implies that "personal data" itself is a dynamic concept. With the development of technology, more and more information can fall under the characteristics of personal data and be subject to personal data protection rules.

The basis on which the evaluation of identifiability should be based remains a point of contention. The question is whether the data subject must be identifiable to the controller to constitute personal data or whether it is sufficient that someone (controller or third party) is able to link the data in question to a natural person[44].

It is, for example, still unclear, whether an Internet Protocol (IP) address is personal data. The Article 29 Working Party, for example, has considered IP addresses as data relating to an identifiable person[45]. A dynamic IP address does not allow everyone to identify the natural person behind the screen, but at a minimum, the access provider is able to link the IP address to this person. It is possible to consider the IP address as personal data, because someone (the access provider) is able to identify the person; but it is also an option to consider the IP address as personal data only for the access provider, because he is the only one

---

[41] Ibid., p. 14.

[42] Ibid., p. 15.

[43] Ibid., p. 15.

[44] See in more detail Bergt, 'Die Bestimmbarkeit als Grundproblem des Datenschutzrechts', ZD 2015, 365 et seqq.

[45] Article 29 Data Protection Working Party, *Opinion 4/2007 on the concept of personal data*, p. 16.

who is able to carry out the identification. The German Federal Court of Justice (Bundesgerichtshof – BGH) submitted this question to the ECJ[46]. In October 2016 the ECJ ruled that a dynamic IP address registered by an online media services provider when a person accesses a website that the provider makes accessible to the public constitutes personal data, in relation to that provider, where the latter has the legal means which enable it to identify the data subject with additional data which the Internet service provider has about that person[47].

The criterion of a "natural person" clarifies that personal data only include information about living natural persons. Legal persons and decedents are generally outside the scope of protection[48].

However, in some instances information about dead persons can be qualified as personal data. For example, when it also refers to identified or identifiable living persons, as in the case of information on the cause of death where it is a hereditary disease, information about legal persons may fall under the definition of personal data if it relates to a natural person. This can be the case, for example, if the name of a legal person derives from that of a natural person[49].

The Data Protection Directive also contains some provisions on special categories of personal data. According to Art. 8(1) of the directive, special categories of personal data "include data revealing racial or ethnic origin, political opinions, religious or philosophical beliefs, trade-union membership, and the processing of data concerning health or sex life".

1.2.3.2 Anonymous data

Although the term "anonymised data" is not mentioned in the articles of the Data Protection Directive[50], we explain it here due to its importance for the analysis.

Anonymised data are "data rendered anonymous in such a way that the data subject is no longer identifiable" (Recital 26 of the Data Protection Directive). In other words, it is no longer possible for either the controller or any other person to identify the data subject "by all the means likely reasonably to be used". Just like the term "identifiable", used in defining personal data, the concept of anonymised data is very context specific.

Effective anonymisation should prevent "all parties from singling out an individual in a dataset, from linking two records within a dataset (or between two separate datasets) and from inferring any information in such dataset"[51].

---

[46] BGH Case VI ZR 135/13 (28.10.2014).

[47] ECJ Case C-582/14 (19.10.2016), *Breyer v Germany*.

[48] Concerning legal persons see Recital 24 of the Data Protection Directive.

[49] Article 29 Data Protection Working Party, *Opinion 4/2007 on the concept of personal data*, p. 23.

[50] But see Recital 26 Data Protection Directive.

[51] Article 29 Data Protection Working Party, *Opinion 5/2014 on anonymisation techniques*, adopted on 10 April 2014, available at: http://ec.europa.eu/justice/data-protection/article-29/documentation/opinion-recommendation/files/2014/wp216_en.pdf, p.9.

In the context of re-use of PSI the Article 29 Working Party notes that "complete" anonymisation (and a high level of aggregation) of personal data is the most definitive solution to minimise the risks of inadvertent disclosure. Anonymisation should be done at the earliest opportunity prior to making the data available for re-use, by the data controller or by a trusted third party[52].

With reference to case studies and research publications, in its later opinion the Article 29 Working Party warns, however, that creation of a truly anonymous dataset from a rich set of personal data while preserving much of the underlying information is not a simple task, partly because it is possible to combine the anonymous data set with another dataset in a way which will make some individuals identifiable[53]. Thus, anonymisation carries with it a risk factor.

This is especially relevant in the context of sharing both research data and PSI. Having shared data under an open access licence the controller loses control over who can access the data. Thus, the likelihood that "any other person" will have the means and will use those means to re-identify the data subjects increases very significantly[54].

Effectiveness of anonymisation also depends on the type of personal data. Scholars note that anonymisation of human genetic information, due to its uniquely identifiable nature, can hardly guarantee absolute confidentiality to data subjects or their genetically related family members. As long as a reference sample is available, it is possible to re-identify genotyped data subjects and data subjects in pooled mixtures of DNA. New sequencing technology also challenges standard data protection techniques such as encryption[55].

Before making PSI available for re-use, the Article 29 Working Party strongly recommends that controllers carry out a thorough data protection impact assessment[56]. Since, similar to the concept of "personal data" in general, "anonymised data" is also a dynamic concept, which largely depends on the state of the art and availability of technological means, it is also important to carry out periodical assessments of re-identification risks. When anonymised data can no longer

---

[52] Article 29 Data Protection Working Party, *Opinion 3/2013 on purpose limitation*, adopted on 2 April 2013, available at: http://ec.europa.eu/justice/data-protection/article-29/documentation/opinion-recommendation/files/2013/wp203_en.pdf, p. 49; Article 29 Data Protection Working Party, *Opinion 5/2014 on anonymisation techniques*, p. 7; Article 29 Data Protection Working Party, *Opinion 6/2013 on open data and public sector information ('PSI') reuse*, adopted on 5 June 2013, available at: http://ec.europa.eu/justice/data-protection/article-29/documentation/opinion-recommendation/files/2013/wp207_en.pdf, p. 12, 14.

[53] Article 29 Data Protection Working Party, *Opinion 5/2014 on anonymisation techniques*, p. 5.

[54] Article 29 Data Protection Working Party, *Opinion 6/2013 on open data and public sector information ('PSI') reuse*, p. 13.

[55] Kaye, 'The Tension Between Data Sharing and the Protection of Privacy in Genomics Research', Annu. Rev. Genomics Hum. Genet., 2012, 415 (423), text available at: http://www.annualreviews.org/doi/pdf/10.1146/annurev-genom-082410-101454.

[56] Article 29 Data Protection Working Party, *Opinion 6/2013 on open data and public sector information ('PSI') reuse*, pp. 6, 19.

qualify as such in the light of new available means of re-identification, non-compliance with data protection rules constitutes an unlawful act. These insights are equally relevant for research data.

With respect to sharing of PSI, the Article 29 Working Party (without aiming at providing a full list) also highlights a number of factors/concepts that may be helpful in assessing the risks of re-identification[57]:

- what other data are available, either to the public at large, or to other individuals or organisations, and whether the data to be published could be linked to other datasets;
- the likelihood of re-identification being attempted (some types of data will be more attractive to potential intruders than others); and
- the likelihood that the re-identification, if attempted, would be successful, considering the effectiveness of the anonymisation techniques proposed.

It is noted that as a part of the overall assessment of re-identification, techniques such as "penetration" or "pen" testing can be used. This test, however, has its limitations. Moreover, re-identification risks can change over time[58].

Besides anonymisation techniques, the Article 29 Working Party identifies additional suitable technical, legal and organisational limitations of re-use (such as appropriate licence terms, technical measures to avoid bulk download of data, limiting search queries, additional security controls such as, for example, a "captcha35" verification system) as appropriate safeguards against re-identification[59]. Adhering to the principle of data minimisation (discussed below) can also mitigate somewhat re-identification risks. This principle ensures that only the data necessary for a particular purpose are released[60].

The Article 29 Working Party concludes that in case of proven re-identification of personal data from an open dataset, shared as a part of PSI (or, in the present context, as a part of research data), the controller must be able to turn off the feed or remove the dataset from the open data website. Where the dataset is removed from the website, the controller must also inform re-users and advise them to stop processing and delete all data coming from the compromised dataset[61].

Codes of conduct (Recital 26 of the Data Protection Directive) can provide extra guidance on ways of anonymising data.

---

[57] Ibid., p. 14.
[58] Ibid., p. 17.
[59] Ibid., pp. 22, 27.
[60] Ibid., p. 16.
[61] Ibid., p. 18.

1.2.3.3 Processing

As the third important term of the directive, "processing of personal data" (*processing*) is described in Art. 2(b). It means:

> *Any operation or set of operations which is performed upon personal data, whether or not by automatic means, such as collection, recording, organisation, storage, adaptation or alteration, retrieval, consultation, use, disclosure by transmission, dissemination or otherwise making available, alignment or combination, blocking, erasure or destruction.*

Processing basically means any operation in connection with personal data. It is irrelevant whether data are processed in digital form or otherwise. In this way, the term "processing" is formulated in a technology-neutral way[62]. Legal scholars note that this term is all embracing and any operation with personal data not qualifying as processing is almost unthinkable[63].

Even though pseudonymisation and anonymisation are not included in this definition, they also constitute processing of personal data and thus fall under the requirements of the data protection framework.

1.2.3.4 Controller

According to Art. 2(d) Data Protection Directive:

> *Controller shall mean the natural or legal person, public authority, agency or any other body which alone or jointly with others determines the purposes and means of the processing of personal data; where the purposes and means of processing are determined by national or Community laws or regulations, the controller or the specific criteria for his nomination may be designated by national or Community law.*

The controller is the norm addressee of the directive. Controllers must comply with the provisions of the directive. They can be either a natural or legal person and determine the purposes and means of the processing of personal data[64]. The directive does not distinguish between public and private persons or institutions. However it does not prohibit Member States from introducing different sets of rules for the public and private sectors[65].

In circumstances where a legal entity or a body processes personal data, such company or body, rather than an individual within the company or body, will qualify as the controller. The situation will be different when an individual acting within a company/body processes data for their own purposes, different from

---

[62] Kühling/Seidel/Sivridis, *Datenschutzrecht*, 2nd edition, Heidelberg, C.F. Müller, 2011, p. 26.

[63] Kuner, *European Data Protection Law: Corporate Compliance and Regulation*, Oxford, Oxford University Press, 2007, p. 75.

[64] See Bygrave, *Data Privacy Law*, Oxford, Oxford University Press, 2014, p. 17.

[65] Gounalakis/Mand, 'Die neue EG-Datenschutzrichtlinie – Grundlagen einer Umsetzung in nationales Recht (I)', CR 1997, 421 (434); Brühann/Zerdick, 'Umsetzung der EG-Datenschutzreichtlinie', CR 1996, 429 (431).

those of the company[66]. In the context of research carried out by a university, the controller would be the body (such as a management board) authorised to legally represent the university and not an individual researcher, unless the latter processes personal data outside of their work for the university.

In each particular case, circumstances play a major part in designating the role of controller. In order to determine who the controller is, it is necessary to assess who determines the purposes and the means of processing personal data[67].

Deciding upon the purpose of the processing of personal data would always trigger the qualification as controller. As regards the means of processing, only determination of essential elements of the means would imply control. Thus, it is possible that the data processor exclusively determines the technical and organisational means[68]. "Essential means" is subject to interpretation and is very context specific. This issue is especially relevant to the circumstances in which cloud service providers process personal data.

The controller also decides on the main parameters of data processing, such as its duration and access rights to personal data[69].

1.2.3.5 Processor

Art. 2(e) of the Data Protection Directive defines the processor in contrast to the controller:

> *Processor shall mean a natural or legal person, public authority, agency or any other body which processes personal data on behalf of the controller.*

The Article 29 Working Party identifies two basic characteristics of a processor following from this definition[70]:

- being a separate legal entity with respect to the controller, and
- processing personal data on behalf of the controller.

The latter characteristic is the crucial factor in distinguishing processor from controller. The role of the processor is much more limited than that of the controller. According to Art. 16 of the Data Protection Directive, the processor themself, as well as any person acting under their authority who has access to personal data, "must not process them except on instructions from the controller". Thus, the parameters of personal data processing by the processor are always limited to those set down by the controller. The processor has no interest

---

[66] Article 29 Data Protection Working Party, *Opinion 1/2010 on the concepts of "controller" and "processor"*, adopted on 16 February 2010, available at: http://ec.europa.eu/justice/policies/privacy/docs/wpdocs/2010/wp169_en.pdf, pp. 15 et seq.

[67] Ibid., p. 12.

[68] Ibid., pp. 13 et seq.

[69] Ibid., p. 15.

[70] Ibid., p. 25.

of their own in processing the personal data of the data subject. They are just acting on behalf of the controller. The processor does not have any power of disposition concerning the data.

It is the controller who must comply with data protection rules and who, in most cases, is liable for data protection violations (Art. 27 of the Data Protection Directive). The controller should also ensure the processor's compliance with data protection law. They are responsible to the data subject for the processing of personal data by the processor.

With a view to security of processing, a processor must have a contract or another legally binding act in writing or in another equivalent form "stipulating, in particular, that the data processor shall act only on instructions from the controller" and implement appropriate technical and organisational measures to protect personal data (Art. 17(3) of the Data Protection Directive).

If the processor exceeds the scope of their mandate from the controller and processes personal data for other purposes on their own behalf, they become a controller of personal data in this part (or a joint controller) for another processing activity with all the consequences.

A contractor can also qualify as controller (or a joint controller) for another processing activity and therefore be obliged to fulfil the obligations of the controller. This will be the case when a contractor has an influence on the purpose of processing and carries out the processing (also) for its own benefit, for example by using personal data received with a view to generating added-value services[71].

1.2.3.6 Third party

A "third party" is "any natural or legal person, public authority, agency or any other body other than the data subject, the controller, the processor, and the persons who, under the direct authority of the controller or the processor, are authorised to process the data" (Art. 2(f) Data Protection Directive).

"Third party" is mentioned in the directive in the context of transfer or disclosure of personal data, which constitutes a form of processing personal data. Upon receipt of personal data, the third party becomes the controller of personal data if other qualifying conditions are met[72].

1.2.3.7 Consent of the Data subject

Art. 2(h) of the Data Protection Directive contains a definition of "the data subject's consent". It

> *shall mean any freely given specific and informed indication of his wishes by which the data subject signifies his agreement to personal data relating to him being processed.*

---

[71] Ibid., p. 14.
[72] Ibid., p. 31.

The data subject's consent is the most important legitimation for the processing of their personal data, especially in the private sector. To have legal effect, the consent to processing personal data must be freely given, specific and informed.

According to the Article 29 Working Party[73]:

> *Free consent means a voluntary decision, by an individual in possession of all of his faculties, taken in the absence of coercion of any kind, be it social, financial, psychological or other.*
>
> *Specific consent must relate to a well-defined, concrete situation in which the processing of … data is envisaged.*
>
> *Informed consent means consent by the data subject based upon an appreciation and understanding of the facts and implications of an action. The individual concerned must be given, in a clear and understandable manner, accurate and full information of all relevant issues, in particular those specified in Articles 10 and 11 of the directive, such as the nature of the data processed, purposes of the processing, the recipients of possible transfers, and the rights of the data subject. This includes also an awareness of the consequences of not consenting to the processing in question.*

A particular form of consent is not required by the directive. Consent can, for example, be given verbally or in writing. However, since consent must be given free of doubt, presumed consent is void. What is required is an unambiguous act of consent[74]. Consent based on an individual's inaction or silence would normally not constitute valid consent, especially in an online context[75].

Withdrawing consent: Although the right of the data subject to withdraw consent is not explicitly mentioned in the Data Protection Directive, the Article 29 Working Party points out that this right is implicit in the directive. If consent has been withdrawn and there is no other legal ground for processing this data subject's personal data, the controller should delete them. Withdrawal of consent can only be exercised for the future and does not undermine the legitimacy of previous data processing[76].

---

73 Article 29 Data Protection Working Party, *Working Document on the processing of personal data relating to health in electronic health records (EHR)*, adopted on 15 February 2007, available at: ec.europa.eu/justice/policies/privacy/docs/wpdocs/2007/wp131_en.pdf, pp. 8 et seq.

74 Ehmann/Helfrich, *EG Datenschutzrichtlinie Kurzkommentar*, Cologne, Dr. Otto Schmidt, 1999, Art. 7 paras 12 et seqq.

75 Article 29 Data Protection Working Party, *Opinion 15/2011 on the definition of consent*, adopted on 13 July 2011, available at: http://ec.europa.eu/justice/policies/privacy/docs/wpdocs/2011/wp187_en.pdf, p. 35.

76 Ibid., p. 33.

1.2.4 Processing of personal data

The Data Protection Directive lays down the standards which have to be met to legitimate the processing of personal data. Principles of processing personal data play a crucial role in the European data protection framework. They largely predetermine the parameters of data processing and are actively used in the assessment of compliance with data protection rules.

1.2.4.1 Fair and lawful processing

The main principle of data protection law is that personal data must be processed fairly and lawfully[77] (Art. 6(1)(a) Data Protection Directive). This provision basically requires data controllers to comply with all relevant data protection rules, especially those of the directive.

1.2.4.2 Informing the data subject

Related to the principle of fair and lawful processing is the requirement to keep the data subject informed about the use of their data. As can be seen from the wording of Arts 10 and 11 Data Protection Directive, personal data must principally be obtained from the data subject themself. Before personal data are obtained, the data subject must be informed about:

> *(a) the identity of the controller and of his representative, (b) the purposes of the processing for which the data are intended, (c) information such as the recipients or categories of recipients of the data, whether replies to the questions are obligatory or voluntary, as well as the possible consequences of failure to reply and the existence of the right of access to and the right to rectify the data concerning him.*

Where personal data have not been obtained from the data subject, Member States shall provide that the controller must at the time of undertaking the recording of personal data or, if a disclosure to a third party is envisaged, no later than the time when the data are first disclosed, provide the data subject with similar information. Secret data collection is excluded on principle[78].

1.2.4.3 The purpose limitation for processing personal data

The principle of purpose limitation stipulates, in short, that personal data should be collected for specified, legitimate purposes and not used in ways that are incompatible with those purposes[79].

---

[77] Bygrave, *Data Privacy Law*, Oxford, Oxford University Press, 2014, p. 146.
[78] Hatt, *Konfliktfeld Datenschutz und Forschung*, Baden-Baden, Nomos, 2012, p. 156.
[79] Bygrave, *Data Privacy Law*, Oxford, Oxford University Press, 2014, p. 153.

Art. 6(1)(b) Data Protection Directive states that:

personal data must be collected for specified, explicit and legitimate purposes and not further processed in a way incompatible with those purposes.

Art. 6(1)(b) Data Protection Directive contains the key principle that personal data may only be collected for a specific purpose. To comply with this principle it is necessary to define the purpose of collecting personal data and the institutions which process the data before the data are actually collected[80]. After the collection, the data must be used for the intended purpose and not for any other purpose. Changing of a purpose is only possible within very narrow limits and requires the further processing to be compatible with the purposes for which the personal data was originally collected[81].

The Article 29 Working Party has clarified requirements with respect to the specification of data processing purposes. The purpose should be "specified" in the sense that it should be sufficiently defined to allow delimitation of the scope of each processing operation[82]. To be "explicit" the purpose must be sufficiently unambiguous and clearly revealed, explained or expressed in some intelligible form[83]. The purpose is "legitimate" if it is compliant not only with data protection rules, but also with other applicable laws in general[84].

Regarding the definition of the purpose of processing it is important to note that the purpose needs to be defined as precisely as possible. The degree of detail depends on the particular context in which the data are collected and the personal data involved[85]. However, to guarantee informed consent from the data subject it is necessary to give them all the information needed to understand the scope of their decision[86]. Within the field of scientific research, especially complex research projects, this can lead to difficulties. On the one side the research team has to describe the use of the data within the complex project in as much detail as possible to legitimise all intended uses of the collected data. On the other side the

---

80 See Dammann/Simitis, *EG-Datenschutzrichtlinie Kommentar*, Baden-Baden, Nomos, 1997, Art. 6 para. 5; see also Recital 28 of the Data Protection Directive.

81 See Hatt, *Konfliktfeld Datenschutz und Forschung*, Baden-Baden, Nomos, 2012, p. 152.

82 Article 29 Data Protection Working Party, *Opinion 3/2013 on purpose limitation*, p. 12.

83 Ibid., pp. 12, 17.

84 Ibid., p. 20.

85 Ibid., p. 16.

86 See Rogosch, *Die Einwilligung im Datenschutzrecht*, Baden-Baden, Nomos, 2013, p. 69; Holznagel/Sonntag, in Roßnagel, *Handbuch Datenschutzrecht*, Munich, C.H. Beck, 2003, chapter 4.8 para. 48.

description needs to be simple enough for the data subject to understand[87]. Against this background it is worth thinking about deeming the notification of the data subject on core information as sufficient to guarantee an informed consent[88].

After personal data have been collected they can be further processed only for those purposes which are "not incompatible" with the original ones. "Further processing" implies *any* processing following collection, whether for the purposes initially specified or for any additional purposes[89]. What further processing is considered as compatible is not defined in the Data Protection Directive and should be assessed on a case-by-case basis. The Article 29 Working Party formulates the following cumulative key factors to be considered in assessment of compatibility:[90]

- the relationship between the purposes for which the data have been collected and the purposes of further processing;
- the context in which the data have been collected and the reasonable expectations of the data subjects as to their further use;
- the nature of the data and the impact of the further processing on the data subjects; and
- the safeguards applied by the controller (such as technical and/or organisational measures to ensure functional separation) to ensure fair processing and to prevent any undue impact on the data subjects.

If the purpose has changed it is recommended that an additional notice be given to the data subject or even that they be offered an opt-in or opt-out, depending on the circumstances[91].

It is also explicitly noted that a new legal ground does not help to rectify incompatibility of further processing. However, a separate consent could compensate the change of purpose to some extent[92].

1.2.4.4 Further processing for historical, statistical or scientific purposes

Art. 6(1)(b) Data Protection Directive specifies that:

> *Further processing of data for historical, statistical or scientific purposes shall not be considered as incompatible provided that Member States provide appropriate safeguards.*

---

[87] See Hatt, *Konfliktfeld Datenschutz und Forschung*, Baden-Baden, Nomos, 2012, p. 58; Rogosch, *Die Einwilligung im Datenschutzrecht*, Baden-Baden, Nomos, 2013, p. 73.

[88] Wiebe, 'Datenschutz in Zeiten von Web 2.0 und BIG DATA – dem Untergang geweiht oder auf dem Weg zum Immaterialgüterrecht?', ZIR 2014, 35 (39); cf. also Eidenmüller, 'Liberaler Paternalismus', JZ 2011, 814 (818 et seq.).

[89] Article 29 Data Protection Working Party, *Opinion 3/2013 on purpose limitation*, p. 21.

[90] Ibid., p. 24 et seqq.

[91] Ibid., p. 26.

[92] Ibid., p. 27.

Recital 29 of the Data Protection Directive states that the further processing of personal data for historical, statistical or scientific purposes is not generally to be considered incompatible with the purposes for which the data have previously been collected, provided that Member States furnish suitable safeguards; these safeguards must in particular rule out the use of the data in support of measures or decisions regarding any particular individual.

The term "rule out" suggests that the safeguards should be strong enough to exclude or at least minimise any risks to the data subjects; but this exemption should not be read as providing an overall exemption from the requirement of compatibility. Thus, it does not generally authorise further processing of data for historical, statistical or scientific purposes in all cases[93].

The term "measures or decisions" regarding any particular individual should also be interpreted in the broadest sense, irrespective of whether they are taken by the controller or by anyone else; national law, professional codes of conduct and/or further guidance by data protection authorities (DPAs) can further specify what particular safeguards may be considered as appropriate[94].

Among factors relevant in choosing appropriate safeguards, the Article 29 Working Party refers to the possibility of identification of the data subject, the nature of personal data, and the potential impact on the data subject[95]. It also identifies different scenarios requiring different safeguards[96]:

- Scenario 1: unidentifiable personal data – data are anonymised or aggregated in such a way that there is no remaining possibility of (reasonably) identifying the data subjects.
- Scenario 2: indirectly identifiable personal data – lower level of aggregation, partial anonymisation, pseudonymisation or key-coded data.
- Scenario 3: situations where directly identifiable personal data are needed due to the nature of the research.

A few possible safeguards are discussed, such as full anonymisation (the most definitive solution), specific additional security measures (such as encryption) in case of pseudonymisation, making sure that data enabling the linking of information to a data subject (the keys) are themselves also coded or encrypted and stored separately, etc.[97].

---

[93] Ibid., p. 28.
[94] Ibid., p. 28.
[95] Ibid., pp. 31 et seq.
[96] Ibid., p. 30.
[97] Ibid., pp. 31 et seq.

In the context of sharing PSI for re-use, the Article 29 Working Party recommends a rigorous licensing regime in order to limit re-use of personal data for incompatible purposes[98]. Arguably, this recommendation is also applicable in a situation in which it is important to "rule out" that the data processed for historical, statistical and scientific purposes will be used "in support of measures or decisions regarding any particular individual or for other incompatible purposes", as prescribed in Recital 29 of the Data Protection Directive.

Opening up personal data (as a part of PSI) for re-use under an open licence without any technical and legal restrictions on re-use should generally be avoided[99]. The licence conditions should clearly define the limits of the use of such data. This can be done by explicitly mentioning the purposes for which data were first published and giving an indication of compatible and non-compatible uses[100].

In respect of anonymised public sector data intended for sharing and re-use, the Article 29 Working Party outlines the following requirements of the licence conditions[101], which must:

- reiterate that the datasets have been anonymised;
- prohibit licence-holders from re-identifying any individuals;
- prohibit licence-holders from using the data to take any measure or decision with regard to the individuals concerned;
- contain an obligation on the licence-holder to notify the licensor in case it is detected that individuals can be or have been re-identified;
- contain a procedure for recalling the compromised dataset in the event an increased risk of re-identification is discovered (the right of the licensor to suspend or terminate accessibility of data).

With regard to the scope of "historical, statistical, or scientific purposes", these purposes should not necessarily serve the public interest. In particular, "statistical purposes" include a wide range of processing activities, from commercial purposes (e.g. analytical tools of websites or big data applications aimed at market research) to public interests (e.g. statistical information produced from data collected by hospitals to determine the number of people injured as a result of road accidents)[102].

---

98 Article 29 Data Protection Working Party, *Opinion 6/2013 on open data and public sector information ('PSI') reuse*, p. 19.
99 Ibid., p. 19.
100 Ibid., p. 26.
101 Ibid., pp. 25 et seq.
102 Article 29 Data Protection Working Party, *Opinion 3/2013 on purpose limitation*, p. 29.

The Article 29 Working Party also emphasises that it is necessary to distinguish between situations where further processing is carried out by the initial data controller and where personal data will be transferred to a third party. In the opinion of the Article 29 Working Party, some research projects may require very precise protocols (rules and procedures) to guarantee strict functional separation between participants in the research and outside stakeholders. These may include technical and organisational measures, such as securely key-coding the personal data transferred and prohibiting outside stakeholders from re-identifying data subjects (as in the case of clinical trials and pharmaceutical research) and other possible measures[103].

1.2.4.5 Principle of proportionality or data minimisation

Art. 6(1)(c) Data Protection Directive outlines the principle of proportionality or the principle of data minimisation, respectively. Personal data must be

> *adequate, relevant and not excessive in relation to the purposes for which they are collected and/or further processed.*

This regulation clarifies that the processing of personal data should be limited to the minimum amount necessary[104].

Further expressions of this principle are mentioned in Art. 6(1)(d) and (e), according to which the data controller has to keep personal data accurate, where necessary up to date and in a form which permits identification of data subjects no longer than is necessary for the purposes for which the data were collected.

This implies that personal data must be destroyed after the purpose of their collection has been achieved[105]. This restriction, however, does not apply to data kept in a form that does not permit identification of data subjects, in other words, to anonymised data[106].

Compliance with the limited data retention requirement, according to the European Commission, can be ensured by automatic anonymisation of data after a certain lapse of time[107]. However, it should be recalled here that in the case of longer storage of anonymised data the risks of re-identification of anonymised data should be taken into account and regularly assessed.

---

[103] Ibid., p. 29.

[104] Kuner, *European Data Protection Law: Corporate Compliance and Regulation*, Oxford, Oxford University Press, 2007, p. 74.

[105] European Union Agency for Fundamental Rights, *Handbook on European Data Protection Law*, Council of Europe, 2014, text available at: http://fra.europa.eu/sites/default/files/fra-2014-handbook-data-protection-law_en.pdf, p. 73.

[106] Article 29 Data Protection Working Party, *Opinion 5/2014 on anonymisation techniques*, p. 7.

[107] Communication from the Commission to the European Parliament and the Council on Promoting Data Protection by Privacy Enhancing Technologies (PETs), Brussels, 2 May 2007, COM(2007) 228, p. 3.

Analysing this principle in the context of sharing PSI for re-use, the Article 29 Working Party concludes that it is difficult or sometimes impossible to ensure that data are deleted or removed after they have been published and made available for re-use, and thus to comply with the requirement of Art. 6(1)(e) of the Data Protection Directive; one of the ways to mitigate this difficulty is by not making data available in a downloadable form or only making them available via a customised application programming interface (API) and subject to certain restrictions and security measures[108].

1.2.4.6 Longer-term storage of personal data for scientific use

Keeping data for future scientific, historical or statistical use is explicitly exempt from the principle of limited data retention in the Data Protection Directive (Art. 6(1)(e)). Special safeguards laid down by the Member States should accompany such ongoing storage and use.

The scope of "scientific, historical or statistical" purposes should be understood in the same way as in relation to exemptions from the principle of purpose limitation[109].

1.2.4.7 Prohibition with the reservation of permission

According to Art. 7 of the Data Protection Directive, personal data may be processed only if one of the reasons for processing mentioned is applicable. The Data Protection Directive is based on the principle that every collection or processing of personal data is generally forbidden; it is only allowed if the data subject consents to the collection or processing of their data or the collection or processing is permitted or required by law[110]. As long as there is no consent for the processing of personal data given by the data subject, or any other justification, the processing of personal data is illegal.

The Data Protection Directive contains two sets of rules for lawful processing of personal data: rules for general categories of personal data (Art. 7) and special stricter rules for sensitive data (Art. 8).

1.2.4.7.1 Processing of general categories of personal data

An exhaustive list of legal grounds for processing of general categories of data is outlined in Art. 7 of the Data Protection Directive. The most relevant legal ground in the context of sharing research data (at least as long as there is no

108 Article 29 Data Protection Working Party, *Opinion 6/2013 on open data and public sector information ('PSI') reuse*, p. 22.

109 See above Section 1.2.4.4.

110 Hatt, *Konfliktfeld Datenschutz und Forschung*, Baden-Baden, Nomos, 2012, p. 137; Gounalakis/Mand, 'Die neue EG-Datenschutzrichtlinie – Grundlagen einer Umsetzung in nationales Recht (I)', CR 1997, 421 (433).

special legislation on this issue) is unambiguous consent given by the data subject (Art. 7(a) Data Protection Directive). For the consent[111] to be "unambiguous", the procedure to seek and to give consent must leave no doubt as to the data subject's intention to deliver consent[112].

It should be kept in mind that obtaining the data subject's consent does not free the controller from compliance with other data protection rules[113].

1.2.4.7.2 Processing of special categories of personal data

Processing of special categories of personal data is prohibited unless one (or more) of the five legal grounds for processing such data outlined in Art. 8(2) of the Data Protection Directive is present. The legal grounds most relevant in the context of this study are explicit consent of the data subject (Art. 8(2)(a)) and when "the processing relates to data which are manifestly made public by the data subject" (Art. 8(2)(e)).

"Explicit consent" should be understood as having the same meaning as express consent. This implies that to comply with this requirement there should be an opt-in consent in the form of an affirmative act by the data subject, clearly indicating the data subject's assent to processing of special categories of data[114]. Opt-out solutions will not meet this requirement[115].

Explicit consent cannot be applied as a legal ground for processing special categories of personal data in a Member State if its national law provides that the prohibition on processing special categories of personal data may not be lifted by the data subject's consent (Art. 8(2)(a) of the directive).

If the data subject manifestly made their personal data public, it is presumed that this action must be interpreted as implying their consent to the processing of their personal data[116]. However, making special categories of data manifestly public would not always and in itself be a sufficient condition to allow any type of data processing without an assessment of the balance of interests and rights at stake, as is required in Art. 7(f) of the Data Protection Directive in respect of processing general categories of data for the purposes of legitimate interests of the

---

[111] The term consent is defined above in Section 1.2.3.7.

[112] Article 29 Data Protection Working Party, *Opinion 15/2011 on the definition of consent*, p. 21.

[113] Ibid., p. 7.

[114] Kuner, *European Data Protection Law: Corporate Compliance and Regulation*, Oxford, Oxford University Press, 2007, p. 102.

[115] Article 29 Data Protection Working Party, *Opinion 15/2011 on the definition of consent*, p. 25; Kuner, *European Data Protection Law: Corporate Compliance and Regulation*, Oxford University Press, 2007, p. 102.

[116] European Union Agency for Fundamental Rights, *Handbook on European Data Protection Law*, Council of Europe, 2014, text available at: http://fra.europa.eu/sites/default/files/fra-2014-handbook-data-protection-law_en.pdf, p. 88.

controller of the third party[117]. Furthermore, given the nature of the data involved, the phrase "manifestly made public" should be interpreted narrowly to mean an "obvious and conscious readiness by the data subject to make the data available to any member of the general public"[118].

In accordance with Art. 8(4) of the Data Protection Directive, Member States may lay down exemptions in addition to those mentioned in Art. 8(2) of the directive, either by national law or by decision of the supervisory authority, for reasons of substantial public interest in areas such as scientific research and government statistics. This possibility is, however, subject to the provision of specific and suitable safeguards by the Member States to protect the fundamental rights and the privacy of individuals (see also Recital 34 Data Protection Directive). This implies that there will be a certain variation of legitimate grounds for processing special categories of personal data for purposes which may be considered to serve the public interest by each of the EU Member States.

1.2.4.8 Transparency of personal data processing

Transparency is an important principle of data processing. It is aimed at empowering the data subject to make informed choices in respect of processing of their personal data, in particular, to grant informed consent for data processing.

The scope of the controller's obligation to provide information to the data subject depends on the way in which the controller obtains personal data: directly from the data subject or in any other way (e.g. from third parties). In the present context, further recipients of research data will always qualify as controllers that obtained personal data not from data subjects. The research organisation that initiates data sharing may, depending on the circumstances, qualify both as a controller who obtained data directly from the data subject and as a controller who obtained data from other sources.

If personal data are collected directly from the data subject the controller or their representative must provide the data subject with at least information about the identity of the controller and of their representative and the intended purposes of the processing, unless the data subject already has this information (Art. 10 Data Protection Directive).

---

[117] Article 29 Data Protection Working Party, *Opinion 6/2014 on the notion of legitimate interests of the data controller under Article 7 of the Directive 95/46/EC*, adopted on 9 April 2014, available at: http://ec.europa.eu/justice/data-protection/article-29/documentation/opinion-recommendation/files/2014/wp217_en.pdf, p. 15.

[118] Bygrave, in Becker/Buhse/Grünnewig/Rump, *Digital Rights Management*, Berlin et al., Springer, 2003, p. 435.

The controller (or their representative) is also required to provide further information, such as the recipients or categories of recipients of the data, to the extent that such further information "is necessary, having regard to the specific circumstances in which the data are collected, to guarantee fair processing in respect of the data subject" (Art. 10(c) Data Protection Directive).

Where personal data have not been obtained from the data subject, the controller or their representative must provide the data subject with at least information about the identity of the controller and of their representative and the purposes of the processing, unless the data subject already has such information (Art. 11(1) Data Protection Directive). Thus, the minimum scope of required information is the same as when data are obtained directly from the data subject.

The controller should provide further information, such as information on the recipients or categories of recipients, in so far as such further information is necessary, having regard to the specific circumstances in which the data are processed, to guarantee fair processing in respect of the data subject (Art. 11(1)(c) Data Protection Directive).

All information should be provided to the data subject either at the time when personal data are recorded or, if the controller intends to disclose personal data to a third party, no later than the time of the first disclosure of the data (Art. 11(1) and Recital 39 of the Data Protection Directive).

The Data Protection Directive provides for certain exemptions from the obligation to provide the data subject with the above-mentioned information when personal data have not been collected from the data subject.

According to Art. 11(2) Data Protection Directive, this obligation shall not apply where:

- *in particular* for processing for statistical purposes or for the purposes of historical or scientific research, the provision of such information proves impossible or would involve a disproportionate effort, or
- if recording or disclosure is expressly laid down by law.

In these cases, Member States must provide appropriate safeguards.

It is worth noting that processing for statistical purposes or for the purposes of historical or scientific research is just one of the cases when informing the data subject could prove impossible or would involve disproportionate efforts (Recital 40 Data Protection Directive). In assessing impossibility or disproportionality of efforts to inform the data subject, "the number of data subjects, the age of the data, and any compensatory measures adopted may be taken into consideration" (Recital 40 Data Protection Directive).

A core principle of data protection law is that persons should be able to participate in, and have measures of influence over, the processing of data on them by others[119].

The Data Protection Directive provides some rights for the data subject. Art. 12(a) of the directive includes rights of access:

> *Member States shall guarantee every data subject the right to obtain from the controller without constraint at reasonable intervals and without excessive delay or expense:*
>
> - *confirmation as to whether or not data relating to him are being processed and information at least as to the purposes of the processing, the categories of data concerned, and the recipients or categories of recipients to whom the data are disclosed,*
> - *communication to him in an intelligible form of the data undergoing processing and of any available information as to their source,*
> - *knowledge of the logic involved in any automatic processing of data concerning him ....*

Art. 12(b) of the directive additionally adds the rights of rectification, erasure or blocking of data if the processing of personal data does not comply with the provisions of the directive, in particular because of the incomplete or inaccurate nature of the data.

Art. 12(c) of the directive gives the data subject the right to obtain from the controller the notification to third parties to whom the data have been disclosed of any rectification, erasure or blocking carried out in compliance with Art. 12(b) unless this proves impossible or involves a disproportionate effort.

Subject to adequate legal safeguards, these rights of the data subject can be restricted by a legislative measure of national law (Art. 13(2) Data Protection Directive):

> *When data are processed solely for purposes of scientific research or are kept in personal form for a period which does not exceed the period necessary for the sole purpose of creating statistics*

and

> *There is clearly no risk of breaching the privacy of the data subject.*

Art. 13(2) Data Protection Directive gives an example of appropriate safeguards – it must be ensured that no measures or decisions regarding any particular individual are taken in the context of such data processing. Member States may provide for other safeguards.

---

[119] Bygrave, *Data Privacy Law*, Oxford, Oxford University Press, 2014, p. 158.

1.2.4.10 Measures to ensure security of processing

Art. 17(1) in conjunction with Recital 46 Data Protection Directive requires the controller to "implement appropriate technical and organisational measures to protect personal data against accidental or unlawful destruction or accidental loss, alteration, unauthorised disclosure or access" and "against all other unlawful forms of processing".

When a controller authorises a processor to process personal data on their behalf, the controller must ensure that the processor takes sufficient technical and organisational measures to guarantee the security of data processing (Art. 17(2) Data Protection Directive).

Art. 17(1) Data Protection Directive names the following factors as relevant for the choice of appropriate security measures[120]:

- the state of the art, i.e. the security features available in the market for any particular type of processing,
- the costs of their implementation,
- sensitivity of the data processed, and
- risks represented by the processing.

In the light of these factors, security measures must ensure an appropriate level of security.

Data security cannot be fully achieved by technical measures of protection such as software and hardware. It also requires appropriate organisational measures such as clear distribution of rights and competences among employees, regular information to employees about security rules, protection of access to locations, data security training, and education[121].

1.2.4.11 Trans-border data flows

The harmonisation of data protection law within the EU aims at establishing a single European market for the processing of personal data. Within this single market, Member States shall neither restrict nor prohibit the free flow of personal data between Member States for reasons connected with the protection of personal data (see Art. 1(2) Data Protection Directive).

---

[120] See also European Union Agency for Fundamental Rights, *Handbook on European Data Protection Law*, Council of Europe, 2014, text available at: http://fra.europa.eu/sites/default/files/fra-2014-handbook-data-protection-law_en.pdf, p. 90.

[121] Ibid., p. 92.

Concerning the transfer of personal data to third countries, the directive contains some special rules. According to Art. 25(1):

> *The transfer to a third country of personal data which are undergoing processing or are intended for processing after transfer may take place only if, without prejudice to compliance with the national provisions adopted pursuant to the other provisions of this Directive, the third country in question ensures an adequate level of protection.*

If no adequate level of data protection is guaranteed, the transfer to a third country is not allowed. In this respect Art. 25(1) implies a general prohibition of data transfers to third countries[122]. Art. 25(2)–(6) and Art. 26 Data Protection Directive stipulate some rules on how an adequate level of protection is assessed and ensured and define some exceptions to that principle.

Although the US does not ensure an adequate level of protection, the European Commission has adopted a decision[123] that the transfer of personal data to an entity in the US is allowed if such entity undertakes to comply with the Safe Harbour principles laid down by an agreement between the EU and the US. However, this decision was recently quashed by the ECJ[124] and is therefore invalid. Thus the transfer of personal data to the US can no longer be justified by the Safe Harbour principles.

In order to solve this problem, the US and the EU agreed on a new framework for transatlantic exchanges of personal data known as the "EU-US Privacy Shield". The Commission decided that those new rules guarantee an adequate level of data protection in the US[125]. Nevertheless, the Commission's decision has been harshly criticised and it is questioned whether those rules are really sufficient to ensure adequate data protection.

According to Art. 26(1)(a) Data Protection Directive unambiguous consent of the data subject for the proposed transfer is a derogation from the rule that the transfer to a third country without an adequate level of data protection is not allowed. However, in the event of repeated or structural transfers (which may be the case in the context of research data sharing) consent is "unlikely to provide an adequate long-term framework for data controllers"[126]. There is always a risk that one or more data subjects will subsequently withdraw their consent.

---

122 See Dammann/Simitis, *EG-Datenschutzrichtlinie Kommentar*, Baden-Baden, Nomos, 1997, Art. 25 para. 4.

123 Commission Decision 2000/520/EC of 26 July 2000, text available at: http://eur-lex.europa.eu/legal-content/EN/TXT/PDF/?uri=CELEX:32000D0520&from=en.

124 ECJ Case C-362/14 (6.11.2015), *Schrems v Data Protection Commissioner.*

125 See Commission Implementing Decision (EU) 2016/1250 of 12 July 2016, available at: http://eur-lex.europa.eu/legal-content/DE/TXT/?uri=uriserv:OJ.L_.2016.207.01.0001.01.DEU.

126 Article 29 Data Protection Working Party, *Working document on a common interpretation of Article 26(1) of Directive 95/46/EC of 24 October 1995*, adopted on 25 November 2005, available at: http://ec.europa.eu/justice/data-protection/article-29/documentation/opinion-recommendation/files/2005/wp114_en.pdf, p. 11.

Other derogations for data transfer to third countries not ensuring adequate levels of protection are:

- the transfer is necessary for the performance of a contract between the data subject and the controller or the implementation of precontractual measures taken in response to the data subject's request (Art. 26(1)(b) Data Protection Directive); or
- the transfer is necessary for the conclusion or performance of a contract concluded in the interest of the data subject between the controller and a third party (Art. 26(1)(c) Data Protection Directive); or
- the transfer is necessary or legally required on important public interest grounds, or for the establishment, exercise or defence of legal claims (Art. 26(1)(d) Data Protection Directive); or
- the transfer is necessary in order to protect the vital interests of the data subject (Art. 26(1)(e) Data Protection Directive); or
- the transfer is made from a register which, according to laws or regulations, is intended to provide information to the public and which is open to consultation either by the public in general or by any person who can demonstrate legitimate interest, to the extent that the conditions laid down in law for consultation are fulfilled in the particular case (Art. 26(1)(b) Data Protection Directive).
- authorisation of data transfer or a set of transfers by a competent authority of the state, complemented by adequate safeguards on the part of the controller (Art. 26(2) Data Protection Directive);
- standard contractual clauses approved by the Commission included in the contract with each recipient of data (Art. 26(4) Data Protection Directive); and
- binding corporate rules as a means to provide adequate safeguards within the meaning of Art. 26(2) Data Protection Directive[127].

Cross-border transfer of data means the transfer of personal data from a country falling under the Data Protection Directive to another country outside this area. The way in which the data are transferred is generally irrelevant. A transfer can be made, for example, by delivering a data carrier to a person outside the EU or by transmitting the data online via the Internet to such person.

---

[127] Article 29 Data Protection Working Party, *Working document on a common interpretation of Article 26(1) of Directive 95/46/EC of 24 October 1995*, adopted on 25 November 2005, p. 9.

The Commission has so far recognised Andorra, Argentina, Canada (commercial organisations), Faroe Islands, Guernsey, Israel, Isle of Man, Jersey, New Zealand, Switzerland and Uruguay as providing adequate protection[128].

Online sharing of data raises the question of whether such sharing can be qualified as cross-border transfer of data. In the *Lindqvist* case the ECJ concluded that uploading materials onto an Internet page, which can be consulted and which is hosted by a person established in a third country, thereby making those data accessible worldwide, does not constitute transfer of data to a third country within the meaning of Art. 25 Data Protection Directive[129].

However, this conclusion should be applied with care. The judgment concerns a fact-specific particular case and may not have a universal application to all cases of online data sharing. There is an opinion, which is supported by some of the national DPAs (e.g. the Dutch Authority) that making personal data available online can be viewed as cross-border data transfer if it involves "granting access to the data of other parties on a large scale for business purposes"[130]. As a result, it is not clear whether the *purpose* (business or non-profit) of intentionally making data available online is crucial for its qualification as cross-border transfer. Nevertheless, it can be admitted that online data sharing, for example for the purposes of scientific research, may still qualify as cross-border data transfer if such sharing is done with a clear intention to make data available to third parties located in one or several other countries.

1.2.4.12 Data protection control

In order to guarantee compliance with the provisions of the Data Protection Directive, independent public supervisory authorities must be established. Art. 28(1) of the directive requires each Member State to:

> *provide that one or more public authorities are responsible for monitoring the application within its territory of the provisions adopted by the Member States pursuant to this Directive.*
>
> *These authorities shall act with complete independence in exercising the functions entrusted to them.*

---

[128] See http://ec.europa.eu/justice/data-protection/international-transfers/adequacy/index_en.htm.

[129] ECJ Case C-101/01 (6.11.2003), *Lindqvist*, para. 4.

[130] Kuner, *European Data Protection Law: Corporate Compliance and Regulation*, Oxford, Oxford University Press, 2007, p. 83.

It is for the individual Member State to ensure the independence of the supervisory authorities[131]. However, the ECJ has ruled on numerous occasions that the authorities need complete independence:

> *The establishment in Member States of independent supervisory authorities is thus an essential component of the protection of individuals with regard to the processing of personal data*[132].
>
> *The second subparagraph of Article 28(1) of the Data Protection Directive must be interpreted as meaning that the supervisory authorities responsible for supervising the processing of personal data must enjoy an independence allowing them to perform their duties free from external influence. That independence precludes inter alia any directions or any other external influence in whatever form, whether direct or indirect, which may have an effect on their decisions and which could call into question the performance by those authorities of their task of striking a fair balance between the protection of the right to private life and the free movement of personal data*[133].

The head of a supervisory authority cannot be appointed solely by an executive authority and may only be dismissed in certain cases. With respect to the performance of their duties, the supervisory authorities are not subject to any instructions[134].

The competences of the supervisory authorities are set out in Art. 28(3) Data Protection Directive. Each authority shall in particular be endowed with:

> *- investigative powers, such as powers of access to data forming the subject-matter of processing operations and powers to collect all the information necessary for the performance of its supervisory duties,*
>
> *- effective powers of intervention, such as, for example, that of delivering opinions before processing operations are carried out … and ensuring appropriate publication of such opinions, of ordering the blocking, erasure or destruction of data, of imposing a temporary or definitive ban on processing, of warning or admonishing the controller, or that of referring the matter to national parliaments or other political institutions,*
>
> *- the power to engage in legal proceedings where the national provisions adopted pursuant to this Directive have been violated or to bring these violations to the attention of the judicial authorities.*

---

131 Dammann/Simitis, *EG-Datenschutzrichtlinie Kommentar*, Baden-Baden, Nomos, 1997, Art. 28 para. 6.

132 ECJ Case C-288/12 (8.4.2014), *European Commission v Hungary*, para. 48.

133 ECJ Cases C-288/12 (8.4.2014), *European Commission v Hungary*, para. 51; C-518/07 (9.3.2010), *European Commission v Germany*, para. 30; C-614/10 (16.10.2012), *European Commission v Austria*, paras 41 and 43.

134 Kühling/Seidel/Sivridis, *Datenschutzrecht*, 2nd edition, Heidelberg, C.F. Müller, 2011, p. 34.

In addition to the national supervisory authorities, Art. 29 Data Protection Directive set up a Working Party on the Protection of Individuals with Regard to the Processing of Personal Data. The "Article 29 Working Party" shall be composed of a representative of the supervisory authority designated by each Member State and of a representative of the authority established for the Community institutions and bodies, and of a representative of the Commission.

The Article 29 Working Party has advisory status and acts independently. Its task is to contribute to the uniform application of the Data Protection Directive, to analyse the level of protection in the Community and in third countries, and generally to advise the Commission on data protection matters[135].

1.2.4.13 Room for manoeuvre for Member States

According to Art. 288 TFEU, a directive shall be binding, as to the result to be achieved, upon each Member State to which it is addressed, but shall leave to the national authorities the choice of form and methods. Apart from this inherent flexibility in the choice of form and methods in implementing its provisions, the Data Protection Directive explicitly identifies points on which Member States can create special rules or exemptions as compared to the provisions of the directive.

In the relevant context, the following points are worth mentioning:

- Art. 5 allows Member States to "determine more precisely the conditions under which the processing of personal data is lawful," within the limits of the provisions of Chapter II of the directive.
- Arts 7 and 8 in conjunction with Art. 5 allow Member States "to provide for special processing conditions for specific sectors and for the various categories of data covered by article 8" (see also Recital 22 of the directive).
- Art. 8(4) allows Member States to lay down exemptions from the prohibition of processing special categories of data, in addition to those mentioned in Art. 8(2) of the directive, subject to the provision of suitable safeguards, either by national law or by decision of the supervisory authority for reasons of substantial public interest in areas such as scientific research and government statistics (see also Recital 34 of the directive).

1.2.5 Other directives

There are two other directives of the European Parliament and the Council with relevance to the fundamental right of data protection.

Directive 2006/24/EC on the retention of data generated or processed in connection with the provision of publicly available electronic communications services or of public communications networks (Data Retention Directive)

---

[135] See also Recital 65 of the Data Protection Directive.

required providers of publicly available electronic communications services or communications networks to store certain data in order to ensure the availability of the data for the purpose of investigation, detection and prosecution of crimes. However, this directive was recently quashed by the ECJ[136] and is therefore invalid.

The second directive is Directive 2002/58/EC concerning the processing of personal data and the protection of privacy in the electronic communications sector (Directive on privacy and electronic communications). The aim of this directive is to ensure an equivalent level of protection of fundamental rights and freedoms, and in particular the right to privacy, with respect to the processing of personal data in the electronic communication sector and to ensure the free movement of such data and of electronic communication equipment and services in the Community. Since the focus of this directive is the communication sector, it is of minor relevance in the context of the development of an electronic infrastructure such as OpenAIRE and the Open Research Data Pilot.

1.3 Implementation in different Member States

The following section will evaluate how different Member States have implemented the Data Protection Directive and what differences still exist.

1.3.1 The Netherlands

At the core of the Dutch data protection framework is the Dutch Data Protection Act (*Wet bescherming persoonsgegevens*; DDPA) of 6 July 2000[137], which transposes the EU Data Protection Directive into Dutch law.

The DDPA follows the structure of the directive. While the Act accurately implements the provisions of the directive, the Dutch legislator has exercised its freedom to choose methods of implementation of the directive by elaborating certain provisions in greater detail and has used the room for manoeuvre offered in Arts 5, 7 and 8 of the directive.

The following analysis of relevant aspects of Dutch data protection law is mainly based on the provisions of the DDPA, as interpreted in the Explanatory Memorandum (*Memorie van Toelichting*) to the Act and various guidelines of the Dutch Data Protection Authority (*College bescherming persoonsgegevens*, hereinafter referred to as the "Dutch Authority"). References are also made to the relevant case law and literature, as well as to the opinions of the Dutch Authority.

---

136 ECJ Joined Cases C-293/12 and C-594/12 (8.4.2014), *Digital Rights Ireland.*

137 An unofficial translation of the DDPA is available at: https://www.akd.nl/t/Documents/17-03-2016_ENG_Wet-bescherming-persoonsgegevens.pdf.

1.3.1.1.1 Personal data

The DDPA defines personal data in almost identical terms as in Art. 2(a) Data Protection Directive. According to Art. 1(a) of the Act, "personal data" means "any information relating to an identified or identifiable individual".

However, this definition does not include the definition of "identifiable person" contained in the second part of the European definition. Nevertheless, the interpretation of personal data given in the Explanatory Memorandum is very much in line with that provision of the directive, as well as with the approach taken by the Article 29 Working Party.

According to the Explanatory Memorandum, "information" should be understood in a broad sense. It embraces not only information in written text, but also pictures and sound[138]. Data relating to properties or things are generally not personal data. However, under certain conditions information about a product or process, phone numbers, car number plates and postcodes with house numbers can be considered as personal data. This is the case whenever the information is traceable to a particular person or provides some information about a particular person, for example allowing the assessment of a person's performance at work or the amount of tax levied against the owner of a house[139].

Which information "relates to" an individual is context specific; depending on the context in which it is processed, information can be qualified as personal data if it affects the way in which a person is assessed or treated in society[140]. For example, information is recognised as personal data when it can be used for a purpose focused on a person. Information that is a result of a decision taken with respect to a particular person can also be considered as personal data of this person.

Information which does not directly relate to an individual, and also does not – in the context in which it is processed – influence the way in which the person is assessed or treated in society, is not personal data.

---

138 Memorie van Toelichting, Kamerstukken II 1997/98, 25 892, nr. 3 (Explanatory Memorandum, Parliamentary Papers II 1997/98, 25 892, nr. 3), hereinafter "Explanatory Memorandum DDPA", available at: https://zoek.officielebekendmakingen.nl/kst-25892-3.pdf, p. 45 et seq.

139 Explanatory Memorandum DDPA, pp. 46 et seq.; the Dutch Authority Publication of Personal Data on the Internet, December 2007, available at: https://cbpweb.nl/sites/default/files/downloads/mijn_privacy/en_20071108_richtsnoeren_internet.pdf, section I, para. 4, p. 11.

140 Explanatory Memorandum DDPA, p. 46.

In defining which person is identifiable, two factors play a role: (1) the nature of the personal data and (2) the possibilities of the controller to bring about identification[141]. A person is identifiable if data alone or in combination with other data are so characteristic of a particular person that such person can be identified[142].

In relation to the nature of personal data, the Explanatory Memorandum distinguishes between directly and indirectly identifying data. Directly identifying data are data concerning a person, whose identity can be clearly determined with the help of such data without many detours. Such data include name, address and date of birth, which in combination are unique to and characteristic of a particular person so that this person in the wide sense can be identified with certainty or with a high degree of probability. It should, however, be kept in mind that removal of directly identifying characteristics as such does not always offer sufficient guarantee that the data are not personal data.

Indirectly identifying data do not directly lead to identification of a person. They may not contain a name, but through combination with other data can be associated with a particular person. These are unique in such a way that they are also identifying, such as social security number or unique biometric data, such as voice, fingerprints or DNA profiles[143].

In assessing the possibilities of the controller to identify the data subject, it is necessary to take into account all means from which it can reasonably be assumed that they can be used by the controller or any other person in order to identify the person. Hence, the controller should be reasonably equipped to make such a judgement. The standard of reasonableness correlates with Recital 26 of the Data Protection Directive. Account should be taken of special expertise and technical facilities of the controller. Thus, both the objective standard of a reasonable controller and the subjective measure of the particular controller's expertise should be applied[144].

The same set of standards applies to the recipient of data in the case of transfer of data to a third party. The controller should ask themself whether particular data in the hands of the recipient should be recognised as identifying. The deciding factor is what can reasonably be expected in a given situation. The more the sender has the possibility to foresee or to limit the risks of identification of the data subject by the recipient, the more careful behaviour may be expected[145].

---

141 Ibid., p. 47.

142 Ibid., p. 48.

143 Dutch Supreme Court, decision 03-03-2009, 07/13565 B, LJN BG9218 – health information on a patient can constitute indirectly identifying personal data.

144 Explanatory Memorandum DDPA, pp. 48 et seq.

145 Ibid., p. 49.

Thus, it could be that data do not qualify as personal data when handled by one person, and can be potentially qualified as such when transferred to a third party or shared with a broader public.

The conclusion as to what an "unreasonable" effort is can also change over time given the progress of information technologies. With the availability of new techniques an effort that used to be "unreasonable" may no longer be recognised as such. Therefore, data that are not considered personal data may be qualified as such in the future. The same is true of anonymous data[146]. As soon as data can be qualified as personal data, controllers can be subjected to legal action under the terms of the DDPA.

The long or undetermined lifetime of a publication on the Internet, according to the Dutch Authority, creates the risk that information that does not qualify as personal data or anonymised data can become personal data in the future. Therefore the Dutch Authority recommends that controllers who do not wish to act in contravention of the DDPA consider these risks and ensure that they apply a limited term of publication even to data that do not appear to be personal data. The Dutch Authority also recommends that immediate action be taken upon realising that the data can be used to identify persons[147]. This advice is also relevant with respect to research data shared online.

In principle, personal data include only information about living natural persons. Therefore data about dead persons do not fall under the definition of personal data unless they relate to a living natural person (e.g., a surviving relative, in the case of information relating to a hereditary disease) and can influence the way in which the latter can be assessed or treated in society[148].

Data relating to organisations, such as companies or foundations, are not per se considered as personal data either. However, the DDPA applies to companies if the data identify a person, such as in the case of a one-man business, or if they relate to the individual directors of a company or foundation[149].

1.3.1.1.2 Pseudonymised and anonymised data

Like the Data Protection Directive, the DDPA does not explicitly mention pseudonymised data. The Dutch Authority considers encoded or pseudonymised data as identifiable – and thus as personal data – in relation to actors who have means

---

146 Ibid., p. 49.

147 The Dutch Authority Publication of Personal Data on the Internet, December 2007, section I, para. 6, p. 12.

148 Explanatory Memorandum DDPA, p. 47; The Dutch Authority Publication of Personal Data on the Internet, December 2007, section I, para. 4, p. 11.

149 Ibid.

(the "key") to re-identify the data, but not in relation to other persons or entities[150]. Thus, in certain circumstances pseudonymised data can also be qualified as anonymous and, hence, as not personal data.

Following the logic of the Data Protection Directive, the DDPA does not mention anonymised data. As clarified in the Explanatory Memorandum, data are not personal data (i.e. anonymised) if effective measures were taken in order to reasonably exclude actual identification of an individual. An example of such measures is data coding in combination with additional adaptation or specific organisational measures. A controller can, for example, strip the data of directly identifying data and transfer those data or the key, thereby giving access to those data to a third party. Whether or not such data are considered as personal data depends on the extent to which it can be reasonably expected from the employees of the third party to cooperate with the controller. If this third party is subject to an obligation of confidentiality, which is actually enforced in practice, then it can be concluded that there are insufficient factual possibilities for factual identification of the data subject. It is factual circumstances rather than legal constructions that play a decisive role here[151].

According to the Dutch Authority, the question of whether an item of data is in fact anonymous is specifically raised during the publication of aggregated statistical information on the Internet. Although aggregation can reduce the distinctiveness of data[152], the Dutch Authority clarifies that aggregated information may still contain personal data if the number of data subjects is small and other information is available, for example by means of search engines, enabling identification of individual persons. The data must be treated as personal data in so far as the controller, or a third party, can still use the data to identify natural persons, without the deployment of disproportionate efforts[153].

Dutch scholars express similar concerns with respect to results of research data, which are usually presented in an aggregated way so that they can in no way be related to individual natural persons. Even if there is no risk for an individual,

---

150 Annex 2, "Evaluation of the implementation of the Data Protection Directive" to the Commission Staff Working Paper, Impact Assessment Accompanying the document, Regulation of the European Parliament and of the Council on the protection of individuals with regard to the processing of personal data and on the free movement of such data (General Data Protection Regulation) and Directive of the European Parliament and of the Council on the protection of individuals with regard to the processing of personal data by competent authorities for the purposes of prevention, investigation, detection or prosecution of criminal offences or the execution of criminal penalties, and the free movement of such data SEC(2012) 72 final Brussels, 25.1.2012 (Commission Working Paper SEC(2012) 72), available at: http://ec.europa.eu/justice/data-protection/document/review2012/sec_2012_72_en.pdf, p. 15.

151 Explanatory Memorandum DDPA, p. 49.

152 Ibid., pp. 49 et seq.

153 Explanatory Memorandum DDPA, p. 47; Dutch Authority Publication of Personal Data on the Internet, December 2007, section I, para. 5, pp. 11 et seq.

group privacy can be at stake because the aggregated, anonymous data can have consequences for groups of persons participating in research. The smaller the group, the higher the risk is[154].

1.3.1.1.3 Special categories of personal data

The scope of special categories of personal data is broader in Dutch law than in the Data Protection Directive. Besides personal data concerning a person's religion or philosophy of life, race, political persuasion, health and sexual life, and trade union membership, the DDPA also covers personal data information on a person's criminal behaviour, or unlawful or objectionable conduct connected with a ban imposed with regard to such conduct to special categories of personal data (Art. 16 DDPA).

According to the Explanatory Memorandum, the term "health life" should be understood in a broad sense. It includes not only data processed in the framework of medical research or medical treatment by a doctor, but also all data which concern the mental or physical health of a person[155]. Thus, data about IQ and socio-emotional problems in particular circumstances can be personal data too[156].

Processing of special categories of data is prohibited unless one or more exemptions from this prohibition are present.

1.3.1.1.4 Processing of personal data

The definition of "processing of personal data" in the DDPA closely repeats that of Art. 2(b) Data Protection Directive. According to Art. 1(b) of the Act, processing of personal data means any operation or a set of operations concerning personal data, including in any case collection, recording, organisation, storage, updating or modification, retrieval, consultation, use, transfer by means of transmission, distribution or making available in any other form, merging, linking, as well as blocking, erasure or destruction of data.

As clarified in the Explanatory Memorandum, the list of operations that count as processing of personal data is not exhaustive and the term "processing of personal data" should be interpreted in a broad sense. It includes the whole process that the data undergoes from the moment of collection to the moment of destruction[157].

---

[154] Holvast, *Wetenschappelijk onderzoek en privacy*, in Prins/Berkvens, *Privacyregulering in theorie en praktijk*, Deventer, Kluwer, 2002, p. 356.

[155] Explanatory Memorandum DDPA, p. 109.

[156] See Letter of the Dutch Data Protection Authority to the Dutch Ministry of Education, Culture and Science, 22 April 2003, No. z2003-00284, available at: https://cbpweb.nl/sites/default/files/downloads/adv/z2003-0284.pdf.

[157] Explanatory Memorandum DDPA, pp. 51 et seq.

Even though anonymisation is not explicitly named in the definition, it constitutes processing of personal data as a form of destruction of personal data, at least in cases when the deletion of the name also results in the fact that the data subject can no longer be traced[158].

Processing of personal data takes place as long as there is a possibility to exercise any influence over personal data. It is not relevant whether such influence is actually exercised. Thus, fully automated forms of processing personal data fall under the definition of processing too[159].

Unlike the Data Protection Directive, the DDPA explicitly mentions "transfer by means of transmission, distribution, or making available in any other form" as forms of data processing. Dutch law, however, does not define the concept of "transfer of personal data". According to the Explanatory Memorandum, "transfer of personal data" should be interpreted in a broad sense. The term includes any form of making available or providing personal data, irrespective of the way in which this happens. It can be oral, written or by electronic means, but also by means of transfer of a data storage device. Consulting the data, for example on a CD-ROM, also falls under transfer[160].

Although the Explanatory Memorandum qualifies the making available in any form as a form of transfer of personal data, the Department of Administrative Law of the Dutch Council of State[161] (*Afdeling Bestuursrechtspraak Raad van State*) held that access, whether or not authorised, to a system of electronic files of patients to consult digital medical files does not qualify as transfer of personal data, but as consultation or retrieval of such personal data[162].

The interpretation of "transfer of personal data" is crucial for assessing the lawfulness of publication of information containing personal data on the Internet. As soon as publication (or making available) qualifies as data transfer it can also be qualified as cross-border transfer, and thus be subject to a special set of rules and procedures.

1.3.1.1.5 Controller

Art. 1(d) DDPA defines the "controller"[163] as the natural person, legal person, administrative body or any other entity which, alone or in conjunction with others, determines the purpose and means of processing personal data.

---

158 Memorie van Antwoord, I, nr. 92c, p. 13.

159 Explanatory Memorandum DDPA, p. 52.

160 Explanatory Memorandum DDPA, p. 68.

161 Serves as the highest court of appeal in administrative law cases.

162 ABRvS, 30 November 2011, ECLI:NL:RVS:2011:BU6383, available at: http://uitspraken.rechtspraak.nl/inziendocument?id=ECLI:NL:RVS:2011:BU6383.

163 For the purposes of consistency with the text of the Data Protection Directive the term "controller" is used instead of the term "responsible party" as proposed in the unofficial translation of the DDPA.

The term "controller" implies that only a subject of law (having the capacity to realise rights and juridical duties) can be accountable for the processing of personal data.

To determine which person is the controller it is necessary to proceed from the formal legal powers to determine the purpose and means of processing of data. Moreover, the functional content of the term should be taken into account. The latter is especially important where different actors are involved and their legal powers are not very clearly determined.

The person who decides on the purpose of processing is the one who determines whether the data are processed and if so, which processing, of which personal data and for what purpose takes place. Deciding on the means of processing implies determining the ways in which the processing of personal data takes place. If these powers are not concentrated in the same hands then there are co-controllers[164].

1.3.1.1.6 Processor

The processor of personal data is the person or body that processes personal data for the controller, without coming under the direct authority of that party (Art. 1(e) DDPA). This definition is similar to that of Art. 2(e) Data Protection Directive, with the main difference being that the processor is not explicitly required to be subject to the direct authority of the controller. This means that the processor is a person or institution separate from the organisation of the controller. In most cases, this is a person or institution that has no hierarchal relation with the controller[165].

Unlike the controller, the processor processes personal data without having a say with respect to the purpose and the means of such processing. He takes no decisions about the use of the data, transfer of data to third parties and other recipients, the length of storage, etc. If he acquires the possibility to have a say on these issues, they should be recognised as the controller[166].

For delimitation of the terms "controller" and "processor" the terms of the agreement between the controller and processor are of particular importance[167]. It is important that processing of personal data is the subject matter of the services provided by the processor. If processing takes place as a result of provision of other services for the controller, then the provider of such services should be qualified as the controller of personal data[168].

164 Explanatory Memorandum DDPA, p. 55.
165 Ibid., p. 61.
166 Ibid., pp. 61 et seq.
166 Ibid., p. 62.
168 Ibid., p. 62.

1.3.1.1.7 Third party

"Third party" under the DDPA means any party other than the data subject, the controller, the processor or any person under the direct authority of the controller or the processor, who is authorised to process personal data (Art. 1(g) DDPA). The definition follows the same approach as the one taken in Art. 2(g) Data Protection Directive.

1.3.1.1.8 Consent of the data subject

According to Art. 1(i) DDPA "consent of the data subject" means any freely given, specific and informed expression of will whereby data subjects agree to the processing of personal data relating to them.

"Freely given" means that the data subject should be able to express freely their will in respect of relevant data processing in words, writing or behaviour[169]. For the consent to be valid, the data subject should have an actual choice whether or not to give consent. When the data subject is not given a choice (e.g. when there is no "no" button, or refusal to give consent leads to denial of access to a service), consent is not valid. In certain cases the law can exclude the consent of the data subject as a legal ground for processing, for instance in a situation of unequal balance of power between the controller and the data subject[170].

Consent must be "specific". This requires that the expression of will of the data subject must relate to a particular processing of personal data or limited category of personal data. It should be clear which processing, of which personal data, for what purpose will take place, and, if the data will be transferred to third parties, to which third parties. Therefore, a very broad and undetermined authorisation for processing of personal data cannot be recognised as consent[171].

The data subject's consent should also be "informed". Like the Data Protection Directive, Art. 33(1) DDPA, which regulates the provision of information to the data subject, limits the obligation of the controller to provide information to the data subject to the facts that the data subject already knows or should know. Thus, the data subject also has an obligation to investigate. For the degree to which the data controller should inform the data subject or to which the data subject has to do research, decisive is what can reasonably be expected in society in a particular case[172]. For example, when the data subject approaches the controller on their own initiative, they are expected to be better informed about

[169] Ibid., pp. 65 et seqq.

[170] Hooghiemstra/Nouwt, *Sdu Commentaar Wet bescherming persoonsgegevens*, Den Haag, Sdu Uitgevers, 2014, p. 49.

[171] Explanatory Memorandum DDPA, pp. 65 et seq.

[172] Ibid., p. 66.

processing of their data than when the data subject is approached by the controller. Consent which does not meet the above-mentioned requirements is void[173].

Since protection of privacy is an individual right, collective solutions will never be completely satisfactory. Agreements with interest groups cannot be a substitute for individual consent[174].

Withdrawing consent: Unlike the Data Protection Directive, where the right of the data subject to withdraw consent is merely implied, Art. 5 DDPA provides for an explicit right of the data subject to withdraw their consent to process personal data at any time. Such withdrawal can only have consequences for future processing of personal data and not for processing that has taken place prior to the moment of withdrawal[175].

In the Dutch Authority's opinion, this means that if personal data are published on the Internet controllers must introduce technical measures in relation to such publication, so far as this is based on consent, so that personal data can actively be deleted if a data subject withdraws their consent[176].

1.3.1.2 Principles of personal data processing

As compared to the Data Protection Directive, the DDPA does not include a special article on principles relating to data quality. Principles outlined in Art. 6 of the directive are transposed in a number of provisions of the DDPA discussed below.

1.3.1.2.1 Purpose limitation

The principle of purpose limitation is one of the most important provisions of Dutch data protection law[177]. In line with the provisions and interpretation of the Data Protection Directive, this principle has two components in Dutch data protection law too:

- purpose specification: personal data shall be collected for specific, explicitly defined and legitimate purposes (Art. 7 DDPA), and

---

173 Ibid., p. 67.

174 Beunen/Schiphof, *Juridische Wegwijzer Archieven en Musea online (Legal Companion to Archives and Museums)*, commissioned by the Taskforce Archieven en Museumvereniging (Archives and Museums Association Taskforce), 2006, available at: http://www.nationaalarchief.nl/sites/default/files/docs/juridische_wegwijzer_archieven_en_musea_online_0_0.pdf, para. 1.2.2.4.

175 Explanatory Memorandum DDPA, pp. 67 et seq.

176 Ibid., p. 47; Dutch Authority Publication of Personal Data on the Internet, December 2007, section II, para. 4.1.1, p. 22.

177 Leidraad, *Wet bescherming persoonsgegevens (Guidebook on the Personal Data Protection Act)*, 2011, available at: https://www.rijksoverheid.nl/binaries/rijksoverheid/documenten/richtlijnen/2011/04/29/leidraad-wet-bescherming-persoonsgegevens/leidraad-wet-bescherming-persoonsgegevens.pdf, para. 5.1.3.

compatible use: personal data shall not be further processed in a way incompatible with the purposes for which they have been obtained (Art. 9(1) DDPA).

The provision of Art. 7 DDPA closely repeats that of Art. 6(1)(b) Data Protection Directive.

The "principle of purpose specification" prohibits collection of personal data without a precise description of the purpose of such collection. In order to be "specific" the description of the purpose should be clear and not too vague or too broad. It should offer a framework against which it can be checked whether the particular data are necessary for this purpose. The purpose should be defined before collection and cannot be formulated during the process of collection[178].

"Explicitly defined" means that the controller should describe the purpose for which they process data in the notification sent to the Authority according to the obligation provided for in Art. 27 DDPA. If this obligation is not applicable to the controller based on a general administrative regulation (*Algemene Maatregel van Bestuur*), then the purpose described in the general administrative regulation under Art. 29(2)(a) DDPA shall apply[179].

The purpose is "legitimate" only if it complies not only with one of the legal grounds for processing personal data provided for in Art. 8 DDPA, but also with any written or unwritten law. If the purpose of personal data collection is only achievable when data are stored or transferred to third parties in violation of Art. 8 or any written or unwritten law, it is not compliant with the requirement of "legitimate purpose" and relevant data cannot be collected in accordance with Art. 7 DDPA[180].

The requirement of "compatibility of further processing" set forth in Art. 9(1) DDPA provides a starting point and assessment framework for each form of (further) processing of personal data.

Processing of personal data for purposes other than those for which data were collected is not categorically ruled out but the (in)compatibility of purposes for further processing should be carefully assessed[181]. These other purposes should be compatible with the original purpose. The purpose of obtaining data is the anchor point for regulation of further use. Purposes of further processing should also be specific, explicitly defined, and legitimate.

---

178 Explanatory Memorandum DDPA, p. 79.

179 Ibid., p. 79.

180 Ibid., p. 79; Dutch Supreme Court, decision of 09-09-2011, 10/03988, para. 3.3c) where the Court stated: "Even if the data is in principle allowed on any of the Art. 8 Data Protection Act exhaustively listed grounds, the requirement remains that the processing must be necessary in the case in view of the defined purpose of the processing. The presence of a legal justification therefore makes superfluous interests on the basis of the principles set out above under (a). The circumstances of the case must be taken into account".

181 Leidraad, *Wet bescherming persoonsgegevens (Guidebook on the Personal Data Protection Act)*, 2011, para. 5.1.5.

The requirement of compatible use applies both inside and outside the organisation of the controller, which means that it also concerns third parties[182]. This requirement is also applicable to combining personal data[183].

With respect to re-use of personal data available on the Internet, the Dutch Authority warns that the availability of personal data on the Internet does not mean that they can simply be re-used in another context for a different purpose. The purpose of such re-use should be compatible with the original one. Moreover, the person re-using such data should have an independent legal ground for such re-use and must comply with the requirements of quality and security of data processing. The Dutch Authority underscores that re-use of data may be unlawful, even when it is done for a compatible purpose, if the data being re-used comprise obsolete, incorrect information about a person[184].

Moreover, in assessing whether (re-)publication of personal data on the Internet is compatible with the original purpose, a controller must account not only for the origin of the data, but also for the risk of others using the data that the controller themself publishes on the Internet. In order to reduce the risks to data subjects, each controller must take adequate security measures against illegitimate re-use of data by third parties[185].

Art. 9 DDPA, as compared to the provision of Art. 6(1)(b) Data Protection Directive, provides for much more detailed requirements with respect to compatibility of further processing of personal data. In particular, Art. 9(2) DDPA explicitly outlines a list of factors which should "at least" be taken into account in the assessment of compatibility of further processing[186].

According to Art. 9(2) DDPA, for the purposes of assessing whether processing is compatible with the purposes for which the data have been obtained, the controller shall at least take account of the following:

- the relationship between the purpose of the intended processing and the purpose for which the data have been obtained (Art. 9(2)(a));
- the nature of the data concerned (Art. 9(2)(b));
- the consequences of the intended processing for the data subject (Art. 9(2)(c));

---

182 Explanatory Memorandum DDPA, pp. 89 et seq.

183 Ibid., pp. 93 et seq.

184 Ibid., p. 47; Dutch Authority Publication of Personal Data on the Internet, December 2007, section II, para. 3.2, p. 20.

185 Dutch Authority Publication of Personal Data on the Internet, December 2007, section II, para. 3.2, p. 20.

186 A similar list of factors with respect to the relevant provisions of the directive was summarised by the Article 29 Working Party, see Article 29 Data Protection Working Party, *Opinion 3/2013 on purpose limitation*, pp. 24 et seqq.

- the manner in which the data have been obtained (Art. 9(2)(d)), and
- the extent to which appropriate guarantees have been put in place with respect to the data subject (Art. 9(2)(e)).

The clarification "at least" indicates that the list of relevant factors is not exhaustive[187]. Each of the factors will be briefly explained below.

Relationship between initial purpose and the purpose of further processing (Art. 9(2)(a)): The closer the relationship between the initial purpose and the purpose of further processing, the more likely the purpose of further processing will be considered as compatible[188]. For establishing compatibility of use, it is irrelevant whether the data are used by the same controller or by a third party.

Nature of the data concerned (Art. 9(2)(b)): The more sensitive the data are, the more likely further use can be considered as incompatible. As will be discussed below, personal data can be sensitive by nature (the list is provided for in Art. 16 DDPA) or sensitive in the context in which they are used, for example data about someone's solvency or wealth. The more sensitive data are the less likely it is to be accepted that their use is compatible, if the purpose of processing differs from the original one[189].

Consequences for the data subject (Art. 9(2)(c)): If personal data are used as a basis for possible decisions relating to the data subject, then it is more likely to be concluded that the use is incompatible than when data are used for the purposes of scientific research or for transmission of particular messages. Where no decision is actually made against the data subject, there is a lower chance of incompatible use[190]. In the case of scientific research, in principle the data subject is not adversely affected by the processing. This, however, may change if someone who knows the data subject as a researcher obtains non-identifiable data about the data subject, or when in a long-lasting piece of research the data subject is approached at later stages of research for further questions[191].

Manner of obtaining data (Art. 9(2)(d)): It is relevant if the data were collected from the data subject directly or from third parties. If the data were collected on the basis of a public law obligation, they cannot be used for private law purposes. Such use is in principle incompatible[192].

---

187 Explanatory Memorandum DDPA, p. 90.

188 Ibid., p. 90.

189 Ibid., p. 90.

190 Hooghiemstra/Nouwt, *Sdu Commentaar Wet bescherming persoonsgegevens*, Den Haag, Sdu Uitgevers, 2014, p. 62 (C3).

190 Explanatory Memorandum DDPA, p. 91.

192 CBP Naslag, *Wet bescherming persoonsgegevens (Handbook of the Dutch Authority on Article 9(2)(d) of the Dutch Data Protection Act)*, available at: https://cbpweb.nl/nl/over-privacy/wetten/wbp-naslag/hoofdstuk-2-voorwaarden-voor-de-rechtmatigheid-van-de-verwerking-v-13, Artikel 9 lid 2 sub d.

Appropriate guarantees (Art. 9(2)(e)): which guarantees are appropriate should be determined in each particular case. It could be appropriate to inform the data subject about the intended use or, going one step further, give them an opportunity to give their opinion about it. The most far-reaching option would be to ask the data subject to consent to the use in question[193].

1.3.1.2.2 Further processing for historical, statistical or scientific purposes

In line with Art. 6(1)(b) Data Protection Directive, Art. 9(3) DDPA provides that further processing of personal data for historical, statistical or scientific purposes shall not be regarded as incompatible where the controller has made the necessary arrangements to ensure that further processing is carried out solely for these specific purposes. This exemption applies to further processing of data initially collected for purposes other than historical, statistical or scientific research.

Art. 9(3) DDPA is not applicable if the result of processing does not concern information traceable to persons. Statistical information may in this case be used for all other purposes[194].

As follows from the discussion in the lower chamber of the Dutch Parliament, this provision is not a general exemption, but rather a sectorial specification of the requirement for consistency in the form of an irrefutable presumption of law. The Article 29 Working Party gave a similar qualification to the related exemption of Art. 6(1)(b) Data Protection Directive. Data processing for these purposes is also governed by rules aimed at enforcing an appropriate level of protection of privacy[195].

According to Dutch scholars, "scientific research and statistics" throughout the DDPA should be understood broadly as including all research which is carried out in a scientifically responsible manner[196]. Thus, "scientific research and statistics" should be defined as generation of knowledge about human populations (as opposed to taking individualised decisions or measures) with the use of scientific and/or statistical methods and techniques[197]. Such a process does not need to contribute to the public interest by establishing new insights in a particular research area. Hence, market research, direct marketing, work of statistical bureaus and data mining can also be recognised as "scientific research and statistics" within the data protection framework, even if they do not aim at new (scientific) insights.

---

193 Explanatory Memorandum DDPA, p. 91.

194 Ibid., pp. 92 et seq.

195 CBP Naslag, *Wet bescherming persoonsgegevens (Handbook of the Dutch Authority on Article 9(2)(d) of the Dutch Data Protection Act)*, Artikel 9 lid 3.

196 Holvast, *Wetenschappelijk onderzoek en privacy*, in Prins/Berkvens, *Privacyregulering in theorie en praktijk*, Deventer, Kluwer, 2002, p. 356.

197 Ploem, *Tussen privacy en wetenschapsvrijheid. Regulering van gegevensverwerking voor medisch-wetenschappelijk onderzoek*, 2004, p. 21.

This approach resonates very well with that of the Explanatory Memorandum, which notes that this exemption applies not only to pure scientific research, but also to contract research by universities. It was considered redundant and undesirable to make a distinction in law between pure scientific research and commercial research as well as policy and market research. In practice, it is difficult to draw a line between the two. It is also not clear in advance that the public interest in the case of non-profit scientific research is greater than in the case of commercial scientific research and should be subject to different rules in the framework of the DDPA[198].

This exemption can only be applied if the controller provides for "necessary arrangements to ensure that the further processing is carried out solely for these specific purposes" (Art. 9(3) DDPA). It should be interpreted together with Recital 29 Data Protection Directive, which requires that measures in particular should prevent data being used for taking measures or decisions which are directed to a particular person.

"Necessary arrangements" could, for instance, take the form of "functional separation" between use of data and research. Such measures can be of a legal nature: more precise description of the use that can be made of the data may be specified in, for example, the application form or a code of conduct or can be agreed by contract. Other organisational or technical measures are also possible. If processing must be notified to the Dutch Authority under Art. 27 DDPA, the controller must describe such measures in the notification[199].

According to the Dutch Authority, in the context of online publication of personal data, such arrangements may include the following measures[200]:

- technical measures – e.g. blocking the publication with a password;
- contractual legal measures – e.g. specification of the permissible use of data in a contract; or
- organisational measures – e.g. setting up a procedure for individual assessment of access requests.

The Dutch Authority also notes that this exemption in practice will only apply to strictly guarded intranets[201]. This indicates its narrow approach to the interpretation of this exemption.

---

198 CBP Naslag, *Wet bescherming persoonsgegevens (Handbook of the Dutch Authority on Article 9(2)(d) of the Dutch Data Protection Act)*, Artikel 9 lid 3.

199 Explanatory Memorandum DDPA, pp. 92 et seq.

200 Ibid., p. 47; Dutch Authority Publication of Personal Data on the Internet, December 2007, section I, para. 7.3, p. 13.

201 Ibid.

1.3.1.2.3 Principle of data minimisation

The principle of data minimisation is envisaged in Arts 10 and 11 DDPA. In line with Art. 6(1)(c) and 6(1)(e) Data Protection Directive, these articles require that:

- personal data shall only be processed where, given the purposes for which they are collected or subsequently processed, they are adequate, relevant and not excessive (Art. 11(1)), and
- personal data shall not be kept in a form which allows the data subject to be identified for any longer than is necessary for achieving the purposes for which they were collected or subsequently processed (Art. 10(1)).

Art. 11 DDPA provides for a generally formulated rule of data minimisation: only those data can be processed which are adequate, relevant and not excessive. According to the Explanatory Memorandum, this rule sets forth an obligation of continuous assessment for those who process personal data. For example, every time data are processed for another purpose that is compatible with the original purpose, the assessment provided for in this article should take place[202].

Processed personal data should be adequate in the sense that the controller should have a correct image of the data subject in the light of the purpose of data processing[203]. Data should also be relevant and not excessive in the light of the purpose of their processing[204].

Art. 11(2) DDPA requires the controller to take necessary measures to ensure that the data are correct and accurate. As shown in the Explanatory Memorandum, "necessary" measures means that the controller should take all measures which can be reasonably expected of them. Reasonableness implies that depending on, for example, the kinds of data that are the subject of processing, measures to be taken are limited by the state of the art, and costs associated with the measures[205].

When the controller publishes personal data online, they should determine the terms of availability of personal data in the light of potential risks for the data subjects. The older the data are, the greater the chance that they are incorrect and could therefore cause unnecessary harm to data subjects[206].

---

[202] Explanatory Memorandum DDPA, p. 96.

[203] Ibid., p. 96.

[204] Ibid., pp. 96 et seq.

[205] Ibid., p. 97.

[206] Ibid., p. 47; Dutch Authority Publication of Personal Data on the Internet, December 2007, section II, para. 7.1, p. 30.

The purposes of collecting data and (further) processing are crucial for the determination of the duration of storage[207]. Duration of storage and processing of personal data should be determined by the controller. In certain cases, specific terms of storage are established by law. For example part 3 of Art. 7:454 of the Dutch Civil Code (*Burgerlijk Wetboek*) specifies that medical treatment records of healthcare providers should be stored for 15 years or for as long as reasonably arises from the care of a good healthcare provider.

After the term of storage has expired the controller may no longer lawfully process personal data unless this is done for another compatible purpose, for example statistical archiving[208].

The Dutch Authority recommends that controllers introduce a method whereby personal data can be converted automatically into anonymous data following the expiry of a specified period[209]. Such a procedure was also recommended by the European Commission[210].

1.3.1.2.4 Longer-term storage of personal data for scientific use

Similar to Art. 6(1)(e) Data Protection Directive, Art. 10(2) DDPA allows storage of personal data for longer periods than may be allowed by the requirement of limited personal data retention, if this is done for historical, statistical or scientific purposes.

This article concerns personal data that are collected (or further processed) for historical, statistical, or scientific purposes[211].

In order to comply with the requirement of special safeguards envisaged in Art. 6(1)(e) Data Protection Directive, the DDPA demands that the data controller should make necessary arrangements to ensure that the data concerned are used solely for these specific purposes. The requirement to make necessary arrangements relates to that discussed with respect to Art. 9(3) DDPA in Section 1.3.1.2.2[212].

---

207 Leidraad, *Wet bescherming persoonsgegevens (Guidebook on the Personal Data Protection Act)*, 2011, para. 5.3.

208 Explanatory Memorandum DDPA, p. 95.

209 Ibid., p. 47; Dutch Authority Publication of Personal Data on the Internet, December 2007, section II, para. 7.1, p. 30.

210 Communication from the Commission to the European Parliament and the Council on Promoting Data Protection by Privacy Enhancing Technologies (PETs), Brussels, 2 May 2007, COM(2007) 228, text available at: http://eur-lex.europa.eu/legal-content/EN/TXT/?uri=CELEX:52007DC0228.

211 Explanatory Memorandum DDPA, p. 96.

212 Kranenborg/Verhey, *Wet bescherming persoonsgegevens in Europees perspectief*, Deventer, Kluwer, 2011, p. 100 (para. 3.4.8).

1.3.1.2.5 Legal grounds for lawful processing of personal data

The DDPA repeats the logic of the Data Protection Directive and provides for two blocks of legal grounds for lawful processing of personal data: general rules for general (non-sensitive) categories of personal data (Art. 8) and special stricter provisions with respect to special categories of personal data (*bijzondere persoonsgegevens*, Art. 17–23).

1.3.1.2.5.1 Processing of general categories of personal data

Legal grounds for the processing of general categories of personal data provided for in Art. 7 Data Protection Directive are transposed in Art. 8 DDPA. The most relevant of these legal grounds in the context of open research data sharing is unambiguous consent.

The term "consent" is explained above in Section 1.3.1.1.8. For the consent to be "unambiguous" any doubt should be excluded about the question whether the data subject has given their consent and the particular processing of personal data to which this consent applies. If there is doubt, the controller bears the burden of proving that the data subject has given their consent[213].

Obtaining the data subject's consent does not free the controller from compliance with other rules of personal data processing. The Supreme Court of the Netherlands (*De Hoge Raad der Nederlanden*) ruled that the DDPA should be interpreted in accordance with the ECHR. Each data processing should comply with the principles of proportionality and subsidiarity. An infringement of the interests of the data subject should not be disproportionate in relation to the purpose of the processing, and this purpose should not be reasonably possible to achieve in another manner less harmful for the data subject. The consent provided by the data subject in accordance with Art. 8(a) DDPA does not free the controller from the obligation to balance interests[214].

1.3.1.2.5.2 Processing of special categories of personal data

The processing of special categories of data is prohibited unless one or several exemptions from this prohibition are present. The structure and the scope of these exemptions are different from those of the Data Protection Directive.

The DDPA contains two types of exemptions from the prohibition on processing special categories of personal data: (1) exemptions with respect to a certain type of special categories of data (Arts 17–22) and (2) a residual general provision on exemptions from the prohibition applicable to all sorts of special categories of personal data (Art. 23).

---

213 Explanatory Memorandum DDPA, pp. 66 et seq.

214 HR 9 September 2011, ECLI:NL:HR:2011:BQ8097.

If processing of special categories of personal data cannot be justified based on one of the grounds specified in Arts 17–22, then it should be checked whether respect to Art. 9(3) DDPA the general exemptions in Art. 23 offer such a possibility. If one of the exemptions in Arts 17–22 is applicable, the matter should not be assessed from the perspective of Art. 23[215].

The scope of exemptions offered by the DDPA is also broader. The Netherlands have thus used the discretion provided for in Art. 8(4) Data Protection Directive, according to which, subject to the provision of suitable safeguards, Member States may, for reasons of substantial public interest, lay down additional exemptions to the prohibition on processing special categories of data by national law or by decision of the supervisory authority.

For convenience, exemptions relevant in the given context can be divided into two blocks: (I) relevant general exemptions and (II) exemptions specifically oriented at scientific research and statistics.

(I) General exemptions most relevant in the given context are cases where (1) the processing is carried out with the express consent (*uitdrukkelijke toestemming*) of the data subject (Art. 23(1)(a)); or (2) the data have manifestly been made public by the data subject (Art. 23(1)(b)). Both of these exemptions almost literally repeat those envisaged in Art. 8(2) Data Protection Directive.

Other exemptions can be provided in other Dutch laws or can be granted by order of the Dutch Authority on the basis of the above-mentioned Art. 8(4) Data Protection Directive. This can be done according to Art. 23(1)(e) DDPA, pursuant to which the prohibition on processing of personal data does not apply where this is necessary with a view to an important public interest, where appropriate guarantees have been put in place to protect individual privacy and this is provided for by law or else the Data Protection Authority has granted an exemption. When granting an exemption, the Authority can impose rules and restrictions.

(1) As opposed to the "unambiguous" consent required as a legal ground for processing of general categories of personal data, the prohibition on processing of special categories of personal data can only be lifted by express consent of the data subject.

"Express" consent means that the data subject should communicate their will to the controller about processing of data explicitly in words, writing or behaviour. Silent or implicit consent is not sufficient[216].

---

[215] Leidraad, *Wet bescherming persoonsgegevens* (*Guidebook on the Personal Data Protection Act*), 2011, para. 4.7.5; Explanatory Memorandum DDPA, pp. 23 et seq.

[216] Explanatory Memorandum DDPA, p. 67.

(2) That the data are made public must follow from the conduct of the data subject, which explicitly shows the intention to disclose[217]. Where particular data are open, but the data subject did not explicitly express their will to make such data public, the exemption does not apply. This would be the case, for example, when a person has a visible disability[218].

When the data subject has manifestly made their personal data public, their consent for processing such data is presupposed[219]. Data that were manifestly made public by the data subject can only be processed within the framework of data protection law[220].

(II) The DDPA sets forth two exemptions from the prohibition on the processing of special categories of personal data for the purposes of scientific research or statistics: (1) exemption with respect to the processing of inherited characteristics about a person's health (Art. 21(4)); and (2) exemption relevant for all special categories of personal data (Art. 23(2)).

It is characteristic of both exemptions that they do not explicitly mention historical research, unlike special provisions regarding purpose limitation and longer storage of data.

(1) According to Art. 21(4) DDPA, personal data concerning inherited characteristics may only be processed where this processing takes place with respect to the data subject from whom the data concerned have been obtained.

An essential difference between genetic data and other data is that they do not exclusively concern health conditions of an individual person from whom they originate in the first place, but also concern family members of such a person. Genetic data by definition concern others[221].

Data concerning inherited characteristics may be processed with respect to persons other than those from whom the data have been obtained when the processing is necessary for the purpose of scientific research or statistics (Art. 21(4)(b)). In this case processing of such data should take place with the express consent of the data subject (Art. 21(1)(a)). Processing can be carried out without express consent only if scientific research or statistics meet the requirements specified in Art. 23(2) DDPA. The latter will be discussed below.

---

[217] Ibid., p. 123.

[218] Ibid., p. 123.

[219] Letter of the Dutch Data Protection Authority on privacy aspects of digitising cultural heritage (CBP brief over privacyaspecten digitalisering cultureel erfgoed), 13 November 2006, No. z2006-00869, available at: https://cbpweb.nl/sites/default/files/downloads/adv/z2006-00869.pdf, para. 8, page 5.

[220] Explanatory Memorandum DDPA, p. 123.

[221] Hooghiemstra/Nouwt, *Sdu Commentaar Wet bescherming persoonsgegevens*, Den Haag, Sdu Uitgevers, 2014, p. 99.

Special legislation, such as, for example, the Medical Examinations Act (*Wet medische keuringen*) gives further details that provide for the conditions under which inherited characteristics can be requested from the data subject[222].

As long as scientific research is carried out with inherited characteristics obtained in the field of healthcare, Art. 7:458 of the Civil Code is also applicable. This provision should be considered as clarification of the DDPA[223].

It should be kept in mind that where prohibition of processing of data concerning inherited characteristics does not apply under provisions discussed above, medical professional secrecy nevertheless may hinder such processing[224].

(2) There are two ways in which the processing of special categories of data for scientific or statistical purposes can be legal. In the first place processing is possible based on express consent of the data subject. According to the Explanatory Memorandum, this option is preferable. However, if express consent for the use of special categories of personal data for scientific purposes cannot be obtained, the controller should comply with paragraphs (a) to (d) of Art. 23(2) DDPA, cumulatively[225]. In this case, the controller may process special categories of personal data without a data subject's express consent. These paragraphs require that relevant scientific or statistical research meet all of the following requirements:

- the research serves a public interest (a);
- the processing is necessary for the research or statistics concerned (b);
- it appears to be impossible or would involve a disproportionate effort to ask for express consent (c); and
- sufficient guarantees are provided to ensure that the processing does not adversely affect the individual privacy of the data subject to a disproportionate extent (d).

If the data are used for medical scientific research, Art. 7:458 of the Civil Code also applies as a specific legal provision[226].

---

222 Explanatory Memorandum DDPA, pp. 115 et seqq.; Wet van 5 juli 1997, houdende regels tot versterking van de rechtspositie van hen die een medische keuring ondergaan (Wet op de medische keuringen) (Act of 5 July 1997 laying down rules to strengthen the legal status of those who undergo medical examination (Act on Medical Examinations)).

223 Explanatory Memorandum DDPA, pp. 115 et seq.

224 Ibid., pp. 108 et seq.

225 Ibid., p. 126.

226 Hooghiemstra/Nouwt, *Sdu Commentaar Wet bescherming persoonsgegevens*, Den Haag, Sdu Uitgevers, 2014, p. 115, (C 9); Explanatory Memorandum DDPA, p. 126.

The criterion of necessity further requires that the data may only be processed to the extent and as long as they are necessary in the framework of the relevant research. When the necessity of the data for the research is no longer present, they should be deleted or should be processed in such a way that they can no longer be traced to individuals (i.e. be anonymised)[227].

The requirement in paragraph (c) limits the application of Art. 23(2) to cases when a request for consent cannot be expected[228].

Under the requirement in paragraph (d), the exemption specified in Art. 23(2) is only applicable if in the course of research or statistics guarantees are provided which ensure that processing does not adversely affect the individual privacy of the data subject to a disproportionate extent. This provision is borrowed from Art. 7:458 of the Civil Code and is also linked to the requirement of creating "appropriate safeguards" in Art. 8(4) Data Protection Directive[229].

Which safeguards (guarantees) are appropriate depends on the circumstances. For example, they could be conditions relating to access to the data, confidentiality or presentation of the results of the research. Although the exemption does not explicitly mention historical research, the Explanatory Memorandum notes that personal data can be made public in the communication of results in the case of historical research. The general standard of assessment for all types of cases is that privacy of the data subject should not be unreasonably harmed[230].

In its guidelines on the publication of data on the Internet the Dutch Authority explicitly acknowledges the possibility of constructing an archive with special categories of personal data for scientific purposes and making it available via terminals in libraries to a restricted group of scientists. However, each request for access to such archive for the purposes of scientific research should be assessed against the four requirements of Art. 23(2) DDPA[231]. This requirement makes it clear that not every scientist will get access to such an archive.

The Dutch Authority also refers to the conclusion of the *Legal Companion to Archives and Museums online* (*Juridische Wegwijzer Archieven en Musea*) that the processing of sensitive data in the context of making cultural heritage available electronically cannot be easily reconciled with the DDPA. The Authority notes

---

227 Explanatory Memorandum DDPA, p. 126.
228 Ibid., pp. 127 et seq.
229 Ibid., pp. 127 et seq.
230 Ibid., pp. 127 et seq.
231 Dutch Authority Publication of Personal Data on the Internet, December 2007, section I, para. 7.3, p. 14.

that making sensitive data available to a broad public is "problematic" and the exemption of Art. 23(2) DDPA "does not accommodate institutes that wish to publish their material widely"[232].

The *Legal Companion to Archives and Museums* also notes that to be able to apply an exemption from Art. 23 DDPA for processing special categories of personal data for scientific research, the controller should actively assess whether the research of a person who wants to gain access meets all the requirements. Therefore it is surely not sufficient for visitors to a website, before gaining access to special categories of personal data, to click to agree to use these data only for scientific research. Only after an active assessment can the new user be granted a password to be able to access such data[233].

The *Legal Companion to Archives and Museums* concludes that processing of special categories of personal data in the context of digital accessibility of cultural heritage can be at odds with the DDPA. Making available special categories of data to an indefinite public is problematic. The exemption for the purposes of scientific research does not give any relief to institutions which want to make their material broadly available[234].

1.3.1.2.6 Transparency of personal data processing

The principle of transparency of data processing is elaborated in Arts 33 and 34 DDPA, which contain the controller's obligation to provide information about processing of personal data to the data subject. The above-mentioned articles implement Arts 10 and 11 Data Protection Directive. This obligation is also an important element of the principle of "lawful processing" set forth in Art. 6 DDPA. Breaches of this obligation lead to unlawful processing[235].

The obligation to provide information to the data subject exists whenever the controller can exercise control over personal data because they have saved them. The way in which data were collected is not important[236]. Art. 33 DDPA applies to cases where data have been obtained directly from the data subject, Art. 34 DDPA where data have been obtained in any other manner, for example from third parties or by observation.

---

232 Beunen/Schiphof, *Juridische Wegwijzer Archieven en Musea online (Legal Companion to Archives and Museums)*, commissioned by the Taskforce Archieven en Museumvereniging (Archives and Museums Association Taskforce), 2006, p. 44; Dutch Authority Publication of Personal Data on the Internet, December 2007, section I, para. 7.3, p. 14.

233 Beunen/Schiphof, *Juridische Wegwijzer Archieven en Musea online (Legal Companion to Archives and Museums)*, commissioned by the Taskforce Archieven en Museumvereniging (Archives and Museums Association Taskforce), 2006, para. 1.2.2.4.

234 Ibid.

235 Explanatory Memorandum DDPA, pp. 149 et seq.

236 Ibid., p. 193.

As regards the content of information, the controller should provide to the data subject, at least information about the controller's identity and the purposes of processing (Arts 33(2) and 34(2) DDPA).

Arts 33(3) and 34(3) DDPA regulate the provision of more detailed information. Unlike Arts 10 and 11 Data Protection Directive, these articles do not clarify the types of detailed information the controller may be obliged to provide. The controller shall provide the data subject with more detailed information where, given the type of data, the circumstances in which they have been obtained or the use to be made thereof, this is necessary in order to guarantee with respect to the data subject that the processing is carried out in a proper and careful manner in accordance with Art. 6 DDPA[237].

If the controller makes changes to the information communicated to the data subject in accordance with Arts 33(3) or 34(3) DDPA, for example because the controller intends to send the data to persons other than the categories of recipients communicated to the data subject, then the controller should inform the data subject of such changes[238].

To sum up, the DDPA does not require information about recipients of personal data to be provided to the data subject in all cases. This information, however, should be provided as a part of "more detailed information" under certain circumstances.

Irrespective of the way in which the controller obtained personal data, the obligation to provide information to the data subject is limited by information already known or that should be known to the data subject (Arts 33(1) and 34(1) DDPA). According to the Explanatory Memorandum, the data subject surely has an obligation to investigate (*onderzoeksplicht*) before he makes a decision[239].

To determine the extent to which the controller should inform the data subject or the data subject should do their own investigation, the standard of what can reasonably be expected in the light of the circumstances of a particular case is applied. Factors which can play a role in such weighing are the relevant types of data, the processing intended by the controller and the context of processing, and the third parties to which the data can be sent, etc., but also societal position and mutual relation between the controller and the data subject, as well as the manner in which they came into contact with each other[240].

In principle, the controller has an extra responsibility to inform the data subject if they have taken the initiative to approach the data subject. The data subject who approaches the controller will often be informed about the identity and the objectives of the controller[241].

---

237 Ibid., p. 154.
238 Ibid., p. 154.
239 Ibid., p. 66.
240 Ibid., p. 66.
241 Ibid., pp. 150 et seq.

The DDPA does not regulate the form in which the information should be provided. According to the Explanatory Memorandum, the information should be provided to the data subject in such a manner that the data subject really possesses the information. If the data subject has the information, for example because it has been transferred or sent to them, then the data subject is considered to be informed, irrespective of whether or not they took the initiative to make themself familiar with it[242].

In relation to a particular data subject, information should be provided specifically to this data subject. If more data subjects are involved in a certain type of processing, the method of informing them can be more general. However, data subjects cannot be addressed as a part of the general public[243].

With respect to the publication of personal data on the Internet, the Dutch Authority notes that the controller intending to publish personal data on the Internet must inform all data subjects in advance about such publication. The controller must also provide them with as much additional information as "is necessary in order to ensure that the data subjects understand the purpose and how they can oppose publication if they wish to do so"[244].

The Dutch Authority admits that in certain circumstances provision to the data subject of passive information, for example in the form of a privacy statement indicating the controller's identity and purposes of publication, would be enough to comply with the transparency requirement. But this is only the case when publication creates low risks for the data subjects and the latter "are reasonably aware of the context in which specific personal data about them are published"[245].

According to the Explanatory Memorandum, the obligation to provide information under Arts 33 and 34 DDPA is, in principle, a one-off obligation. If the controller has once informed the data subject, they can further process the data. If such further processing includes transfer of the data to third parties, the controller is not once again obliged to inform the data subject. The controller may be obliged to provide further information, for example of later developments which should have been communicated to the data subject had they been known at the time when the data subject was initially informed[246].

When personal data are obtained directly from the data subject, the information should be communicated to them prior to obtaining personal data. The Dutch Authority notes that if the controller is planning to publish personal data on the Internet on the basis of the data subject's consent, a good way to provide

---

242 Ibid., pp. 150 et seq.

243 Ibid., p. 153.

244 Dutch Authority Publication of Personal Data on the Internet, December 2007, section II, para. 5, p. 26.

245 Ibid.

246 Explanatory Memorandum DDPA, p. 157.

information to the data subjects prior to obtaining such consent would be the publication of a privacy statement. Such privacy statement must be "drawn up in clear, comprehensible language" and "be easily retrievable and preferably accessible from within each section of the publication"[247].

If personal data are not obtained from the data subject, the data subject should be informed about the identity of the controller and the purposes of processing at the moment of recording of data or when it is intended to supply the data to a third party, at the latest on the first occasion that the said data are so supplied (Art. 34(1) DDPA). The Explanatory Memorandum clarifies that the latter option is applicable in cases where transfer of data to third parties is intended to take place at the moment of data collection[248].

The obligation to inform under Art. 34 DDPA implies that any new recipient of personal data who qualifies as a new controller is obliged to inform the data subjects involved that they have obtained personal data. This obligation does not apply if the data subject has already been informed that the new controller will receive their data. This is the case, for example, when the controller from whom such data were obtained has already informed the data subjects about future transfers of their data to third parties in accordance with Art. 33(3) DDPA. This proposition holds if such transfer was done for a purpose compatible with that for which the data were initially collected[249].

The obligation to inform the data subject about the new data processing (where personal data were not obtained from the data subject) is not absolute. According to Art. 34(4) DDPA, this obligation does not apply if it appears to be impossible or would involve a disproportionate effort to provide the said information to the data subject.

Whether an effort to provide information is "disproportionate" depends, among other things, on the extent to which there are other ways to provide adequate information to the data subject and the medium from which it can be assumed that it largely reaches the data subject[250].

The controller should record from whom and in what way the data were obtained. This is important for reconstructing the chain of transfers of personal data, which can afterwards be requested by a data subject based on Art. 35 DDPA[251].

---

247 Dutch Authority Publication of Personal Data on the Internet, December 2007, section II, para. 5.3, p. 27.

248 Explanatory Memorandum DDPA, p. 155.

249 Hooghiemstra/Nouwt, *Sdu Commentaar Wet bescherming persoonsgegevens*, Den Haag, Sdu Uitgevers, 2014, p. 150 (C.6).

250 Explanatory Memorandum DDPA, pp. 155 et seq.

251 Hooghiemstra/Nouwt, *Sdu Commentaar Wet bescherming persoonsgegevens*, Den Haag, Sdu Uitgevers, 2014, p. 150 (C.5); Explanatory Memorandum DDPA, p. 156.

Art. 44(1) DDPA contains an express exemption from the obligation to comply with Art. 34 DDPA where processing is carried out by institutions or services for the purposes of scientific research or statistics, and the necessary arrangements have been made to ensure that the personal data can only be used for statistical or scientific purposes.

According to the Explanatory Memorandum, this article transposes Art. 11(2) and Art. 13(2) Data Protection Directive, and contains a concretisation of the two in accordance with Art. 5 of the directive. Art. 11(2) Data Protection Directive envisages an exemption from the obligation to inform the data subject when personal data have not been obtained from them, so far as the provision of such information proves impossible or would involve a disproportionate effort. Processing for statistical, historical or scientific purposes are cited in this provision of the directive as examples of the exempted situations.

Unlike Art. 11(2) Data Protection Directive, the exemption specified in Art. 44(1) DDPA is not linked to the general exemption relating to impossibility or disproportionate effort (specified in Art. 34(4) DDPA) and is narrower in two ways.

First, the exemption of Art. 44(1) DDPA is limited to institutions or services for scientific research or statistics and in so far as data are used by them for statistical or scientific purposes. The exemption in Art. 11(2) Data Protection Directive, on the other hand, is applicable to any sort of controller as long as they process personal data for statistical, historical or scientific purposes.

Secondly, the scope of purposes for processing personal data exempted under Art. 44(1) DDPA is limited to scientific research and statistics and does not include historical research.

Although the exemption of Art. 44(1) DDPA is narrower than that of Art. 11(2) Data Protection Directive, it is still possible that controllers other than organisations for scientific research or statistics can be exempt from the obligation to provide information under Art. 34 DDPA under general conditions of impossibility or disproportionate effort discussed above.

In line with Art. 11(2) Data Protection Directive the exemption of Art. 44(1) DDPA is backed by the obligation of the controller to make necessary arrangements to ensure that the personal data can only be used for statistical or scientific purposes. According to the Explanatory Memorandum, the term "necessary" indicates the proportionality between the importance of protecting personal data on the one hand, and the costs and efforts connected with the provision of information on the other hand[252].

Examples of "necessary arrangements" are separation of data about the data subject's identity from other data. The possibility of establishing a connection between the two when this is necessary for statistical or scientific purposes should,

[252] Explanatory Memorandum DDPA, p. 156.

in compliance with the rules of self-regulation, be subject to specific verifiable processes. It is decisive that no use of personal data is made, and given compliance with security measures, no use can be made, aimed at any investigation or measure in relation to individual data subjects. A 'measure' is understood as a decision to approach the data subject, either in order to bring to their attention information which may be of interest to them, or in order to ask further questions, for example for additional scientific research. The nature of the required arrangements is dynamic and will change with the developments in the state of the art[253].

In designing the exemption of Art. 44(1) DDPA, the Dutch government assumed that if all conditions specified in this article were met, there would be no risk of breach of privacy: implementation of the necessary arrangements would prevent data about individual persons being (or possibly being) used[254]. Whenever conditions set forth in Art. 44(1) DDPA cannot be complied with (e.g. when the data subject is still being approached for additional information) the rights of the data subject to information revive[255].

Although, as mentioned above, the DDPA does not contain an exemption from the obligation to provide information to a data subject, when personal data are processed for historical purposes Art. 44(2) DDPA provides for an exemption for data which are processed as a part of archival records.

According to Art. 44(2) DDPA, where personal data which form part of archive records transferred to an archive storage place under Arts 12 or 13 of the Archives Act 1995 (*Archiefwet* 1995) are processed, the controller shall not be required to provide the information referred to in Art. 34 DDPA. This article refers to archival records which, after the process of selection, were considered worth being preserved, in particular for reasons of administration of justice, science or history of culture[256]. The Archives Act itself contains a procedure which is focused on informing interested persons about the manner in which the government intends to deal with archival records about them[257].

---

253 Ibid., p. 156.
254 Ibid., pp. 172 et seq.
255 Ibid., pp. 100, 172 et seq.
256 Ibid., pp. 172 et seqq.
257 Ibid., pp. 172 et seqq.

1.3.1.2.7 Data subject's right of access to data

In accordance with the Data Protection Directive, the DDPA grants data subjects, in particular, the following rights of access to their personal data against the controller:

- the right to obtain from the controller information about the processing of personal data, including information about the recipients or categories of recipients (Art. 35(2) DDPA, implements Art. 12(1) Data Protection Directive);
- the right to request that the controller correct, supplement, delete or block the data in the event that it is factually inaccurate, incomplete or irrelevant to the purpose or purposes of the processing, or is being processed in any other way which infringes a legal provision (Art. 36(1) DDPA, implements Art. 12(2) Data Protection Directive);
- notification to third parties to whom the data has previously been supplied about the correction, addition, deletion or blocking, unless this appears to be impossible or would involve a disproportionate effort (Art. 38(1) DDPA, implements Art. 12(3) Data Protection Directive).

The Dutch Authority clarified with respect to the publication of personal data online that the way in which requests for correction are dealt with depends on the legal ground for publication.

If the publication is based on consent of the data subject which has been withdrawn, the controller must always comply with a request for deletion and consider this possibility beforehand in the technical design of its systems. If the publication is based on one of the other legitimate grounds, a data subject may request that data be deleted or corrected in the event that the data are factually incorrect, incomplete or irrelevant for their purpose, or have been published in some other way that contravenes a statutory regulation. If the request is justified, the publication becomes unlawful and the controller is obliged to comply[258].

It is customary in the archives world, in cases where the request for correction is accepted, not to delete or destroy data but to offer the data subject the possibility to add their own reading of the relevant information. This may also be

---

[258] Dutch Authority Publication of Personal Data on the Internet, December 2007, section III, para. 3, p. 40.

possible where archives are made available in digital form[259]. The Dutch Authority underscores that the DDPA does not limit controllers of Internet publications to maintaining a separate list of data that are evidently incorrect[260].

Unlike the provision of Art. 13(2) Data Protection Directive, which allows Member States to restrict all rights of access cited in Art. 12 of the directive (the rights to request information about processing and to request rectification, erasure or blocking; controller's obligation to inform third parties about the latter), restrictions introduced by the DDPA are more nuanced. The DDPA contains an explicit exemption with respect to the data subject's right to request information (Art. 44(1) DDPA) and with respect to the controller's obligation to notify third parties about correction, deletion or blocking of personal data (Art. 38 DDPA), but does not provide for a general exemption applicable to all the data subject's rights.

Art. 44(1) DDPA sets forth the conditions under which the controller may refuse to comply with the data subject's request for information about processing of data, including information about the recipients or categories of recipients, as provided for in Art. 35 DDPA. Refusal to provide information to the data subject is allowed if:

- the controller is an institution or service for scientific research or statistics; and
- the controller has made the necessary arrangements to ensure that the personal data can only be used for statistical or scientific purposes.

The interpretation of "necessary arrangement" as referred to in Art. 44(1) has been discussed above in Section 1.3.1.2.2.

Thus, the limitation of the right to receive information provided for in Dutch data protection law is narrower than is allowed under the Data Protection Directive in the sense that in Dutch law it is limited not only by a special type of activity (which is scientific research or statistics in both cases), but also by special types of controllers.

Unlike Art. 13(2) Data Protection Directive, the DDPA does not provide for an explicit limitation of the data subject's right to correction, deletion, blocking, etc. of data provided for in Art. 36 of the Act. However, according to Art. 36(1) DDPA the rights granted by this article can be requested by "a person who has been informed about personal data in accordance with Art. 35". This means that if the controller refuses the data subject's request under Art. 35 DDPA, the data subject will not be able to exercise the rights under Art. 36 DDPA.

---

[259] Beunen/Schiphof, *Juridische Wegwijzer Archieven en Musea online (Legal Companion to Archives and Museums)*, commissioned by the Taskforce Archieven en Museumvereniging (Archives and Museums Association Taskforce), 2006, para. 1.2.2.7.

[260] Dutch Authority Publication of Personal Data on the Internet, December 2007, section III, para. 9.1, p. 36.

The controller who has corrected, supplemented, deleted or blocked personal data in response to a request under Art. 36 DDPA need not comply with the obligation to notify third parties when this appears to be impossible or would involve a disproportionate effort (Art. 38 DDPA).

Notification of third parties in the sense of this provision is not possible if the controller no longer has information as to which third parties they have transferred personal data. Notification may also be omitted if it requires a disproportionate effort[261].

The provision of Art. 38 DDPA clearly presupposes a trade-off between the interests of the data subject and those of the controller. The data subject must have an actual interest in notifying third parties about the correction of certain personal data. If the data subject has no such interest, than it is more likely to be concluded that a disproportionate effort is required on the part of the controller[262].

Following the logic applied above with respect to Art. 36 DDPA, it can also be argued that since the obligation to notify exists only in cases where data were corrected, supplemented, deleted or blocked in accordance with Art. 36 DDPA, institutions and services for scientific research and statistics, which do not have to comply with the request under Arts 35 and 36 DDPA, are automatically exempt from the obligation under Art. 38 DDPA.

1.3.1.2.8 Measures to ensure security of processing

Art. 13 DDPA obliges the controller to implement appropriate technical and organisational measures to secure personal data against loss or against any form of unlawful processing. These measures must guarantee an appropriate level of security, taking into account the state of the art and the costs of implementation, and having regard to the risks associated with the processing and the nature of the data to be protected. These measures must also aim at preventing unnecessary collection and further processing of personal data. This article implements Art. 17(1) Data Protection Directive.

In the given context, it is particularly relevant that the controller should implement appropriate security measures against any form of unlawful processing and prevent *unnecessary further processing* of personal data.

The term "appropriate" points at the proportionality between the security measures and the nature of data to be protected. If processing involves sensitive data, or the context in which data are used constitutes a serious threat to privacy, more serious requirements are set for the security of the data. There is, however, no obligation to take the most serious security measures. Measures should be adequate to the risks of processing and the nature of the data[263].

---

261 Explanatory Memorandum DDPA, p. 161.
262 Ibid., p. 162.
263 Ibid., p. 99.

The criterion of "appropriate" measures is a dynamic one. The required level of security is higher when more possibilities are available to ensure such level. In the light of technological developments, a periodical assessment of security measures is required[264].

According to the Explanatory Memorandum, the obligation to take technical and organisational security measures is a cumulative requirement[265]. If computer software makes it actually impossible to process personal data in a way other than is compliant with the law, the control of behaviour of individual subordinates is less necessary[266].

In the Guidelines of 2007 on publication of personal data on the Internet, the Dutch Authority identifies privacy-enhancing technologies (PET) as an efficient measure to prevent unnecessary processing without the loss of functionality of data[267]. More recent Guidelines of the Dutch Authority on data security of 2013 clarify that PET is a collective term for a number of techniques which the controller can apply in the course of processing personal data to limit the risks for the data subject[268].

The central principle of PET is reduction of the degree to which personal data are traceable to the data subject. The most severe form of PET is anonymisation of personal data. A lighter form of PET is separation of the processed personal data into (very well-protected) identifying data and non-identifying data (pseudonymisation). The identity of the data subject can be reconstructed only with the help of identifying data[269].

In its Guidelines of 2007, the Dutch Authority outlines five obligations of controllers publishing personal data on the Internet which ensure compliance with security measures[270]:

a) avoid unnecessary publication of personal data;

b) block specific pages containing personal data from search engines;

---

264 Eerste Kamer der Staten-Generaal, Memorie van Antwoord, I, 25 892, nr. 92c, (Explanatory response of the first chamber of the Dutch Parliament), available at: https://zoek.officielebekendmakingen.nl/kst-19992000-25892-92c.pdf, p. 15.

265 Explanatory Memorandum DDPA, p. 99.

266 CBP Naslag, *Wet bescherming persoonsgegevens* (*Handbook of the Dutch Authority on Article 13 of the Dutch Data Protection Act*), Article 13.

267 Dutch Authority Publication of Personal Data on the Internet, December 2007, section II, para. 8.1, p. 32.

268 CBP Richtsnoeren, *Beveiliging van Persoonsgegevens (Dutch Data Protection Authority Guidelines on the Security of Personal Data)*, February 2013, available at: https://cbpweb.nl/sites/default/files/downloads/rs/rs_2013_richtsnoeren-beveiliging-persoonsgegevens.pdf, para. 1.4.

269 Ibid.

270 Dutch Authority Publication of Personal Data on the Internet, December 2007, section II, para. 8.1, p. 32.

c) use passwords or another appropriate method to restrict the target group;

d) ensure that data transfer is secure by means of the SSL (Secure Sockets Layer) protocol;

e) secure machine(s) and underlying databases against unauthorised access by third parties.

The Dutch Authority warns that the use of login and password would not be enough to protect sensitive data. Thus, when a publication contains special categories of personal data, additional technical measures capable of restricting access to such data only to authorised persons are required[271].

The Dutch Authority also recommends that "a strict separation" be established between the database where special categories of personal data are processed and the server enabling the publication of data on the Internet, especially when sensitive data are processed. Such separation also implies that special categories of personal data are sent to the server only in an encrypted format and are decrypted at the recipient's level[272].

It is sensible to apply the recommendations of the Dutch Authority of 2007 bearing in mind that new, more advanced technical security measures could have developed since that time.

According to Art. 14 DDPA, when data are processed by a processor on behalf of the controller the latter shall make sure that the processor provides adequate guarantees concerning the technical and organisational security measures for the processing to be carried out. The controller shall ensure compliance with these measures. This requirement reflects the provision of Art. 17(2) Data Protection Directive.

If the processor fails to provide appropriate security measures, this can lead to the loss or unlawful processing of the personal data[273]. As already mentioned, it is the controller who is accountable to the data subject for the processing of data by the processor.

Besides sufficient security, the controller should also ensure sufficient transparency on the part of the processor. Insufficient transparency may lead to non-compliance of the controller with the legal requirements too. For example, the controller must ensure that the processor takes sufficient technical and organisational security measures and must monitor compliance. If the controller has

---

271 Ibid., section II, para. 8.4, p. 34.

272 Ibid., section II, para. 8.6, p. 35.

273 *CBP Richtsnoeren, Beveiliging van Persoonsgegevens* (*Dutch Data Protection Authority Guidelines on the Security of Personal Data*), February 2013, para. 4.1.

insufficient knowledge of the security level offered or if they are not able to assess whether the processor really complies with the agreed security measures, then the controller is not compliant with these legal obligations[274].

1.3.1.2.9 Cross-border data transfer

The issue whether online publication of information containing personal data so that they become accessible in countries outside the EU and the European Economic Area (EEA)[275] constitutes cross-border transfer of such data is unclear not only at the EU level, but also at the level of the Dutch legal system.

According to the Explanatory Memorandum, the term "transfer" refers to bringing personal data to the attention of a person who is located outside the EU. It includes the use of personal data within a group of companies which are located in- and outside the EU, the transfer to third parties located outside the EU, and making personal data available with the aim of processing them[276].

The Dutch Authority follows the line of the *Lindqvist* judgment of the ECJ[277]. According to this judgment, the provisions regarding transfer to other countries that do not have an adequate level of protection do not apply if it is *not explicitly the intention* of the controller to export the data to such countries and make personal data available to a specific group of persons in a country outside the EU[278]. This, according to the Dutch Authority (and in line with the Explanatory Memorandum), may be the case when a multinational company that has several branches across the world makes personal data available to employees in all of the branches by means of an intranet[279].

The Dutch Authority also notes that the *Lindqvist* judgment is restricted to the case presented, in which the specific conditions are taken into consideration. In particular, the ECJ refers to "action of a person in Mrs. Lindqvist's position" and "actions such as those of Lindqvist"[280].

It is not yet clear how "explicit intention" of the controller to make personal data available to persons outside the EU/EEA will be interpreted, and how it can be deduced from the controller's actions. Arguably, if data are made available with the intention of providing open access to anyone and anywhere, such publication can be qualified as cross-border transfer.

---

274 Ibid.

275 The EEA consists of the EU and the EFTA (European Free Trade Area) states Iceland, Liechtenstein and Norway.

276 Explanatory Memorandum DDPA, p. 193.

277 ECJ Case C-101/01 (6.11.2003), *Lindqvist.*

278 Dutch Authority Publication of Personal Data on the Internet, December 2007, section V, paras 3 and 5, pp. 49 et seq.

279 Ibid., section V, para. 5, p. 50.

280 Ibid.

Provisions of the DDPA on cross-border transfer of data closely resemble those of Arts 25 and 26 Data Protection Directive. According to Art. 76(1) DDPA, personal data can only be transferred to a country outside the EU if that country guarantees an adequate level of protection. The European Commission or the European Council establishes which countries meet such a level.

Derogations from the prohibition on transferring data to countries that do not provide for an adequate level of protection are envisaged in Art. 77 DDPA in line with Art. 26 Data Protection Directive. In particular, an operation or category of operations to transfer personal data to a country not providing an adequate level of protection may take place if the data subjects have unambiguously given their consent thereto (Art. 77(1)(a) DDPA).

Besides, in accordance with Art. 26(2) Data Protection Directive, according to Art. 77(2) DDPA, the Dutch Minister of Justice, after consulting the Authority, may issue a permit for a personal data transfer or category of transfers to a third country that does not provide guarantees for an adequate level of protection. This permit must be accompanied by more detailed rules required to protect the individual privacy and fundamental rights and freedoms of persons and to guarantee implementation of the associated rights.

Derogations in the form of standard contractual clauses approved by the Commission (Art. 26(4) Data Protection Directive) and binding corporate rules (BCRs) can also be applied in the Netherlands, even though they are not explicitly mentioned in the DDPA. In respect of the latter the Dutch Authority, together with data protection authorities of 15 other EU Member States and three EEA countries (Iceland, Liechtenstein and Norway), has joined a mutual recognition procedure aimed at speeding up the procedure for analysing and approving BCR to ensure that they provide the necessary data protection safeguards[281].

With respect to the online publication of personal data, the Dutch Authority also mentions an obligation of controllers to inform data subjects about the possibility that their personal data may be accessed in countries that do not guarantee an adequate level of personal data protection. This obligation is especially relevant when processing involves a substantial risk – for example when processing involves special categories of personal data. The Dutch Authority deduces this obligation from the provision of Art. 6 DDPA, which requires that personal data be processed in accordance with the law and in a proper and careful manner[282].

1.3.1.2.10 Codes of conduct

Art. 25(1) DDPA, which implements Art. 27(2) Data Protection Directive, provides that an organisation or organisations planning to draw up a code of conduct may request the Dutch Authority to declare that the rules contained in the said

[281] Commission Working Paper SEC(2012) 72, p. 38.

[282] Dutch Authority Publication of Personal Data on the Internet, December 2007, section V, para. 6, p. 50.

code properly implement this Act or other legal provisions on the processing of personal data. The declaration of the Dutch Authority is valid for the duration of the code of conduct, but no longer than five years from the date on which the declaration was announced (Art. 25(5) DDPA).

According to the Explanatory Memorandum, a "code of conduct" includes any type of self-regulation relating to the handling of personal data[283]. The above-mentioned declaration of the Dutch Authority in relation to the code of conduct is optional and does not influence the validity of the code of conduct.

The extent to which a code of conduct is binding can be determined by relevant organisations. Thus, different codes of conduct can have different status. It is also possible that a code of conduct is not legally binding, but only contains recommendations. In most cases, compliance with codes of conduct is a membership obligation and a legal obligation based on the law of associations[284].

In the field of scientific research and statistics, the following Dutch codes of conduct are relevant:

- Code of conduct for the use of personal data in scientific research adopted by the Association of universities in the Netherlands (*VSNU Gedragscode voor gebruik van persoonsgegevens in wetenschappelijk onderzoek*, hereinafter referred to as the "VSNU Code") (December 2005)[285]; and
- Code of conduct for research and statistics (*Gedragscode voor Onderzoek en Statistiek*)[286] (approved by the Dutch Authority on 21 June 2010, approval published on 24 June 2010).

The VSNU Code explains the provisions of Dutch data protection law applicable to scientific research.

According to the VSNU Code, if scientific research is carried out by a university, the controller is its executive board (*College van Bestuur*, paragraph 7 ad. 4 of the Preamble).

---

283 Explanatory Memorandum DDPA, p. 130.

284 *CBP Naslag, Wet bescherming persoonsgegevens (Handbook of the Dutch Authority on Articles 25(1) and 25(2) of the Dutch Data Protection Act)*, Article 25 lid 1 and 2.

285 Declaration by the Dutch Authority (*Goedkeuring Gedragscode voor gebruik van persoonsgegevens in wetenschappelijk onderzoek van VSNU Vereniging van Universiteiten*, decision of 22 December 2005, published 2 January 2006) expired 1 January 2011 (five years after its publication). The text of the code in Dutch is available at: http://www.vsnu.nl/files/documenten/Domeinen/Accountability/Codes/Gedragscode%20persoonsgegevens.pdf.

286 Declaration by the Dutch Authority, decision of 1 June 2010, published 24 June 2010, expired 23 June 2015 (five years after its publication). The text of the code in Dutch is available at: https://www.windesheim.nl/~/media/files/windesheim/over-windesheim/gedragscode-voor-onderzoek-en-statistiek.pdf?la=nl-nl.

In the field of scientific research, personal data are collected by means of surveys in the form of interviews or questionnaires. Data can be collected in the course of repeated measurements, where a group of people is followed in time (cohorts) or measurements collected when (groups) of individuals are followed over time (panels) (paragraph 4 of the Preamble).

Paragraph 7 ad. 1 summarises the privileges for researchers provided for in the DDPA as follows:

- Personal data not covered by professional confidentiality, which were collected for another purpose, can be used anew for the purposes of scientific research.
- Personal data may be stored longer for purposes of scientific research than for the purposes for which they were originally collected.
- The prohibition on processing special categories of personal data other than for special purposes set forth in the DDPA or with express consent of the data subject can, under certain conditions, be lifted for the purposes of scientific research.
- In some cases, an exemption applies for scientific research in respect of the obligation to provide information and the right of access of the data subject to personal data.

The VSNU Code also contains provisions on the transfer of personal data to third parties (Art. 5). The Code contains separate provisions with respect to transfer to institutions for scientific research and statistics (Art. 5.1) and with respect to transfer to other third parties.

According to Art. 5.1, the controller, or researchers in the name of the controller, can transfer personal data obtained in accordance with the provisions of the Code to institutions for scientific research and statistics, exclusively in accordance with the Code and thus exclusively for the purposes of scientific research carried out by these third parties and even then to the extent it is sufficiently ensured that the recipient knows it is bound by the provisions of the Code and must process data in accordance with it.

Art. 5.2 provides that the controller, or researchers in the name of the controller, can transfer personal data obtained in accordance with the provisions of the Code to other third parties exclusively in accordance with the Code and if it is sufficiently ensured that the data will be used by those third parties exclusively for the purposes of scientific research and moreover in compliance with the DDPA.

The commentary to these provisions explains that the use of data exclusively for scientific research exempts the controller from the obligation to comply with the principle of purpose limitation, which would normally apply. It also allows reliance on the exemption for scientific research to process special categories of data without express consent[287].

According to the commentary, Art. 5 consists of two parts because there are some exemptions for institutions for scientific research, which do not apply to others. In the case of research by an institution for scientific research and statistics the data subject should not be informed that their personal data are being processed (Arts 34 and 44 DDPA). In this case the right of the data subject to information and correction is limited too (Arts 35 and 44 DDPA). These exemptions apply exclusively to institutions for scientific research and statistics. According to Art. 5.1 they are, however, required to comply with the VSNU Code after the file with personal data has been sent to them[288].

With respect to Art. 5.2, the commentary notes that files with personal data can also be sent to others. It should be required that such others use the data they receive exclusively for the purposes of scientific research. The other exemptions mentioned above with respect to institutions for scientific research do not apply to them. Thus when other third parties process data for the purposes of scientific research and statistics (but do not qualify as institutions for scientific research), they should inform the data subject about processing of their data; the right of the data subject to access their data is applicable without limitations[289].

The term "sufficiently ensured" used in both paragraphs of Art. 5 refers to the agreement between the sender and the third party[290].

Art. 7 of the VSNU Code addresses the issue of publication of personal data. According to this article, publication of research results takes place in such a way that tracing data subjects is not possible in any way, unless the data subject gave their unambiguous consent or express consent if personal data belongs to special categories. Such consent should only be sought if publication of research results is not possible without tracing data subjects.

The Code of conduct for research and statistics was adopted by a number of (market) research organisations (namely *Vereniging voor Beleidsonderzoek* (VBO) (Association for Policy Research), *de Vereniging voor Statistiek en Onderzoek* (VSO) (Association for Statistics and Research) and *de Marktonderzoekassociatie.nl* (MOA) (Association for Market Research)).

This code is much less elaborate than the VSNU Code. The most important substantial difference between the two is that the VSNU Code regulates universities' (or other research institutions') own research when they act as controller. The

---

287 VSNU Code, p. 30.

288 Ibid.

289 Ibid.

290 Ibid.

Code of conduct for research and statistics focuses more on two different settings of research: research carried out by an organisation as contractor for the client (i.e. as processor) and research carried out by an organisation as controller.

The scope of the Code of conduct for research and statistics is very broad: it embraces all research where scientifically accepted methods are applied and amount to results not traceable to persons (or aggregated results). It can thus apply to both qualitative and quantitative research (surveys, opinion- and market research, censuses and/or monitoring)[291].

The Code of conduct for research and statistics does not contain any provisions relevant to the framework of online sharing of research data.

1.3.2 Germany

The world's first privacy Act was adopted in Germany in 1970. However, it was not a federal Act, but the Data Protection Act of the federal state of Hessen[292]. The Federal Data Protection Act (BDSG) came into force some years later in 1977. The BDSG has been amended several times and today it is strongly influenced by the Data Protection Directive. In fact, the Data Protection Directive in large part forms the basis of the BDSG.

1.3.2.1 Constitutional basis

It is helpful for understanding the German data protection legislation to have a look at the constitutional basis.

There is a fundamental right of data protection recognised in Germany[293]. However, unlike in the EU Charter and the regulations in some other Member States data protection is not explicitly mentioned in the German Constitution[294]. On the federal level, the right to data protection is derived from the general right to personality in conjunction with the fundamental rights of human dignity and has its basis in Art. 2(1) and Art. 1(1) of the German Constitution. Nevertheless the fundamental right of data protection is explicitly included in most of the Constitutions of the federal states[295].

---

291 Ploem, Tussen privacy en wetenschapsvrijheid. Regulering van gegevensverwerking voor medisch-wetenschappelijk onderzoek, 2004, p. 112.

292 See Gola/Schomerus, *Bundesdatenschutzgesetz*, 11th edition, Munich, C.H. Beck, 2012, Einleitung para. 1; Kühling/Seidel/Sivridis, *Datenschutzrecht*, 2nd edition, Heidelberg, C.F. Müller, 2011, p. 5.

293 Taeger, *Einführung in das Datenschutzrecht*, Frankfurt am Main, Deutscher Fachverlag, 2014, chapter II para. 1.

294 See Schrader, 'Datenschutz in den Grundrechtskatalog', CR 1994, 427.

295 See Gola/Schomerus, *Bundesdatenschutzgesetz*, 11th edition, Munich, C.H. Beck, 2012, Einleitung para. 3.

In this context the Federal Constitutional Court (BVerfG) recognised the "right to informational self-determination". This right comprises the protection of intimacy and privacy[296]. The fundamental decision of the BVerfG on this right was given in 1983[297].

The Court ruled in its judgment on the census that every individual has the right to decide, as a basic principle, on the surrender and use of their own personal data. Free development of the personality requires the protection of individuals against unlimited data collection, recording, use and transfer of their personal data.

It should be noted that the BVerfG uses a rather broad definition of the term "personal data". It ruled as early as 1983 that under the existing conditions for automated data processing there were no irrelevant data[298]. This must apply a fortiori under the conditions of today's information society.

Like all other fundamental rights, the right to informational self-determination is primarily a right of defence against the state. Interference with the right by a public authority requires a sufficient legal basis[299]. However, the application of the right to informational self-determination is not limited to actions of the state, but has effect in civil law too[300]. The state has the duty to guarantee that fundamental rights of the individual are not infringed by private parties[301]. In this respect, the fundamental rights of the Constitution – such as the right to informational self-determination – also guarantee an objective order of values which are deemed to govern civil law relations[302].

1.3.2.2 Aim of the data protection legislation

The aim of the BDSG is defined in its Art. 1(1). According to Art. 1(1) BDSG the objective of the law is to protect the individual against interference with their right to privacy due to dealing with their personal data. It is remarkable that the provision does not explicitly identify the protection of the right to informational self-determination as its aim, but it is recognised that the protection of this right is the main object of the general data protection legislation[303].

---

296 Tinnefeld/Buchner/Petri, *Einführung in das Datenschutzrecht*, 5th edition, Munich, Oldenbourg Verlag, 2012, p. 68.

297 BVerfG Case 1 BvR 209/83 et al. (15.12.1983), *Volkszählungsurteil.*

298 Ibid.

299 Ibid.

300 Taeger, *Einführung in das Datenschutzrecht*, Frankfurt am Main, Deutscher Fachverlag, 2014, chapter II para. 6.

301 See Grimm, 'Der Datenschutz vor einer Neuorientierung', JZ 2013, 585 (587 et seq.).

302 BVerfG Case 1 BvR 400/57 (15.01.1958).

303 See Simitis, in Simitis, *Bundesdatenschutzgesetz*, 8th edition, Baden-Baden, Nomos, 2014, § 1 para. 25.

Moreover, many federal state data protection laws explicitly mention the right to informational self-determination. Art. 1 of the Data Protection Act of the federal state of Lower Saxony (NDSG), for example, defines the aim of the law as being to guarantee the right of the individual to decide for themselves about release and use of their personal data (right to informational self-determination).

Thus the general objective of all German data protection legislation is the protection of the individual's right to informational self-determination.

1.3.2.3 Scope of application

Germany is a federal state. This means that there is federal law and state law on data protection in each of the 16 federal states. Moreover, and unlike the Data Protection Directive, German data protection legislation distinguishes between the processing of data by a public or private person or entity. This leads to some difficulties when determining the applicable law.

To decide which law is applicable in an individual case it is necessary to consider who is collecting or processing what kind of data[304]. For some areas there are field-specific regulations, for example the rules of the Telecommunications Act (TKG) or Telemedia Act (TMG) in the area of electronic communications and services. If no specific regulation exists, the general data protection law is applicable.

If a private person or entity is collecting or processing personal data, the relevant provisions of the federal law, the BDSG, are applicable (Art. 1(2) no. 3 BDSG). If a public authority is using personal data, which law applies depends on what kind of public authority is acting. Where a public body of the federal government is acting, the federal law, the BDSG, is applicable (Art. 1(2) no. 1 BDSG); where the acting body is that of a federal state, the federal state law on data protection is applicable (see e.g. Art. 2(1) NDSG)[305]. Due to the fact that it is impossible to analyse 16 different state laws within this study, the following analysis is mainly based on the BDSG.

Data protection regulations are applicable where personal data are concerned[306]. The BDSG, for example, shall apply to the collection, processing and utilisation of personal data (Art. 1(2) BDSG)[307]. Unlike the Data Protection Directive, the BDSG does not distinguish between automatic and non-automatic processing of personal data, at least in the field of public bodies[308]. Thus in the

---

304 Kühling/Seidel/Sivridis, *Datenschutzrecht*, 2nd edition, Heidelberg, C.F. Müller, 2011, p. 71.

305 See for a more detailed description of the scope of application: Taeger, *Einführung in das Datenschutzrecht*, Frankfurt am Main, Deutscher Fachverlag, 2014, chapter III paras 2 et seqq.; Simitis, in Simitis, *Bundesdatenschutzgesetz*, 8th edition, Baden-Baden, Nomos, 2014, § 1 paras 48 et seqq.

306 Brink/Eckhardt, 'Wann ist ein Datum ein personenbezogenes Datum?', ZD 2015, 205.

307 Likewise the NDSG, see § 2(1) in conjunction with § 3(2) NDSG.

308 Simitis, in Simitis, *Bundesdatenschutzgesetz*, 8th edition, Baden-Baden, Nomos, 2014, § 1 para. 71.

case of non-automatic processing, the BDSG shall apply not only if the data are stored or are intended to be stored in a filing system, but in every case of non-automatic data processing. Hence the scope of application is slightly broader.

However, if personal data are processed by a private person or entity the BDSG is only applicable when data are stored or processed by a data processing system or the data are taken from or stored in non-automated data files.

1.3.2.4 Definitions

Art. 3 BDSG contains some important definitions for the understanding of the Act.

1.3.2.4.1 Personal and anonymous data

Art. 3(1) BDSG defines personal data as individual items of data relating to the personal or professional circumstances of a specific or specifiable natural person (person concerned)[309].

The term "personal data" should be understood very broadly[310]. The definition covers, for example, name, address, age, profession, hair colour, bank account number, health-related data, finances, leisure behaviour – generally any data related to a concrete person[311].

Just as in the Data Protection Directive, but unlike the legislation in other states, for example Austria, Denmark or Luxembourg, only natural persons are protected by the BDSG; the Act is not applicable to data of legal persons[312] and decedents[313].

Personal data can be anonymised. Anonymised data fall outside the scope of the BDSG since those data are no longer related to an individual person. According to Art. 3(6) BDSG anonymisation means to modify personal data in such a way that details of personal or professional circumstances can no longer, or only with disproportionate investment of time, cost and labour, be attributed to an identified or identifiable natural person.

---

[309] The same definition is used in § 3(1) NDSG.

[310] See Buchner, in Taeger/Gabel, *BDSG*, Frankfurt am Main, Deutscher Fachverlag, 2013, § 3 para. 3.

[311] See Taeger, *Einführung in das Datenschutzrecht*, Frankfurt am Main, Deutscher Fachverlag, 2014, chapter III para. 36; Gola/Schomerus, *Bundesdatenschutzgesetz*, 11th edition, Munich, C.H. Beck, 2012, § 3 paras 3 et seqq.

[312] Gola/Schomerus, *Bundesdatenschutzgesetz*, 11th edition, Munich, C.H. Beck, 2012, § 3 para. 11.

[313] Ibid., para. 12.

As can be seen from this provision, the legislator accepts that there is no absolute anonymity. Data are deemed anonymous when the attribution to an identifiable person is possible but disproportionate (relative anonymity). In this respect the question is not whether data are anonymous but whether they are sufficiently anonymous[314].

1.3.2.4.2 Collecting, processing and using personal data

Unlike the Data Protection Directive, the BDSG does not use just the term "processing of personal data" as a relevant act, but distinguishes between collecting, processing and use of personal data.

"Collecting" is the acquisition of data of a person concerned (Art. 3(3) BDSG). Collecting is a prerequisite for the subsequent processing[315]. Collecting requires an active action of the responsible body[316].

"Processing" means the storage, modification, transmission, blocking and deletion of personal data (Art. 3(4) BDSG). The terms "storage", "modification", "transmission", "blocking" and "deletion" are further specified in Art. 3(4) BDSG.

"Use" is any use of personal data which is not processing (Art. 3(5) BDSG). This term serves as a catch-all element[317].

Within the BDSG, the relevant actions according to data protection law are more precisely described than in the directive. But effectively the provisions of the directive and the BDSG have the same content. Any operation which is performed upon personal data constitutes a relevant act according to data protection legislation.

1.3.2.4.3 Responsible body

Art. 3(7) BDSG defines the responsible body as every person or entity that collects, processes or uses personal data for and by themselves or through a third party.

The BDSG refers to the responsible body and does not use the term "data controller" as in the Data Protection Directive[318]. "Responsible body" is the collective term for all norm addressees mentioned in Art. 2 BDSG[319]. These are public and private entities, and natural and legal persons. The meaning is similar to the meaning of the term "data controller".

---

314 Dingledine, *The Free Haven Project*, 2012, text available at: http://www.freehaven.net/doc/freehaven.pdf, p. 13.

315 See Gola/Schomerus, *Bundesdatenschutzgesetz*, 11th edition, Munich, C.H. Beck, 2012, § 3 para. 24.

316 Tinnefeld/Buchner/Petri, *Einführung in das Datenschutzrecht*, 5th edition, Munich, Oldenbourg Verlag, 2012, p. 230.

317 Ibid., p. 232.

318 The Netherlands does not use the term "controller" either, see above Section 1.3.1.1.5.

319 Gola/Schomerus, *Bundesdatenschutzgesetz*, 11th edition, Munich, C.H. Beck, 2012, § 3 para. 48.

1.3.2.4.4 Special categories of personal data

German data protection law provides for special categories of personal data. According to Art. 3(9) BDSG, these special categories of personal data are information about a person's racial or ethnic origins, political opinions, religious or philosophical beliefs, trade union membership, health or sex life.

These special categories of data are considered to be particularly sensitive. There are some special provisions regarding the processing of these categories of personal data in the BDSG[320]. As a general principle, special categories of personal data may not be processed. This provision is in line with Art. 8(1) Data Protection Directive, which requires Member States to prohibit the processing of personal data revealing racial or ethnic origin, political opinions, religious or philosophical beliefs, trade union membership, and concerning health or sex life.

Whether the distinction between personal data and special categories of such data is useful can be questioned. It is generally the context in which data are used that makes them sensitive. For example, the name of a person in a register of a drug counselling office can be very sensitive although a name itself does not belong to the special categories of personal data in terms of the BDSG or the Data Protection Directive[321].

1.3.2.4.5 Order data processing

Art. 11 BDSG contains provisions on order data processing. Where a contracted data processor collects, processes or uses data on behalf of the responsible body, the contracting authority and not the contracted processor is responsible for compliance with the BDSG and other data protection regulations. The responsible body has to choose the contracted data processor carefully and ensure that they fulfil data security standards, and is entitled to issue instructions to the processor[322]. The agreement on order data processing must be in writing.

The contracted data processor has no interest of its own in collecting, processing or using the data. It is just the contracting authority that wants the data to be processed. Examples of such order data processing are the outsourcing of payroll accounting or e-mail services through subcontracting them to external computer centres or the use of external call centres as an instrument for consumer acquisition[323].

---

[320] Ibid., para. 56.

[321] See Tinnefeld/Buchner/Petri, *Einführung in das Datenschutzrecht*, 5th edition, Munich, Oldenbourg Verlag, 2012, p. 240.

[322] See Taeger, *Einführung in das Datenschutzrecht*, Frankfurt am Main, Deutscher Fachverlag, 2014, chapter III para. 65.

[323] Tinnefeld/Buchner/Petri, *Einführung in das Datenschutzrecht*, 5th edition, Munich, Oldenbourg Verlag, 2012, pp. 258 et seq.

1.3.2.4.6 Consent

Art. 4a BDSG contains the central provision on consent for the processing of personal data. Consent is only effective if it is based on the free decision of the person concerned. The person concerned must be informed about the purpose of the collection, processing or use of the personal data. Furthermore, the responsible body has to indicate to the person concerned the consequences of the refusal of consent.

The Data Protection Directive does not require a particular form of consent. Consent can be given verbally or in writing[324]. The German legislation requires written consent. According to Art. 4a(1) BDSG, consent must in principle meet the requirements of written form, except where due to exceptional circumstances another form than the written form is appropriate. Thus the present German standards on consent are stricter than the provisions of the European directive. In fact no other EU Member State requires a written form of consent[325].

Art. 4a(2) BDSG contains a special provision concerning scientific research. In the area of scientific research, a written form of consent is not required if it would significantly affect the intended research purpose.

Concerning the collecting, processing or use of special categories of personal data, Art. 4a(3) BDSG requires the consent to be explicitly given with regard to these data. Consistently this requires written form and the naming of the data in the text of the expression of consent[326].

1.3.2.5 Processing of personal data

The BDSG implements the Data Protection Directive into national German legislation. It lays down general conditions to legitimise the processing of personal data.

[324] Ehmann/Helfrich, *EG Datenschutzrichtlinie Kurzkommentar*, Cologne, Dr. Otto Schmidt, 1999, Art. 2 para. 67; Drewes/Siegert, 'Die konkludente Einwilligung in Telefonmarketing und das Ende des Dogmas von der datenschutzrechtlichen Schriftform', RDV 2006, 139 (144).

[325] Drewes/Siegert, 'Die konkludente Einwilligung in Telefonmarketing und das Ende des Dogmas von der datenschutzrechtlichen Schriftform', RDV 2006, 139.

[326] Gola/Schomerus, *Bundesdatenschutzgesetz*, 11th edition, Munich, C.H. Beck, 2012, § 3 para. 57.

1.3.2.5.1 Binding to the purpose of processing

From the recognition of the constitutional right of data protection follows the obligation to allow the processing of personal data only for specific and legitimate purposes[327]. The binding of the processing to its purpose is not explicitly mentioned in the BDSG[328] but it is generally accepted. Furthermore, several provisions of the Act imply this principle[329].

Even before personal data are collected, processed or used, the purpose of such use must be fixed[330]. For the processing of data through private entities, this requirement is even explicitly mentioned in Art. 28(1) BDSG. After the collection of data for a specific purpose, such data are only allowed to be used for the intended purpose. The ability of personal data to be processed is thus restricted permanently[331]. Only in certain cases determined by law, or if extended consent has been obtained, is the changing of the intended purpose permitted[332]. Data retention without the binding to a purpose is not permitted[333].

1.3.2.5.2 Principle of necessity

Administrative actions must always comply with the principle of proportionality[334]. The principle of necessity is part of proportionality. According to this principle, interference with a person's fundamental right is only justifiable if it is necessary to achieve a legitimate objective. It is not justifiable if the objective can be achieved just as well by other less intrusive alternative measures.

In the field of data protection law, Art. 13(1) BDSG emphasises this principle. According to this provision, the collection of personal data by a public authority is permitted if knowledge of the data is necessary for the responsible body to perform its tasks. The task in question must be assigned to the public body which is collecting the data. The public body is only allowed to collect the minimum of

---

[327] See BVerfG Case 1 BvR 209/83 et al. (15.12.1983), *Volkszählungsurteil.*

[328] Gola/Schomerus, *Bundesdatenschutzgesetz*, 11th edition, Munich, C.H. Beck, 2012, § 14 para. 9; Helbing, 'Big Data und der datenschutzrechtliche Grundsatz der Zweckbindung', K&R 2015, 145 (147).

[329] See e.g. Art. 4(3), Art. 4a(1), Art. 4b(6), Art. 14, Art. 28 BDSG.

[330] Gola/Klug, *Grundzüge des Datenschutzrechts*, Munich, C.H. Beck, 2003, pp. 48 et seq.

[331] Simitis, in Simitis, *Bundesdatenschutzgesetz*, 8th edition, Baden-Baden, Nomos, 2014, Einleitung para. 38.

[332] Taeger, *Einführung in das Datenschutzrecht*, Frankfurt am Main, Deutscher Fachverlag, 2014, chapter III para. 114.

[333] Tinnefeld/Buchner/Petri, *Einführung in das Datenschutzrecht*, 5th edition, Munich, Oldenbourg Verlag, 2012, p. 237.

[334] See Maurer, *Staatsrecht I*, Munich, C.H. Beck, 2010, § 8 paras 55 et seqq.

data it requires for its tasks, it is not sufficient for the collection of data to be merely practical, useful or appropriate[335]. Data collection without a specific reason is generally not permitted[336].

If the responsible body is a private person or entity, such body generally has no assigned tasks. Hence the principle of necessity can only be applied in a limited way. As a rule, the use of the data must be covered by the consent of the person concerned. Additionally the BDSG contains some balancing clauses which are applicable for the use of personal data by private responsible bodies[337].

1.3.2.5.3 Principle of data avoidance and data economy

Art. 3a BDSG contains an important goal of data protection law. The collection, processing and use of personal data and of data processing systems shall be oriented towards the goal of collecting, processing or using as little personal data as possible. In particular, personal data shall be anonymised or pseudonymised as far as this is possible within the scope of the intended use.

Technical data protection and privacy-friendly system structures must contribute to a high level of protection of personal data[338]. Art. 3a BDSG highlights once again that even before a privacy-relevant action is carried out, the responsible body – irrespective of whether public or private – shall decide whether the action is necessary at all. The principle of data avoidance and data economy is a legal duty. A violation of this duty is not enforced by a penalty; nevertheless it is binding[339].

1.3.2.5.4 Direct survey and transparency

The fundamental right to informational self-determination requires the handling of personal data to be transparent[340]. The BVerfG explicitly ruled in its judgment on the census that every citizen has the right to know what is known about them, by whom, at what time and on what occasion[341]. Only when the individual knows who knows what about them are they able to decide for themself about the use of their data. Moreover, the person concerned is only able to exercise their rights of rectification, erasure or blocking of personal data according to Art. 20 or Art. 35

---

335 Wedde, in Däubler/Klebe/Wedde/Weichert, *Bundesdatenschutzgesetz*, 4th edition, Frankfurt am Main, Bund, 2014, § 13 para. 15.

336 Sokol/Scholz, in Simitis, *Bundesdatenschutzgesetz*, 8th edition, Baden-Baden, Nomos, 2014, § 13 para. 26; Gola/Klug, *Grundzüge des Datenschutzrechts*, Munich, C.H. Beck, 2003, p. 48.

337 See e.g. § 28(1) no. 2 BDSG.

338 Kühling/Seidel/Sivridis, *Datenschutzrecht*, 2nd edition, Heidelberg, C.F. Müller, 2011, p. 112.

339 Kühling/Bohnen, 'Zur Zukunft des Datenschutzrechts – Nach der Reform ist vor der Reform', JZ 2010, 600 (603).

340 Wedde, in Däubler/Klebe/Wedde/Weichert, *Bundesdatenschutzgesetz*, 4th edition, Frankfurt am Main, Bund, 2014, § 19a para. 2.

341 BVerfG Case 1 BvR 209/83 et al. (15.12.1983), *Volkszählungsurteil.*

BDSG if they have information about who is using their data[342]. Additionally, the principle of direct survey best guarantees the authenticity and correctness of the collected data[343].

In line with this principle of transparency, Art. 4(2) BDSG states that personal data are to be collected directly from the person concerned. Without their participation, personal data may only be collected if this is required by law, the administrative task or business objective requires indirect collection, or direct collection involves a disproportionate effort. Where personal data are collected, the responsible body is required to inform the person concerned about the identity of the responsible body, and the purpose of collection, processing or use, and provide information on the categories of recipients of the data (Art. 4(3) BDSG).

1.3.2.5.5 Prohibition with the reservation of permission

Art. 4(1) BDSG clarifies that the collecting, processing and use of personal data is only allowed in so far as the BDSG or another legal provision permits it or the person concerned has consented to the use of their data. According to this the collecting, processing and use of personal data is forbidden as a matter of principle. The use of personal data is allowed only as far as there is a legitimisation. Such legitimisation is either provided for by law or the existing consent of the person concerned[344].

The importance of the provision in Art. 4(1) BDSG cannot be overestimated[345] since besides the principle of prohibition with the reservation of permission, it includes one more important rule, namely that collecting, processing and use of personal data is allowed if the person concerned has given their consent. It thus implements the first and probably most important permission for the processing of personal data.

German data protection legislation distinguishes between the processing of data by a public or private person or entity. However, permission through consent is applicable in the public as well as in the private sector. This is logical since the aim of the BDSG is to guarantee the right of the individual to decide for themself about release and use of their personal data. But then the individual must be able to allow the use of their data, irrespective of the nature of the responsible body. Through the consent of the person concerned, the interference with the right to informational self-determination loses its illegal character[346].

---

342 See Taeger, *Einführung in das Datenschutzrecht*, Frankfurt am Main, Deutscher Fachverlag, 2014, chapter III para. 122.

343 Tinnefeld/Buchner/Petri, *Einführung in das Datenschutzrecht*, 5th edition, Munich, Oldenbourg Verlag, 2012, p. 238.

344 Taeger, *Einführung in das Datenschutzrecht*, Frankfurt am Main, Deutscher Fachverlag, 2014, chapter III para. 133.

345 Scholz/Sokol, in Simitis, *Bundesdatenschutzgesetz*, 8th edition, Baden-Baden, Nomos, 2014, § 4 para. 2.

346 Rogosch, *Die Einwilligung im Datenschutzrecht*, Baden-Baden, Nomos, 2013, p. 37.

Although the legitimisation of the processing of personal data through consent is applicable to both sectors, it is more relevant in the private sector[347] as public authorities are not allowed to use consent as an instrument to circumvent the constitutional principal that a legal basis is needed for any interference in the right to informational self-determination[348].

As already mentioned[349], Art. 4a BDSG contains the central provision on consent for the processing of personal data. Consent must be based on the free decision of the person concerned and the person must be informed about the purpose of the collection of personal data. However it can often be called into question whether the persons concerned really have the choice to refuse consent. Often they simply have to consent to be able to use a service, to obtain credit or to order consumer goods[350]. In fact the instrument of consent is often a blunt instrument in the fight for informational self-determination.

1.3.2.5.6 Permissive rules in the public sector

In any case, in order to be legal the collecting, processing and use of personal data by public authorities needs legitimisation. Sector-specific legitimisations for the use of personal data by public authorities can be found in federal as well as state law[351]. However, if no sector-specific provision is applicable, some general provisions which allow the use of personal data can be found in the BDSG.

I. Art. 13(1) BDSG is the central provision concerning the collection of personal data through a public authority. The collection of the data in question by a public authority is permitted if knowledge of the data is necessary for the responsible body to perform its tasks.

First, this requires the public authority to be competent to perform the task in question. Secondly, the performance of the task itself must be lawful. However, in addition to these standard requirements for a public authority to act lawfully, thirdly, the collection of data must be necessary to perform the lawful task[352]. Regarding the collection of special categories of personal data (Art. 3(9) BDSG), Art. 13(2) BDSG lays down some special requirements.

---

347 Däubler, in Däubler/Klebe/Wedde/Weichert, *Bundesdatenschutzgesetz*, 4th edition, Frankfurt am Main, Bund, 2014, § 4a para. 3; Holznagel/Sonntag, in Roßnagel, *Handbuch Datenschutzrecht*, Munich, C.H. Beck, 2003, chapter 4.8 para. 24.

348 See Tinnefeld/Buchner/Petri, *Einführung in das Datenschutzrecht*, 5th edition, Munich, Oldenbourg Verlag, 2012, pp. 323 et seq.

349 See above section 1.3.2.4.6.

350 See Tinnefeld/Buchner/Petri, *Einführung in das Datenschutzrecht*, 5th edition, Munich, Oldenbourg Verlag, 2012, pp. 345 et seqq.

351 An overview can be found in Bergmann/Möhle/Herb, *Datenschutzrecht*, 48th edition, Stuttgart et al., Boorberg Verlag, 2015, chapter I, para. 4.2.2.

352 See Gola/Schomerus, *Bundesdatenschutzgesetz*, 11th edition, Munich, C.H. Beck, 2012, § 13 para. 3; Tinnefeld/Buchner/Petri, *Einführung in das Datenschutzrecht*, 5th edition, Munich, Oldenbourg Verlag, 2012, p. 320.

Special categories of personal data may not be collected, processed or used as a general principle. However, Art. 13(2) no. 9 BDSG allows the collection of special categories of personal data if it is necessary for conducting scientific research and the *scientific* interest in the conduct of the research considerably outweighs the interest of the person concerned in their data not being used, and the research purpose cannot, or only with disproportionate efforts, be achieved by other means.

II. Art. 14(1) BDSG stipulates that storage, modification or use of personal data is permitted if this is necessary for the responsible body to perform its task and the data were collected to perform this task. This means that data which are collected for a specific purpose must generally be used for this purpose and no other. However, the principle of binding the use of data to the purpose of collection requires some exceptions within the administrative process[353]. Therefore Art. 14(2) BDSG allows storage, modification or use for other purposes if certain conditions are met, for example it is required by law or the person concerned consented to the other use.

Art. 14(2) no. 9 BDSG allows the storage, modification or use of personal data if it is necessary for conducting scientific research and the *scientific* interest in the conduct of research considerably outweighs the interest of the person concerned in their data not being used and the research purpose cannot, or only with disproportionate efforts, be achieved by other means.

Art. 14(5) no. 2 BDSG allows the storage, modification or use of special categories of personal data if it is necessary for conducting scientific research and the *public* interest in the conduct of the research considerably outweighs the interest of the person concerned in their data not being used and the research purpose cannot, or only with disproportionate efforts, be achieved by other means. Unlike the provision of Art. 13(2) no. 9 BDSG, Art. 14(5) no. 2 BDSG requires not just a prevailing *scientific* interest, but a prevailing *public* interest. This regulation is therefore slightly stricter[354].

As an example of federal state legislation, Art. 25 NDSG contains a provision on the processing of personal data for scientific purposes. The provision is applicable when a public entity of the federal state of Lower Saxony processes personal data in the context of a research project[355]. According to Art. 25(2) NDSG, the processing of personal data which were initially collected or stored for other purposes can be processed for a specific research project if:

- the persons concerned have consented to such use;
- a legislative provision provides for such use; or

353 Gola/Schomerus, *Bundesdatenschutzgesetz*, 11th edition, Munich, C.H. Beck, 2012, § 14 para. 12.

354 See in more detail Dammann, in Simitis, *Bundesdatenschutzgesetz*, 8th edition, Baden-Baden, Nomos, 2014, § 14 para. 120.

355 See above Section 1.3.2.3.

- owing to the kind of data and the manner in which they are processed it is unlikely that the legitimate interests of the person concerned are affected or the *public* interest in the conduct of the research considerably outweighs the interest of the person concerned in their data not being used.

Additionally, the personal data must be pseudonymised or anonymised or deleted as soon as the research purpose allows this (Art. 25(4) NDSG).

Sector-specific regulation of scientific use of personal data is, for example, included in the German Social Code (Sozialgesetzbuch; SGB X). Art. 75(1) no. 1 SGB X allows the transmission of social data if such transfer is necessary for a particular purpose of scientific research in the area of social welfare or labour market research or occupational research, and the legitimate interests of the person concerned are not affected or the *public* interest in the conduct of the research considerably outweighs the interest in confidentiality of the person concerned.

III. According to Art. 15(1) BDSG the transfer of personal data to another public authority is permitted if the transfer is necessary to perform the task of the transmitting party or the recipient and the requirements of Art. 14 BDSG are met. The transmitting party is responsible for compliance of the transfer with data protection law (Art. 15(2) BDSG).

Art. 16 BDSG deals with the transfer of personal data by a public authority to a private person or entity. Such transfer is permitted if the transfer is necessary to perform the task of the transmitting party and the requirements of Art. 14 BDSG are met or the recipient has a legitimate interest in knowing the data concerned. Again, the transmitting party is responsible for compliance of the transfer with data protection law.

1.3.2.5.7 Permissive rules in the private sector

The legitimisation of data processing through consent is of great importance, especially in the private sector[356]. If the person concerned has not consented to the collecting, processing or use of their data, the use is only legal as far as another legitimisation is applicable[357]. Such legitimisations can be found in sector-specific laws or, if no such legitimisation exists, in Arts 28 et seqq. BDSG.

---

[356] See Tinnefeld/Buchner/Petri, *Einführung in das Datenschutzrecht*, 5th edition, Munich, Oldenbourg Verlag, 2012, p. 341.

[357] Kühling/Seidel/Sivridis, *Datenschutzrecht*, 2nd edition, Heidelberg, C.F. Müller, 2011, p. 136.

The central provision for the use of personal data through private responsible bodies is Art. 28 BDSG[358]. According to Art. 28(1) BDSG, collecting, storage, modification, transmission or use of personal data for the performance of one's own business is allowed, if:

a) it is necessary for the establishment, performance or termination of a contractual obligation to which the person concerned is party with;

b) it is necessary to maintain the responsible body's legitimate interests and there are no grounds for assuming that the person concerned has an overriding legitimate interest in precluding the processing or use of the data; or

c) the data are generally accessible and the person concerned has no obvious overriding interest in precluding the processing or use of the data.

Art. 28(1) no. 1 BDSG requires a contractual or quasi-contractual relationship between the responsible body and the person concerned and in addition the necessity to process or use the data to perform the contract[359]. Art. 28(1) no. 2 BDSG requires a balancing of the interests of the responsible body and the person concerned. This implies a decision on a case-by-case basis[360]. The Data Protection Directive does not prescribe the legitimisation of data processing where the data are generally accessible. However, Art. 28(1) no. 3 BDSG introduces such a legitimisation. Data such as those found in phone books, newspaper articles or public registers such as the commercial register or register of associations are generally accessible.

Art. 28(1) sentence 2 BDSG emphasises once again the principle of binding the use of data to the purpose of collection. If data are collected, the purpose of processing and use shall be specified.

Nevertheless, Art. 28(2) BDSG allows the transmission or use of data for other purposes in some cases. For example, Art. 28(2) no. 3 BDSG allows the transmission or use if this is necessary in the interests of a research institution for undertaking its research and the *scientific* interest in the conduct of research considerably outweighs the interest of the person concerned in their data not being used for this other purpose and the research purpose cannot, or only with disproportionate efforts, be achieved by other means.

---

[358] Buchner, in Taeger/Gabel, *BDSG*, Frankfurt am Main, Deutscher Fachverlag, 2013, § 27 paras 4 et seqq.

[359] Taeger, *Einführung in das Datenschutzrecht*, Frankfurt am Main, Deutscher Fachverlag, 2014, chapter III para. 144.

[360] Gola/Schomerus, *Bundesdatenschutzgesetz*, 11th edition, Munich, C.H. Beck, 2012, § 28 para. 27.

The collecting, processing or use of special categories of personal data for the performance of one's own business is as a matter of principle permitted only if the person concerned has consented thereto. However, Art. 28(6) BDSG contains some exceptions to this principle. Regarding scientific research, Art. 28(6) no. 4 BDSG allows the collecting, processing and use of special categories of personal data if this is necessary for conducting scientific research and the *scientific* interest in the conduct of research considerably outweighs the interest of the person concerned in their data not being used and the research purpose cannot, or only with disproportionate efforts, be achieved by other means. It is worth noting that this provision privileges only in-house research of the respective research institution[361].

There are some provisions in Arts 28 et seqq. BDSG dealing with the use of personal data for advertising purposes, data transfers to credit agencies, scoring and address trading. However, those regulations are of minor relevance in the context of the research carried out in this study.

1.3.2.5.8 Rights of the person concerned

The BDSG provides some rights for the person concerned. To enable the person concerned to exercise their rights they first need to have knowledge of the processing of their personal data[362]. Therefore, Arts 19a(1) and 33(1) BDSG contain an information obligation: where personal data have been obtained without the knowledge of the person concerned, the responsible body has to inform the person about the collection of data, the identity of the responsible body, the intended purpose of the collecting, and other recipients to whom the data are transferred.

There are some exceptions to the duty to inform the person concerned in Arts 19a(2) and 33(2) BDSG. For example, if the person concerned has become aware of the use of their data by other means, or informing them would require a disproportionate effort, or the storing or data transmission is explicitly required by law, the responsible body does not have to inform the person concerned.

In addition to the information duty of the responsible body, the person concerned has a right to information. According to Arts 19 and 34 BDSG, the person concerned can in particular demand information on:

- what personal data relating to them have been stored and how the data were collected;
- the recipients or categories of recipients to whom the data have been disclosed; and
- the purpose of the storage.

---

361 Kühling/Seidel/Sivridis, *Datenschutzrecht*, 2nd edition, Heidelberg, C.F. Müller, 2011, p. 153; Bergmann/Möhle/Herb, *Datenschutzrecht*, 48th edition, Stuttgart et al., Boorberg Verlag, 2015, BDSG § 28, para. 522.

362 Tinnefeld/Buchner/Petri, *Einführung in das Datenschutzrecht*, 5th edition, Munich, Oldenbourg Verlag, 2012, p. 270.

Based on the information on the use of their personal data, the person concerned can exercise their rights of rectification, erasure or blocking. Art. 20(1) and Art. 35(1) BDSG require the responsible body to rectify personal data if they are incorrect. They must rectify the data on their own initiative if they become aware of inaccuracies[363].

According to Arts 20(2) and 35(2) BDSG, personal data must be erased if, for example, their storage is illegal or the knowledge of the data is no longer necessary for the responsible body in order to achieve the purpose for which the data were stored.

Blocking means the marking of personal data in order to restrict their further use (see Art. 3(IV) no. 4 BDSG). Art. 20(3) and Art. 35(3) BDSG require the blocking of data in the event they cannot be erased because:

- they have to be stored due to a legal retention period;
- there are reasonable grounds to assume that by erasing the data legitimate interests of the person concerned would be affected; or
- erasure of the data is not, or only with disproportionate efforts, possible due to the particular type of storage.

Arts 20(5) and 35(5) BDSG entail the right of the person concerned to object against the otherwise legitimate[364] processing and use of their personal data if their legitimate interests, owing to their particular personal situation, outweigh the interests of the body responsible for processing the data.

Art. 6(1) BDSG clarifies that the rights of information, rectification, erasure or blocking of the person concerned cannot be excluded or limited by means of legal transaction.

1.3.2.5.9 Trans-border data flows

The provisions concerning trans-border data flows are strongly influenced by the European Data Protection Directive too.

For transmission of personal data within the European data protection area (consisting of the EU and EEA), the same legal limits shall apply as to transmission within Germany. In this respect Art. 4b(1) BDSG states that the relevant provisions of the BDSG, namely Arts 15(1), 16(1) and 28–30a, are applicable to such transfers. This means that a responsible body which is located in Germany must comply with the relevant German data protection rules, even if the recipient is located in another country of the European data protection area.

---

[363] Mallmann, in Simitis, *Bundesdatenschutzgesetz*, 8th edition, Baden-Baden, Nomos, 2014, § 20 para. 25.

[364] Kühling/Seidel/Sivridis, *Datenschutzrecht*, 2nd edition, Heidelberg, C.F. Müller, 2011, p. 195.

Concerning the transfer of personal data to third countries, Art. 4b(2) BDSG stipulates that such a transfer must not take place in so far as the person concerned has a legitimate interest in not transmitting the data, in particular if the recipient country does not ensure an adequate level of data protection. Art. 4b(3) BDSG specifies some criteria for assessing an adequate level of data protection. Art. 4c BDSG contains some exceptions on the principle of ensuring an adequate level of protection; for example, such a transfer may be legal if the person concerned consented to the transfer.

From a European point of view, the US does not guarantee an adequate level of data protection. However, to enable data transfer to the US, the "Safe Harbour Principle" was created. It is based on a voluntary commitment by US data recipients to comply with stronger data protection rules[365]. In turn the EU accepts those recipients as safe. Whether the commitment of US data recipients is an effective way to guarantee adequate data protection is more than questionable. In fact most of the Safe Harbour participants do not even comply with the basic principles of this agreement[366]. Consequently the ECJ recently quashed the Safe Harbour decision of the European Commission[367].

1.3.2.5.10 Data protection control

In order to ensure compliance with data protection regulations, Germany has implemented a combination of internal and external data protection controls.

The external control for the public sector is exercised by the Federal Commissioner for Data Protection and Freedom of Information and the corresponding Commissioners at the federal state level. According to Art. 22(4) BDSG the Federal Commissioner is independent as regards the performance of their duties.

The Federal Commissioner monitors compliance of federal public bodies with the BDSG and other data protection rules (Art. 24(1) BDSG). If the Federal Commissioner becomes aware of violations of data protection rules, they must make a complaint about the violation (Art. 25(1) BDSG). Every two years the Federal Commissioner must present an activity report to Parliament (Art. 26(1) BDSG).

As far as the private sector is concerned, the federal states are obliged to establish supervisory authorities (Art. 38(6) BDSG). According to Art. 38(3) BDSG the responsible bodies are obliged to provide the supervisory authority with the necessary information. Art. 38(4) BSDG provides the supervisory authority with necessary rights of access and rights of inspection. Art. 38(5)

---

365 Ibid., pp. 31 et seq.

366 Tinnefeld/Buchner/Petri, *Einführung in das Datenschutzrecht*, 5th edition, Munich, Oldenbourg Verlag, 2012, p. 266.

367 ECJ Case C-362/14 (6.11.2015), *Schrems v Data Protection Commissioner*.

BDSG enables the supervisory authority to release official orders to responsible bodies in order to ensure compliance with the BDSG and other data protection rules.

Internal data protection control is exercised by data protection officers. Art. 4d(1) BDSG imposes a duty on responsible bodies to report procedures of automated processing to the competent supervisory authority. But according to Art. 4d(2) BDSG, the reporting is not necessary if a data protection officer is appointed. Art. 4f BDSG describes the cases in which a data protection officer needs to be appointed. In fact, most of the responsible bodies fall under this paragraph. As a result, the reporting obligation under Art. 4d(1) BDSG is the exception rather than the rule[368].

The data protection officer works to ensure compliance with the BDSG and other data protection regulations. Therefore they must, among other things, monitor the proper use of data processing programs and familiarise relevant persons with the provisions of the BDSG and other data protection regulations (Art. 4g (1) BDSG). A data protection officer can be an employee of the responsible body or an external person[369].

It is worth noting that the data protection officer works towards compliance with data protection rules. Nevertheless, it is still the management of the responsible body that is legally responsible for compliance with legal rules[370].

1.3.3 Poland

In Poland personal data are protected under general rules of civil law applying to privacy and other personal rights. In the course of democratic changes initiated in 1989 and harmonisation of law with the acquis, protection has also been provided by administrative law, mainly in the form of the Act of 29 August 1997 on the protection of personal data ("the Act"). Before the introduction of the Act, there had been no specific administrative provisions focusing on the protection of data subjects but there certainly had been provisions regulating the processing of various personal data in public registries, which provided for protection mainly by simple delimitation of authorities' competence in processing the data. The Act has been amended several times since it entered into force.

---

[368] Kühling/Seidel/Sivridis, *Datenschutzrecht*, 2nd edition, Heidelberg, C.F. Müller, 2011, p. 201.

[369] Tinnefeld/Buchner/Petri, *Einführung in das Datenschutzrecht*, 5th edition, Munich, Oldenbourg Verlag, 2012, p. 281.

[370] See Simitis, in Simitis, *Bundesdatenschutzgesetz*, 8th edition, Baden-Baden, Nomos, 2014, § 4g para. 29.

1.3.3.1 Constitutional basis

The Polish Constitution of 1997 does not have a specific provision on personal data protection but it lays down some basic principles for the protection of privacy (right to privacy) and informational self-determination. Naturally, the Constitution is mostly concerned with the protection of citizens vis-à-vis the state and so it focuses on delimiting administrative powers to gather and process data, as well as on obligations to make the data accessible to data subjects and, in particular, to correct data. Following the rule of law, the Constitution explicitly forbids public authorities to process data other than as necessary in the democratic state, and it explicitly authorises the terms of such processing to be specified in an Act of Parliament. However, the Act is not limited to the relationship of data subjects with the state as it also applies to private data controllers and processors.

1.3.3.2 Aim of the data protection legislation

The Act constitutes the implementation of the Data Protection Directive. It is generally agreed that the Act aims at the protection of interests of data subjects but this aim is not explicitly defined in the Act. Rather, it stipulates in Art. 1 everyone's right to protection of their personal data and provides for a closed list of reasons that legitimise processing of personal data (although these general reasons are expressed in very broad terms – i.e., public good, personal good, third-party good). These reasons are further specified in the Act and they may also be specified in separate laws regulating specific areas (e.g. Acts on various public registries).

1.3.3.3 Scope of application

The scope of application of the Act is defined as follows: the Act recognises the right to protection of personal data attributable to everyone (every natural person), which implies that generally there is no protection of personal data of non-living persons. The Act (Art. 2) applies to personal data processed in datasets (with a notable exception where processing takes place in an IT system – then the Act also applies when the processing takes place outside a dataset). Further, according to Art. 3, the Act applies to public authorities (both central and territorial administration) and entities incorporated by them, and private entities that perform public tasks. It also applies to natural and legal persons that process personal data for economic, professional or statutory reasons. In Art. 3 it is further specified that the Act applies to entities processing data that have their seat or residence in Poland, but also to those entities that merely use technical means situated in Poland (unless such technical means are used only to transmit data). For the avoidance of doubt, only processing of personal data by natural persons for personal reasons is explicitly excluded from the scope of the Act (Art. 3a). Further exclusions (Art. 3a.2) apply to journalism and literary and artistic activities, unless freedom of expression and dissemination of information materially infringe the rights and freedoms of data subjects. There is no exclusion for scientific activity but there is special treatment for temporary datasets assembled only for technical reasons, for educational reasons, or in the course of lecturing at high schools if they are immediately removed after use or anonymised – such datasets are subject only to a limited part of the Act.

1.3.3.4 Definitions

There are definitions of important terms, found mainly at the beginning of the Act.

1.3.3.4.1 Personal and anonymous data

According to Art. 6.1, personal data comprise any information pertaining to an identified or identifiable natural person. Thus, there is no provision in the Act for protection of data of legal persons. A person is considered identifiable when it is possible to specify their identity directly or indirectly, in particular using an ID number, or the person's physical, physiological, intellectual, economic, cultural or social characteristics (Art. 6.2). Data is not considered personal when excessive costs, time or activities would be required to ascertain the meaning of the data (Art. 6.3).

The definition above is very broad and highly subjective. There is no limitation on what kind of data may constitute personal data, so they are not just names, addresses, etc. Any information attached to a person that allows that person to be identified is personal data. But this always has to be considered from the point of view of the entity that processes the given piece of data. If such data are meaningless to that entity or the entity would be required to employ excessive costs, time or activities to ascertain the meaning of the data, those data do not constitute personal data for that entity. If the same piece of data is acquired by another entity, it may constitute personal data for the new entity, for example if the costs are no longer excessive.

Anonymous data are not explicitly defined but the definition can be derived from the above using *argumentum a contrario*. The Act uses the term "anonymisation" when specifying its scope, so such a working definition is useful in practice. Generally speaking, anonymisation can be understood as removing information necessary to identify the data subject without having to invest excessive costs, time or activities.

1.3.3.4.2 Processing of personal data

Any activity performed on personal data is "processing" (Art. 7.2). The provision explicitly mentions that collecting, recording, storing, modifying, making available and deleting are types of processing, especially if they are performed in IT systems.

1.3.3.4.3 Data administrator

In the Act the responsible body is called the "administrator danych" (English: "data administrator") and is the equivalent of "data controller" as understood in the Data Protection Directive. "Administrator danych" is defined as any entity within the scope of the Act that undertakes decisions about aims and means of data processing.

1.3.3.4.4 Special categories of personal data

The Act provides for special treatment of "sensitive data", which are personal data that pertain to a person's racial or ethnic origin; political views; religious or philosophical beliefs; membership of religious organisations, political parties or labour unions; health, DNA, addictions and sexual life; and data about sentences and penalties as well as other court or administrative decisions (Art. 27.1).

It is explicitly prohibited to process sensitive data unless one of the enumerated conditions legitimising the processing is met. These conditions are much stricter than the conditions that legitimise processing of non-sensitive data (for example, the data subject's consent has to be given in writing as opposed to consent in any form as long as it is explicit).

1.3.3.4.5 Order data processing

Art. 31 of the Act envisages that data processing can be outsourced by the data controller to a contractor. This has to be the subject of a written contract. The data processor must process the data only within the scope and for the purpose specified in the contract (so it is in the best interests of both parties to negotiate these provisions carefully). The data processor is obliged to employ protective measures specified in the Act, and they will be liable for failure to meet the Act's requirements in this area. However, the data controller remains responsible for observing the Act, which does not exclude contractual liability of the data processor vis-à-vis the controller. Data processors are also subject to administrative control.

Although there is no explicit provision to this end, in practice it is often the case that the data are further outsourced (by data processors to sub-processors). Parties usually try to apply Art. 31 *mutatis mutandis* to such situations.

Outsourcing of data processing is different from changing the data controller. The data processor does not process the data for their own reasons and does not decide which means are used for processing (the ultimate decision lies with the data controller, although the contract may outsource this power to a large extent). It should be noted that the Act does not deal with rights to data such as *sui generis* database rights, so when data processing is outsourced or data are moved to a new data controller, account has to be taken of to whom the *sui generis* right applies.

1.3.3.4.6 Consent

Art. 7.5 determines that consent for the processing of personal data cannot be implied or deduced from a statement with another meaning. Consent may be revoked at any time. Consent of the data subject is one of the possible grounds that legitimise processing of personal data (Art. 23). Consent does not have to be in writing in order to be valid (unless it covers sensitive data). Consent can cover future processing within the same purpose of processing. It is not necessary to obtain consent if the processing is necessary for the protection of material interests of the data subject and consent is impossible to obtain (which is an explicit confirmation that the rule *impossibilia nulla obligatio est* applies in Poland).

Arts 24 and 25 specify information obligations of data controllers towards data subjects but do not describe these obligations as prerequisites for valid consent. But it can still be argued that a person who was not given sufficient information about the data controller could not have given proper consent. Data controllers have to provide information as to their name and address, the purpose of data processing, the data subject's right to access and correct data, and whether there is an obligation to provide the data or not. If data are not obtained from a data subject, the data controller must inform the data subject about the categories of data and their source and some additional rights of data subjects.

1.3.3.5 Processing of personal data

1.3.3.5.1 Binding to the purpose of processing

Data controllers have to stick to the declared purpose of processing, in particular the purpose of which they informed data subjects while gathering their consents. For data controllers which are part of public authorities this already follows from the rule of law – the state cannot do more than it is allowed to in the law. But it is explicitly made clear in the Act that the data are gathered for specific, legal purposes. Processing for other purposes than the purposes for which data are collected, even if these are legal, is only allowed where it does not infringe rights and freedoms of data subjects and is done for scientific, educational, historical or statistical reasons. Otherwise it is possible if there is a reason legitimising processing (e.g., consent to extend purposes of processing) and the data controller performs its information obligations. The above follows from Art. 26 of the Act, which specifies the general obligations of data controllers.

1.3.3.5.2 Principle of necessity

Under Art. 26 of the Act all data controllers, not only public entities, must ensure that the data are adequate for the purposes of processing, not processed for other purposes, and not stored without anonymisation for longer than is necessary for achieving the purpose of processing. With regard to public entities, these obligations may be construed in an even stricter way using rule-of-law arguments prohibiting public authorities from exceeding their statutory powers and competences.

1.3.3.5.3 Principle of data avoidance and data economy

The Act does not elaborate on the principles of data avoidance or data economy. However, they may be derived, from the already described obligations of data controllers under Art. 26.

1.3.3.5.4 Direct survey and transparency

There is no principle of direct survey under the Act, as it explicitly recognises that data may not be collected from data subjects (Art. 25 extends the controller's information obligations in such cases). So indirect collection is possible for any legal purpose, and data controllers do not have to turn to data subjects in the first place if they have an alternative data source.

1.3.3.5.5 Prohibition with the reservation of permission

Under Art. 23 processing of personal data is possible only if at least one of the conditions specified in this article is met (there is a separate list of conditions for sensitive data in an attempt to subject them to more strict rules). The conditions are: consent (consent is not necessary for removal of data or when it is not possible to obtain consent for processing in a person's interest); when processing is necessary for performance of rights or obligations that follow from law; when processing is necessary to perform a contract with a data subject (or if necessary in pre-contractual relations and when requested by the data subject); when processing is necessary for the performance of tasks aimed at the public good that are specified in the law; and when processing is necessary for legitimate purposes of data controllers or data recipients and it does not infringe rights and freedoms of the data subject. Such purposes include direct marketing of the controller's own products or pursuing liability arising from economic activity (Art. 23.4).

1.3.3.5.6 Permissive rules

There is generally no difference between processing in the public and private sectors apart from the already mentioned constraints to which public authorities are subject under the rule of law. However, sector-specific laws, such as Acts that regulate the operation of various public registries, can differentiate the scope of rights and obligations of parties involved in the processing of personal data. They often provide for certain additional obligations for public authorities (e.g., by directly enumerating which data are to be gathered, thus allowing the avoidance of arguments as to whether the scope of data is adequate). Sometimes such sector-specific regulations render whole sections of the Act inapplicable in their area.

But there are some specific permissions in the Act itself. For example, it is not necessary to inform data subjects about the collection of their data from third parties, in particular where the data collected are necessary for scientific research, processing does not infringe rights and freedoms of the data subject and the information obligation performance would require excessive investment or would endanger the purpose of the survey (Art. 25.2.3). This provision applies equally to public and private data controllers as long as they meet its requirements.

When data are processed for scientific reasons it is also possible to change the purpose of processing as already described in relation to Art. 26 (but it is still necessary not to infringe the data subject's rights and freedoms). A similar provision allows for processing sensitive data for scientific research, but it explicitly prohibits publishing non-anonymised data gathered in the course of research (Art. 27.2.9).

1.3.3.5.7 Rights of the person concerned

Art. 32.1 of the Act provides a long list of rights included in the data subject's right to control the subject's personal data. These are mostly informational obligations of data controllers (about data controllers, the datasets in question, and particularities of processing). Data subjects are also authorised to require corrections of personal data, and even to request that data are not processed or deleted if the data are wrong, were collected illegally or are no longer necessary for the intended purpose.

In some cases, exercise of such rights immediately triggers a procedure before the DPA – the General Inspector for the Protection of Personal Data. The General Inspector is separately authorised to control conformance with the Act by data controllers.

As already explained, data controllers may disregard their information obligations if data are processed for scientific reasons and excessive costs, time or activities would be required to ascertain the meaning of the data.

1.3.3.5.8 Trans-border data flows

There are no specific requirements if the data are transmitted within the EEA. Data controllers subject to the Act (those having their seat or residence in Poland or those using technical means situated in Poland apart from mere transmission of data) have to comply with the Act in the same way as if the data were transmitted within Poland only.

Additional requirements apply where data are transmitted to a "third country", which is defined as a country outside the EEA. Such transfer is only possible if the target country guarantees an adequate level of protection of personal data. "Adequacy" is scrutinised using factors specified in Art. 47.1a. This scrutiny is not necessary if the transmission is required by law or in an international treaty that provides for an adequate level of protection.

Art. 47.3 provides a list of exceptions that allow the transmission of data to a third country (arguably even if the protection is not adequate there). It is possible when there is written consent of the data subject or it is necessary to perform a contract or a request of the data subject, to perform a contract between the data controller and a third party in the interest of the data subject, for the public good, in order to provide evidence of a legal claim, or to protect material interests of a data subject, or data are publicly available.

Finally, if the protection is inadequate and the Art. 47.3 exceptions are not applicable, it is still possible to apply to the DPA for consent to transmit the data to a third country, and the DPA may issue individual consent. Consent is given provided that the data controller guarantees adequate protection. Surprisingly, Art. 48.2 states that consent is not required if the data controller employs standard contractual clauses approved by the European Commission or BCRs (the latter, however, have to be approved by the DPA).

1.3.3.5.9 Data protection control

While the protection of the right to privacy is generally exercised by courts, conformance with the Act (being part of administrative law) is controlled by the General Inspector for the Protection of Personal Data ("Generalny Inspektor Ochrony Danych Osobowych", GIODO), who is the Polish DPA in the area of personal data protection. GIODO is appointed by Parliament for a four-year term (renewable only once), subject to a quite strong rule of incompatibilities and having immunity equivalent to other high state officials (the President, Members of Parliament). GIODO is in particular responsible for controlling whether the Act is complied with, and may issue administrative decisions ordering data controllers to comply (even comprising an order to delete personal data), as well as scrutinising complaints of data subjects. Representatives of GIODO may enter in person the premises of data controllers and require access to pertinent documentation, IT systems, etc.

Particularly in order to enable GIODO to know the extent of data processing, data controllers are obliged to register their data sets in a public registry operated by GIODO.

Data controllers are generally obliged to ensure compliance with the Act themselves, but they may also appoint data officers to undertake the performance of such obligations on behalf of the controllers. These officers have special tasks and obligations specified in the Act. They can be employees of the data controller or external subcontractors. Notably, the appointment of a data officer does not relieve the data controller of the obligation to comply with the Act and from liability in the event of failure to comply.

1.3.4 Spain

The following section discusses legal provisions of Spanish data protection law, with special emphasis on those that can potentially create legal barriers for online sharing of research data in the framework of the Open Research Data Pilot.

In Spain the main legal instrument on data protection is the Spanish Data Protection Act enacted in 1999 (Ley Orgánica 15/1999, de 13 de diciembre, de Protección de Datos de Carácter Personal, hereafter the "LOPD")[371], which transposes the Data Protection Directive into Spanish law and establishes the limits and guarantees of the right to data protection. Further, the Spanish legislator has also enacted the Real Decreto 1720/2007, de 21de diciembre, which passes the Reglamento de desarrollo de la ley Orgánica 15/1999 (hereafter the "Regulation"). Sectorial regulations exist in the area of e-commerce, clinical records and telecommunications law etc.[372].

1.3.4.1 Constitutional basis

The Spanish Constitution of 1978 recognised the fundamental right to privacy as well as that of personal data protection. Art. 18.4 of the Spanish Constitution recognises the right to the protection of personal data, separate from the right to privacy[373], by stating that "the law will limit the use of (information) technology in order to safeguard the honour and intimacy, of person and family, of the citizens and the full exercise of their rights". The literal terms of the article, however, do not clarify sufficiently the rationale of this right. Much has been written on the

---

[371] The LOPD came into force on 14 January 2000.

[372] For example, Ley 41/2002, básica, reguladora de los derechos y obligaciones en materia de documentación clínica. Personal data are also regulated in additional instruments, such as Ley 32/2003, de 3 de noviembre, General de Telecomunicaciones or Ley 34/2002, de 11 de julio, de Servicios de la Sociedad de la Información y de Comercio Electrónico. In these the Agencia Española de Protección de Datos (AEPD) is given responsibility for the safeguarding of the rights of users and customers in electronic communication.

[373] Note that the term used in Spanish law is 'intimacy' and not 'privacy'. To avoid confusion, we will refer to 'privacy' unless we are quoting specific legislative provisions or case law.

relationship between these rights and on whether, and to what extent, the relationship between both rights is of a substantive or instrumental (accessory) nature. In this analysis it is generally Art. 10 of the Constitution that, by asserting the dignity of the individual as a governing principle of social cohesion, provides the pillar for the reasoning. The decision of the Spanish Constitutional Court 292/2000 of 30 November shed some light on this relationship by recognising the right to data protection as an autonomous fundamental right destined to preserve the dignity of the individual. This decision, which remained ambiguous in areas such as distinguishing privacy from data protection, ended up also being disputed by some authors, who doubted the excessively static role granted by the Court to the right of privacy.

It was actually largely through doctrinal evolution that the principle of informational self-determination, derived from Art. 18.4 of the Constitution and part of the larger right to privacy, developed in Spain. Beyond the scope of personal and family privacy, the LOPD establishes informational self-determination or informational freedom, expressly recognised as a fundamental right separate from that of *intimacy* (privacy) as per decision 292/2000[374]. Hence, the LOPD not only protects citizens against information technology processing, but also, in a broader sense, protects other fundamental rights and the individual freedom against the automated treatment of their personal data.

1.3.4.2 Fundamental legal terms

Some important legal terms for the understanding of Spanish law will be described below.

1.3.4.2.1 Personal data

The LOPD defines personal data in line with Art. 2(a) Data Protection Directive. According to Art. 3(a) LOPD, personal data means "any information relating to an identified or identifiable natural person". While this definition is identical to that of the directive, the LOPD chooses to leave aside the additional (descriptive) text present in the directive.

The LOPD does not expressly define "information". The Regulation, however, in its Art. 5 (definitions) notes that (f) this information can be "numerical, alphabetic, graphical, photographical, acoustic or any other type, relating to physical persons identified or identifiable". When a person is "identifiable" is again not defined in the LOPD.

It is the Agencia Española de Protección de Datos (Spanish Data Protection Authority – AEPD) that has developed some rules for interpretation. Further, the Regulation offers some guidance in its Art. 5 of what "identifiable" implies.

[374] The first time that informational freedom had been expressly mentioned by Spanish case law was the decision of the Constitutional Court 254/1993, de 20 de Julio.

Section (o) mentions this is the case with "every person whose identity can be determined, directly or indirectly, by means of any available information related to their physical, physiological, psychological, economic, cultural or social identity. A physical person will not be considered identifiable if said identification process requires disproportionate terms or tasks." That is, in the definition, both the nature of the data and the extent to which they allow identification, directly or indirectly (the reasonableness requirement of Recital 26 of the Data Protection Directive) are important. The key point to bear in mind here is that the concept of "reasonableness" is not static and can change over time, thus requiring ongoing monitoring by the controller.

Personal data only include information about living natural persons. Data about dead persons do not fall under the definition of personal data. This is expressly regulated by the Regulation in its Art. 2.4. Two broad exceptions are made. One is contemplated by Art. 2.4 itself, and concerns access of surviving relatives to the dead person's data in order to release a death announcement etc. A second exception concerns situations where the data actually relate to a living natural person who might be legally capable of taking legal action on behalf of the dead party in order to safeguard any constitutionally recognised right. This is the case, for example, when a surviving relative relies on the clinical history of a dead relative in the context of hereditary diseases. The AEPD has produced a legal report, 2020-0523, which confirms this.

Data related to legal persons, such as companies or foundations, are not considered to be personal data. However, the LOPD does apply to legal persons to the extent the data available identifies, or makes it possible to identify, physical individuals. This may be the case with contact names for a foundation or the names of members of a board of directors etc. In other words, the contact data of natural persons are not subject to the LOPD if the use is professional.

1.3.4.2.2 Anonymised data and encoded data

Following the logic of the Data Protection Directive, the LOPD does not mention anonymised data as such. *A contrario*, following Art. 2.3 LOPD, which mentions personal data and, especially, Art. 3(a), which defines them, it can be concluded that anonymised data are those which do not refer to a natural person or which refer to a natural person but this person is not identified or identifiable. Indeed, the concept of anonymised data is later referred to by the Regulation, Art. 2.1(e) as dissociated data, defined as data which do not allow the identification of a data subject or interested party.

It is interesting to note another term, "dissociated data", which is also defined by the Regulation in its section (e). It is said to refer to data that do not permit the identification of a data subject or interested party. Similarly, a "dissociation process" is one whereby dissociated data can be obtained.

The AEPD offers some guidance as to what should be understood as personal data in a moving context. Report 285/2006 concerns the use of a telephone number by means of fixed line. The report concludes that a phone number will be considered as personal data when it appears in connection with the owner of the number or is linked to additional personal identifiable data, such as the address, that is stored with the number in line with what is understood to be "identifiable" (LOPD, Art. 3(a)). As the report says, this criterion has also been ratified by the Audiencia Nacional (Sent. 8 de marzo 2002), which states that "the existence of personal data, as opposed to dissociated data, is not necessary to have full coincidence between the data and the specific person but it is sufficient that the identification can take place without disproportionate efforts". It continues by saying that it is necessary to consider the full set of instruments at the disposal of the controller, or any other person, to identify said person.

Just like the Data Protection Directive, the LOPD does not explicitly mention encoded data. The AEPD has considered encoded data as identifiable and thus as personal data in some cases. Thus, the contrary also applies and encoded data can also be qualified as anonymous and, hence, not personal data.

1.3.4.2.3 Special categories of personal data

Art. 16.2 of the Constitution establishes that no one can be obliged to declare their ideology, religion or belief.

Art. 7 LOPD deals with special categories of personal data, such as ideology, trade union membership, religion and belief, race, health and sexual life.

1.3.4.2.4 Processing of personal data

The definition of "processing of personal data" in the LOPD repeats Art. 2(b) Data Protection Directive. According to Art. 3(c) LOPD, processing of personal data means any operation or technical process, automated or not, that allows the collection, recording, storage, elaboration, modification, consultation, use, cancellation, blocking or erasure, as well as the disclosure, of data resulting from communications, consultations, interrelationships and transfers. This is also found in Art. 5.1(t) LOPD.

1.3.4.2.5 Controller

The figure of the controller (*responsable del fichero o tratamiento*) has been introduced by the LOPD, which defines the term in its Art. 3(d), in line with Art. 2(d) Data Protection Directive. A controller can be a natural person, a legal person, public or private, or an administrative entity responsible for the purpose, content and use of the processing. Hence, a controller can be a private company as regards personal data held in respect of its employees or clients, a freelancer in respect of data of their clients, or a city council in respect of those living in that community.

Among the obligations of the controller, which needs to register the filing system with the AEPD, are those of information, monitoring, updating and safeguarding the right of the data subject, and the accuracy of the data.

The Regulation is slightly more precise than the LOPD in defining the controller. It adds that the responsibility for the definition of purpose, content and use of the processing can be shared with other parties even if that does not make them materially responsible. Further, the Regulation clarifies that the controller can be an entity with no legal personality (Art. 5(q) LOPD).

1.3.4.2.6 Processor

The figure of the processor (*encargado del tratamiento*) in the LOPD, in line with the Data Protection Directive Art. 2(e), is that of a natural or legal person, public or private, or administrative entity, which, alone or together with other parties, processes personal data on behalf of the controller. That is, it can act together with other parties but, unlike the controller, the processor does not decide on the purpose, content or use of the processing (otherwise the processor would become a controller).

Again, it is the Regulation that provides a more precise definition of the processor. In this case, it details the relationship between the controller and the processor. Art. 5(i) explains that the processor acts on the back of a legal relationship established with the controller, which specifies the scope of the activity contracted.

This legal relationship is generally based on a service contract (*contrato de servicios*), which focuses on the provision of personal data processing services and which would therefore exclude those who access the data on the back of an employment relationship with the controller, given that a processor, by definition, does not fall under the direct authority of the controller.

The Regulation also notes that the processor can be an entity with no legal personality.

1.3.4.2.7 Third party

"Third party" is defined by the Regulation as a natural or legal person, private, public, or administrative entity, other than the interested party or data subject, of the controller, the processor, owner of the filing, or anyone authorised to process data under direct authority of the controller or responsible for the processing. Third parties can also be entities without legal personality. It thus follows the approach adopted by Art. 2(g) Data Protection Directive.

1.3.4.2.8 Consent of the data subject

According to Art. 3(h) LOPD "consent of the data subject" means any freely given, unambiguous, specific and informed expression of will whereby data subjects agree to the processing of personal data relating to them.

The AEPD has provided some guidance on the meaning of consent. In its 2000 Report it states that "freely given" refers to the lack of substantive or procedural defects as per the Spanish Civil Code. "Specific" relates to both the treatment and the purpose of the processing itself, which should be specific, legitimate and explicit, per Art. 4.2 LOPD. "Informed" requires that the data subject is aware before the processing takes place of the processing and its purpose in line with Art. 5.1 LOPD. "Unambiguous" means that implicit consent, derived from any act performed by the data subject, is not sufficient, and an explicit act or omission is required to be able to derive the existence of this consent.

It is worth noting that the AEPD offers some guidance on the issue of minors. To that end, it refers to the Spanish Civil Code and the distinction it makes between minors older and younger than 14 because the former are capable of entering into certain legal contracts. In other words, the Spanish legislator establishes a legal presumption of maturity for the provision of consent set at 14 years of age.

Withdrawing consent: Unlike the Data Protection Directive, where the right of the data subject to withdraw consent is merely implied, Art. 6(3) LOPD explicitly contemplates the withdrawal of consent if there is a justified reason for it. There is no retroactive effect. This implies that the required measures need to be implemented to make any future withdrawal technically possible.

1.3.4.3 Principles of personal data processing: Data quality

In line with the Data Protection Directive, the LOPD provides, in its Art. 4, the principles related to data quality. The guiding principles are "data minimisation" and "purpose specification", implemented by the directive.

1.3.4.3.1 Purpose limitation

According to the LOPD, personal data can only be collected when the purpose of the collection is specific, explicit and legitimate (Art. 4.1 LOPD). This is in line with Art. 6(a)–(c) Data Protection Directive.

Again, the Regulation expands the principle of the LOPD. It adds in Art. 8.1 that the data processing needs to be legitimate and lawful. It is prohibited to collect data by fraudulent or illegal means. Further it states in Art. 8.3 that the data cannot be used for purposes that are incompatible with the original purpose.

Besides this, the requirement of compatibility of further processing is set forth in Art. 4.2 LOPD. Report 0078/2005 of the AEPD illustrates the extent of the compatibility. It deals with a situation where the data subject is both an employee and a client of a particular credit entity. In none of the cases, given the existence of a contractual situation under Art. 6.2 LOPD, would the credit entity be obliged to receive consent. However, this rationale also needs to be compatible with Art. 4.1 LOPD, which recognises the principle of proportionality in data processing and compatibility of use (Art. 4.2 LOPD). According to the Spanish Constitutional Court (Sent. 292/2000, de 30 de noviembre) "incompatible purposes should be interpreted as different purposes". Therefore, the AEPD concludes, in the particular case, the controller cannot claim compatibility of purposes. Consent of the data subject is therefore required to use the personal data for a different purpose, in this case for contracting for a financial product or service. Further, Art. 5.1 LOPD on information requirements also plays a part in informing the data subject that their data will be used for other purposes etc. It should be noted, however, that the situation changes, and potentially the outcome too, where a specific product or service is offered to the customer because they are already an employee.

1.3.4.3.2 Further processing for historical, statistical or scientific purposes

In line with Art. 6(1)(b) Data Protection Directive, Art. 4(2) LOPD states that further processing of personal data for historical, statistical or scientific purposes shall not be regarded as incompatible. This exemption applies to processing of data initially collected for purposes other than historical, statistical or scientific research.

Further, Art. 9 of the Regulation adds that these excluded purposes should be interpreted in line with the laws regulating each of them (e.g. on historical heritage, on scientific and technical research etc.). It therefore avoids providing specific guidance.

1.3.4.3.3 Data minimisation

The principle of data minimisation is envisaged in Art. 4 LOPD and deals with the scope of data collection. In line with Art. 6(1)(c) and 6(1)(e) Data Protection Directive, the article requires that:

- personal data shall only be processed where, given the purposes for which they are collected or subsequently processed, they are "adequate", "pertinent" and "not excessive" (Art. 4(1) LOPD), and
- personal data shall not be kept in a form which allows the data subject to be identified for any longer than is necessary for achieving the purposes for which they were collected or subsequently processed (Art. 4(5) LOPD). In fact, personal data should be deleted once they have ceased to be necessary or relevant to the original purpose they had been collected for.

Data minimisation requires an ongoing, continuous assessment. Art. 4(3) LOPD states that the data should be "accurate" and "up to date" so that they correspond to the true situation of the individual. This requires that the controller adopt the necessary measures to ensure that the data are correct and accurate and thus update them if necessary. This is in line with Art. 6(d) Data Protection Directive though the article omits the more subjective reference to "every reasonable step" and the explicit reference to the original purpose of the collection as the only valid benchmark (though this can, arguably, be implied in the Spanish legislation).

Art. 4(4) LOPD continues by explaining that, if the data recorded turn out to be inaccurate, in whole or in part, or are incomplete, the data should be deleted and replaced by the correct data, without prejudice to any of the rights of rectification or blocking contemplated in Art. 16 LOPD. Art. 4(6) LOPD, in line with the dynamic nature of the data collected, obliges the controller to store the data in such a way that allows the right of access.

As the AEPD explains, the processing of personal data is governed by, among other things, the principle of data quality per Art. 4 LOPD. That is, personal data should be deleted once they have ceased to be necessary for the purpose for which they had originally been collected.

Nonetheless, Art. 8.6 of the Regulation provides that, exceptionally, some data can be stored during the time allowed to claim liability under any legal obligation. In this case, cancellation of the data should be done by blocking the data in such a way that they are only available to the public administration and the judiciary for the purposes of legal responsibility (per Art. 16.3 LOPD). Once the term expires, the data should be permanently erased and can only be kept if (i) the data are dissociated or if, exceptionally, (ii) they remain stored in light of their historical, statistical or scientific worth.

Legal Report 0408/2010 of the AEPD deals with a question posed on the duration of the storage with respect to physical filing systems dealing with legal and administrative data. The AEPD again highlights the fact that the cancellation of the data does not imply their automatic erasure. That is, the cancellation should be interpreted, per Art. 5.1(b) of the Regulation, as "ceasing to use the data". That is, cancellation is the blocking of the data with the aim of preventing processing in all cases, except, of course, those dealing with administrative or judicial reasons or, for example, statistical purposes.

To determine the length of the "blocking term", the AEPD requests that consideration be given to the decision of the Constitutional Court Sent. 292/2000 de 30 de noviembre, which expressly establishes the legal reservation principle as regards any limitations to the right to data protection in such a way that any limitation to the right needs to be expressly contemplated by law (e.g. four years for fiscal debt prescription per the Ley General Tributaria).

1.3.4.3.4 Longer-term storage of personal data for scientific use

Art. 9.1 of the Regulation establishes that, as an exception to the general rule whereby personal data cannot be used for incompatible purposes, data processing of personal data for historical, statistical or scientific uses is allowed. The Regulation further explains that these uses have to be interpreted in line with the relevant sectorial regulation.

Further, Art. 9.2 establishes yet another exception to the principle of minimum conservation, for historical, statistical or scientific uses. That is, the AEPD can store personal data for historical, statistical and scientific reasons. The procedure is detailed in Arts 157 and 158 of the Regulation. The AEPD can grant, if formally requested to do so, the storage of certain data, given their historical, statistical or scientific worth[375]. The AEPD decides within three months. Silence is understood as implicit consent. The Regulation provides no further guidance on how these data should be handled.

Legal Report 0120/2010 deals with the question of whether data related to members of the executive board of a [political] party since 1977 can be disclosed to university researchers. Whereas the exclusion of dead members from the LOPD seems to be relatively uncontroversial (except as regards special situations such as that of Art. 2.4 of the Regulation), as explained earlier, the AEPD concludes that the data of any surviving members is indeed covered by the LOPD. At its most general, Art. 11.1 LOPD is applicable if disclosure of the data on the Internet is involved and consent of the data subject is, in principle, required.

Nonetheless, the historical nature of the information requires resort to special legislation, such as that dealing with national documents and official secrets, which states that public disclosure cannot take place without express consent of the data subjects 25 years after the death of the data subject, if known, or 50 years after the date of the document. Despite the ambiguity of the last phrase, the AEPD interpretation is that the data can be treated for historical, scientific or statistical purposes 50 years after the date of the document, whether the data subject is alive or the date of death is uncertain. Otherwise, express consent is needed.

1.3.4.3.5 Legal grounds for lawful processing of personal data

The LOPD follows the Data Protection Directive in its distinction between two blocks of legal grounds for lawful processing of personal data: (i) general rules for general (non-sensitive) categories of personal data (Art. 6 LOPD) and (ii) special stricter provisions with respect to special categories of personal data (Art. 7 LOPD).

1.3.4.3.5.1 Processing of general categories of personal data

Legal grounds for the processing of general categories of personal data provided for in Art. 7 Data Protection Directive are transposed in Art. 6 LOPD.

Art. 6 establishes that the processing of personal data requires the unambiguous consent of the data subject, unless the law provides otherwise.

---

[375] Any application requires information on the purpose of the data, the reasoning, the guarantees, and documentary evidence.

Paragraph 2 contains a series of exceptions to the consent principle, namely: (i) as required by the public administration in the exercise of its tasks, (ii) in the context of a contractual or pre-contractual agreement, (iii) in the context of serious medical or health reasons or (iv) when the data are found in publicly accessible sources and their processing is required.

In this context, it is necessary to point out that the AEPD takes a narrow view of the definition of "required data" per Art. 4.1 LOPD. The collection of additional data, not strictly required to serve the purpose of the contract, would require consent of the data subject. This means, therefore, that the data subject needs to be informed in advance.

The AEPD, responding to a query as to whether consent could, in some cases, be tacit or implicit, defined once more the implications of "freely given" (i.e. as defined by the Spanish Civil Code), specific (in processing and purpose, explicit and legitimate), informed and unambiguous. The AEDP subsequently concluded that these definitions do not necessarily justify the requirement that consent has to be explicit in all situations. Therefore, when explicit consent is required, the law will expressly say so (e.g. Art. 7.2 LOPD regarding specially protected data or Art. 7.3 LOPD regarding data related to health, race and sexual life). In other words, consent can be tacit (implicit) in some cases but, in order to be considered unambiguous, the controller needs to provide the data subject with enough time for them to acknowledge that non-opposition to a particular processing implies consent.

Finally, paragraph 4 establishes a general exception to the no-consent rule: where no consent is required, and no law provides otherwise, the data subject can oppose the processing when there are legitimate and reasonable reasons regarding a personal situation.

It should be noted that the Regulation, in its Art. 10, dictates that the only cases where consent is not required when processing or disclosing personal data are: when a law or EU regulation allows it and (i) the processing would satisfy the legitimate interest of the controller, as long as this is not overridden by the fundamental rights of the data subject or (ii) the processing is necessary in order to comply with an obligation of the controller.

1.3.4.3.5.2 Processing of special categories of personal data

If special categories of personal data are to be collected, the controller needs to inform the data subject in advance of their right not to consent to the collection. That is, the governing principle is the right to non-disclosure of special categories of personal data.

Paragraph 2 of Art. 7 LOPD states that the processing of data revealing ideology, trade union membership, religion and belief requires *express and written consent* of the data subject. Further, paragraph 3 deals with data related to race, health and sexual life, which can only be collected, processed and disclosed as a matter of general interest, if so required by law or if the controller has the express consent of the data subject.

Paragraph 4 contains an express prohibition of filing systems that have been created with the exclusive purpose of storing personal data revealing of ideology, trade union membership, religion, belief, racial or ethnic origin or sexual life.

Finally, paragraph 5 describes personal data in respect of administrative or criminal offences, which can only be incorporated into filing systems of the administration in specific cases contemplated by the relevant law.

Art. 7 LOPD describes all the special categories of data defined in Art. 8.1 Data Protection Directive. However, formally, the Spanish law does not structure it as the directive does, with a general prohibition followed by exceptions to the prohibition (Art. 8.1. and Art. 8.2 respectively).

(I) The general rule states that the processing can only be carried out as regards ideology, trade union membership, religion or beliefs if the data subject has provided their express and written consent. There is an exception in relation to the filing systems kept by political parties, trade unions, churches, religious communities, non-profit foundations or associations, whose aims are political, philosophical, religious or unionistic, relating to the data of their members, without prejudice to the fact that any further disclosure would always require the consent of the data subject (Art. 7.2 LOPD).

Another special case is that of personal data in relation to race and ethnic origin, health and sexual life. These data can only be collected, processed and disclosed when, for reasons of general interest, the law so establishes – unless, of course, the data subject has expressly consented. For the avoidance of doubt, the article, continuing in its paragraph 4, states that filing systems created with the sole and exclusive purpose of storing data revealing ideology, trade union membership, religion, belief, race and ethnic origin or sexual life are strictly prohibited.

(II) However, the aforementioned exceptions of Art. 7 LOPD are not applicable when the processing is required for medical diagnostic, sanitary assistance or the treatment or management of healthcare services, as long as the processing is done by personnel bound by professional confidentiality or by a third party bound by a similar obligation of confidentiality.

Further, the above data can also be processed if the processing is necessary to safeguard the life-sustaining interest of the data subject or other person where the data subject is physically or legally incapable of giving consent.

Art. 8 especially deals with healthcare data and provides that health institutions and hospitals, private or public, and healtcare professionals, can process the data related to the health of those individuals that attend such health centres, per the national or regional legislation on health. Unfortunately, the LOPD does not offer a definition of "healthcare data" (*datos de salud*).

1.3.4.3.6 Transparency of personal data processing

The principle of transparency of data processing is elaborated in Art. 5 LOPD, which contains the controller's obligation to provide information about the processing of personal data to the data subject. Art. 5 LOPD implements Arts 10 and 11 Data Protection Directive as regards what should be considered to be lawful processing.

Art. 5.1–5.3 LOPD applies to cases where data were obtained directly from the data subject; Art. 5.4 LOPD, when data were obtained in any other manner, for example from third parties or by observation.

Art. 5.1 LOPD describes the content of the information that needs to be provided to the data subject:

a) the existence of a filing system or personal data processing, its purpose and the recipients of the information[376];

b) the optional or compulsory nature of the responses;

c) the consequences of the data collection and/or the failure to disclose for the data subject;

d) the rights that assist the data subject;

e) the name and address of the controller or, alternatively, of the controller's representative.

These provisions are almost identical to those of Art. 10 Data Protection Directive.

Art. 5.1 LOPD ends with a provision dealing with the situation where a controller outside the EU uses processing means located in Spain. In this case, the controller requires a representative in Spain.

Art. 5.2 LOPD specifies that if questionnaires are used to collect data, the above requirements need to be met too. However, Art. 5.3 LOPD excludes the requirements of (b), (c) and (d) if the content and purpose can be clearly established from the mere nature and circumstances of the data collection process.

Together with the content of the information itself, Art. 5.1 LOPD also describes how the information should be communicated to the data subject, prior to obtaining personal data, in a manner that is "express", "precise" and "unambiguous".

According to Art. 14.5 of the Regulation, the requirement to obtain consent of the data subject under the above procedure is not required if the purpose and processing are the same and take place within one year of the prior request for consent.

---

[376] "Recipient" is defined by the Regulation as any natural or legal person, public or private, or administrative organ, to whom data are disclosed (Art. 5h).

Under Art. 5.1 LOPD, the obligation to provide information to the data subject when personal data are obtained directly from them should be communicated in the manner described above ("express", "precise" and "unambiguous") and with the content of Art. 5.1 LOPD. These requirements need to be detailed in any questionnaire used to gather data. Some of the information requirements, namely those concerning the nature of the responses, the consequences of data collection or the lack of it, and the rights of the data subject, are not necessary if they are clearly implied in the data collection process and its context.

If personal data are not obtained from the data subject, Art. 5.4 LOPD states that the data subject should be informed "expressly", "precisely" and "unambiguously", by the controller or its representative, within three months of registering the data, unless the data subject has already been informed, of the content of the processing, origin of the data, controller, rights and purpose of the filing system.

Similarly, Art. 5.5 LOPD contains an express exemption from the obligation to comply with Art. 5.4 LOPD where processing is carried out by institutions or services for historical, statistical or scientific research or statistics, and the necessary arrangements have been made to ensure that the personal data can only be used for statistical or scientific purposes. It should be noted that there is no express mention of any such type of institution or service but rather to the purpose itself, regardless of the actor.

The obligation to inform the data subject about further data processing (when personal data are not obtained from the data subject) is not absolute. That is, Art. 5.5 LOPD follows Art. 11(2) Data Protection Directive by contemplating the exceptions derived from (i) scientific, statistical or historical research (as discussed above) and (ii) the impossibility of contact.

There is, however, a slight change in the grammar. The directive mentions statistical, scientific or historical research as a subset (in particular) of the "disproportionate" exercise. The LOPD, on the other hand, uses Art. 5.5 LOPD as a paragraph to contain all the exceptions to the non-directly collected data requirement for information. Thus, it mentions (i) a law specifically providing otherwise, (ii) the processing for historical, statistical or scientific purposes or (iii) impossibility or disproportionate efforts to inform the data subject.

Finally, in a separate paragraph, the legislator mentions another special situation, namely when the data come from publicly accessible sources and are used for marketing purposes, every disclosure to the data subject will indicate the origin of the data and the identity of the controllers and the rights that assist the data subject.

whether an effort to provide information is disproportionate or not depends on the criteria of the AEPD (or its regional representatives) and should take into account the number of interested parties, the date of the data and the potential compensatory measures.

1.3.4.3.7 Disclosure of Data (comunicación or cession)

The governing principle under Spanish data protection law is that whenever a disclosure implies or leads to the identification of specific natural persons, it falls within the disclosure of personal data scenario contemplated by Art. 3.1 LOPD, defined as "any disclosure of data to a recipient other than the data subject". Unfortunately, the LOPD uses the terms *comunicación* and *cession* indistinguishably when referring to the disclosure of data.

Processed personal data can only be disclosed to a third party for purposes directly related to the tasks of the disclosing party and the recipient with the prior consent of the data subject. This is the general rule established by Art 11.1 LOPD.

However, there is a series of exceptions, specified in Art. 11.2 LOPD, where consent is not required:

- when the disclosure of data is contemplated by the law;
- when the data has been collected from publicly accessible sources;
- when the processing responds to the free and legitimate acceptance of a legal relationship that requires interlinking the processing with third-party filing systems (as long as its purpose remains specific and limited);
- when the recipient is part of the judiciary, Defensor del Pueblo[377] or Ministerio Fiscal[378];
- by the public administration for purposes of a historical, statistical or scientific nature;
- urgency reasons per health regulations.

Consent can be withdrawn. The recipient of the disclosure is automatically bound by the LOPD. If dissociation of the personal data has previously taken place the above safeguards are not required.

A legal report of the AEPD of 2002 deals with the interpretation of the above in the context of data disclosure between public universities with the aim of targeting specific interviewees for scientific (sociological) research. Assuming that the universities qualify as members of the public administration, the AEPD seeks

---

377 Defined on its own website as the "High Commissioner of the Parliament responsible for defending the fundamental rights and civil liberties of citizens by monitoring the activity of the Administration and public authorities".

378 "Ministerio Fiscal" is the Spanish Public Prosecutor.

to define the term "scientific" given that, in its broadest interpretation, it could relate to pretty much any area of research. Thus, the AEPD first argues that the term should be interpreted in line with the proportionality and quality of data principles of Art. 4 LOPD. Similarly, it also explains that Art. 11.2(e) LOPD needs to be interpreted according to the doctrine developed by the Spanish Constitutional Court, which treats the protection of personal data as a fundamental right. In this assessment, where "scientific" should be interpreted as restrictively as possible in order not to infringe the fundamental right to data protection, the AEPD concludes that the research in question strictly qualifies under the definition. An important indication is the fact that the type of research is included in the public R&D funding programme. Finally, the AEPD refers to the general aim of the disclosure, which is to be able to assess the identity of the potential interviewees. This means that, once contacted, these parties will still be able to deny consent (and the purpose of the processing would have disappeared altogether leading to cancellation of the data). Thus, the AEPD established that no prior consent was required in this particular case.

Another legal report of some relevance to this section is Report 0243/2010. The query relates to the legality of accessing certain personal data of the Spanish census by individuals for research purposes. The AEPD refers to a prior decision from 2008 and explains that the query also needs to be assessed in the context of Art. 11 LOPD, given that it implies a disclosure. Further, Art. 11.2 LOPD provides an exemption from the requirements of compatibility of use and consent if another law allows for it. The AEPD refers to the regulation of Spanish heritage and documentary heritage whereby access to any such data will rely on privacy, security, healthcare etc. reasons, in which case access will only take place with express consent or 25 years after the death of the data subject or 50 years after the date of the document if death is unknown.

As recalled by the AEPD, data from the census can be shared with other public administrations without consent (per Art. 11 LOPD) when the data are relevant for a specific competence-based use, and can also be used for statistical purposes by the relevant administrations in accordance with the regulation and subject to the *secreto estadistico*[379].

Art. 12 LOPD deals with situations that do not qualify under Art. 11 LOPD, that is, that do not involve disclosure. These basically involve situations where disclosure is required in order to provide a service to the controller, for example. Of course, the law sets forth the requirements of this exception, namely the existence of a contract detailing the instructions to the third party as regards the processing of the data.

[379] Ley 12/1989 de 9 de mayo, de la Funcion Estadistica Publica.

1.3.4.3.8 Data subject's right of access to data

The LOPD grants data subjects a series of rights vis-à-vis the controller in the context of the collection and treatment of their personal data. These rights are described in Title III of the LOPD (*Derechos de las Personas*):

- "Right to object to automated individual decisions" based on the processing of personal data (Art. 13 LOPD)[380].
- "Right of access to the General Register of Data Protection" (*Registro General de Protección de Datos*) (Art. 14 LOPD).
- "Right of access", to request and obtain information about the processing of personal data, including origin and communication of the data (Art. 15.1 and Art 15.2 LOPD). The right of access may not be exercised more than once in any 12-month period except where the interested party can claim a legitimate interest.
- "Rights of rectification and blocking" of the data in the event that the data do not conform to the principles of the LOPD and/or when the data are inaccurate or incomplete. Under Art. 16 LOPD, this should be done within 10 days, after which the data should be deleted. If these data have previously been disclosed to third parties, the controller is obliged to notify the rectification or blocking and act accordingly (Art. 16.4 LOPD).
- "Right to compensation", per Art. 19 LOPD, in the event of harm arising from the infringement of any of the principles of the LOPD.

It is remarkable that the LOPD, which introduces the concept of "opposition" in Spanish legislation, makes little express reference to a right of opposition. Art. 6.4 LOPD states that the data subject can object in some cases where data were collected because no consent was required. It is the Regulation which uses the term "right of opposition" (Art. 34) to refer to different scenarios, including that contemplated by Art. 13 LOPD, which was mentioned above. That is, Art. 34 defines the right of opposition as the right of the data subject to prevent or stop any processing of personal data where (i) no consent was required for the processing in light of the existence of a legitimate interest (unless a law dictates the contrary), (ii) when the filing systems deal with marketing activities or (iii) when the processing seeks a decision based on purely automated data processing as contemplated, among others, by Art. 14 LOPD. In that sense, it should be noted that the Regulation shapes Art. 15 Data Protection Directive on automated individual decisions as a right that falls within the broader right of opposition, finally defined in said Regulation.

---

[380] What the Directive defines in its Art. 15 as "automated individual decisions".

Surprisingly, given that it offers no formal definition, the LOPD mentions the right of opposition in Art. 17 but only as regards the formal enforcement process. Indeed, Art. 17 LOPD explains that the procedure to exercise the rights of opposition, access, rectification or blocking will be detailed via Regulation. Art. 18 LOPD explains that complaints regarding behaviour contrary to any of the articles of the LOPD must be made to the AEPD (or its regional representatives) in line with the procedure detailed in the relevant regulation. The AEPD has six months to produce an express decision. The data subject can appeal against the decision before the administrative courts.

Unlike the provision in Art. 13 Data Protection Directive, the LOPD contains no explicit article enumerating exceptions and limitations generally applicable to the above rights. The Regulation does try, however, to provide specific scenarios rather than broad exceptions.

(I) Instead of detailing the exceptions as a natural consequence of the right of access, the LOPD only contains the exceptions in the description of the different types of filing systems, within the sectorial Title IV. The first breakdown is between public and private and it then proceeds to specify further by content. Thus, Art. 23 LOPD sets forth the conditions under which the controller may refuse to comply with exceptions to the right in the context of state-owned filing systems, in particular those dealing with *Fuerzas y Cuerpos de Seguridad* (armed forces and bodies).

In addition, Art. 30 of the Regulation also deals with scenarios where an access request can be denied by the controller. These include (i) last access request took place within 12 months and there is no legitimate interest, (ii) in accordance with law or EU regulation.

(II) Following a similar structure to that of the right of access, exceptions to the rights to request rectification and blocking are mentioned by the LOPD in the section concerning the different types of filing systems, by ownership and then further by type of content. Thus, the LOPD describes situations where denial of these rights takes place on the back of national security reasons or tax reasons/investigations.

The Regulation, in its Art. 33, establishes some exceptions to the rights, namely (i) when the data need to be stored in accordance with other legislation or in light of the contractual relationship between the data subject and the controller (in line with Art. 16.5 LOPD, which establishes the storage of data in certain situations); (ii) in accordance with law or EU regulation.

1.3.4.3.9 Measures to ensure security of processing

Art. 9 LOPD implements Art. 17(1) Data Protection Directive. It obliges the controller, or the processor if acting on behalf of the controller, to implement appropriate technical and organisational measures to secure personal data against alteration, loss or any form of unlawful processing. This should be done taking into account the nature of the stored data and having regard to the risks associated with the processing, involving human action or arising from it or caused by the physical or natural context. Again, the criteria are dynamic, based on the "state of technology". "Appropriate" also implies a correlation with the nature of the data. In addition, the LOPD states that the Regulation will establish the conditions that filing systems should meet as well as those of the parties involved in the processing of data, as regards security and integrity of the data. The legal flexibility of the Regulation versus that of the LOPD makes the former the better instrument to deal with ongoing technological developments.

The Regulation details extensively the different forms of organisation of security measures, personal and material, that take place in practice in its Title VIII. As such, it includes, for example, a series of measures applicable to both digital (automated) and paper (non-automated) filing systems. The measures are either technical, administrative or organisational in nature. The provisions are aimed at both the controller and the processor and classify the level of security as basic, medium or high, depending on the type of data contained in the filing systems, which is also specified in the relevant articles (Arts 80 and 81).

There is a guide to data security to instruct the responsible parties (*Guía de Seguridad de Datos*). It also includes a model Security Document, basically, the internal document that companies need in order to comply with the Regulation.

For example, in the context of healthcare, the Guide picks on an exception provided by Art. 81.6 of the Regulation, which states that the limited basic level of security can be implemented on the filing systems or processing dealing with healthcare data but only where this deals exclusively with the level of disability or the declaration thereof, in line with what the law provides. The exception, therefore, requires a narrow interpretation, the existence of law that provides for a mandatory collection of this information (e.g. tax or social security files) and specific characteristics (i.e. if this data appears with other clinical files, the security level will be high).

To give an idea of the different levels of security, it might be worth noting some of the considerations found in the Guide. For instance, in relation to the medium level, it is already required, as regards digital filing systems, to:

- appoint someone responsible for the filing system (which does not imply a transfer of responsibility);
- in the case of incidents, compile a detailed log with recovery state, person involved etc.;
- ensure, in terms of access control, that physical access to IT servers is possible.;
- ensure, for identity, a maximum number of access attempts and audit of the data every two years.

High security level implies, for back-up copies, different locations for these copies and recovery processes and servers (equipment).

Art. 44.3(h) LOPD mentions as a serious infraction the maintenance of filing systems with personal data without the proper security measures in place, as determined by the Regulation.

Report 0533/2008 of the AEPD deals with the advice sought by a company as regards the security levels required for (i) the processing of files containing data on employees, clients, candidates and researchers and (ii) the processing of files related to clinical trials (anonymised patient data). The AEPD concludes that regarding the first, if the data are purely those necessary for an employment, professional or commercial relationship there is no need to comply with a medium security level arising from "those personal data that provide a definition of the characteristics or personality of the citizens and that allow the assessment of personality or behavioural traits" per Art. 81.2(f) of the Regulation. As regards the second filing system, the AEPD concludes that the required security level is high given that specially protected data are collected.

The AEPD reaches this conclusion as a result of classifying clinical trials in three categories:

- "Biological sample anonymised or permanently dissociated": a sample that cannot be linked to an identified or identifiable person because the link between both has been eliminated or the association requires a non-reasonable effort;
- "Biological sample non-identifiable or anonymous": a sample with no link to an identified or identifiable person whose origin is, consequently, untraceable;
- "Biological sample codified or reversibility dissociated": a sample with no link to an identified or identifiable person because the informative nexus has been dissociated or replaced but only using a code that allows the inverse operation.

The AEPD reasons that, in the first two categories, the LOPD would not be applicable. Otherwise, it would remain applicable. Given, again according to the AEPD, that the method followed by clinical trials is generally that of the third category, a high level of protection is demanded as per Art. 81.3 of the Regulation and Art. 5.1(g) LOPD, which includes treating healthcare data as a type of specially protected data.

1.3.4.3.10 Cross-border data transfer

The issue of what exactly constitutes cross-border transfer of information containing personal data, so that they become accessible in countries outside the EU and EEA, is still, to a large extent, under discussion.

The LOPD does not define the term "transfer" but a reading of the two articles of Title V on international data transfer indicates that, in geographical terms at least, it refers to countries outside the EU. Further, it mentions countries not offering a comparable level of protection to the data.

In accordance with the *Lindqvist* judgment of the ECJ, the provisions regarding transfer to other countries that do not have an adequate level of protection do not apply if it is not explicitly the intention of the controller to export the data to such countries and make personal data available to a specific group of persons in a country outside the EU[381].

Closer to home, in the *Google Spain SL v Agencia Española de Protección de Datos* (AEPD) decision, the AEPD reasoned that search engine operators were data controllers and thus subject to the Data Protection Directive. The Spanish High Court (Tribunal Supremo), on appeal, referred several questions to the ECJ for a preliminary ruling, among which, whether Google was indeed a data controller and whether, being a non-EU company, was subject to the directive's territorial reach. The ECJ answered both affirmatively. The Court's reasoning on the latter was that even if the data processing takes place outside the EU, the commercial activity of Google, mostly advertising, was also carried out in Spain and hence a close link between the two could be established. Google was thus forced to comply with the applicant's request to delete the personal data. The Court understood that the rights of the person were not superseded by any public interest.

Provisions of the LOPD on cross-border transfer of data closely resemble those of Arts 25 and 26 Data Protection Directive. However, the Spanish legislator has opted for a general norm (Art. 33 LOPD) followed by a series of exceptions (Art. 34 LOPD). According to Art 33 LOPD, as a general rule personal data can only be transferred to a country outside Spain if that country guarantees a comparable level of protection to that of the LOPD, except where the level of protection is met and authorisation has been granted by the Director of the AEPD. This authorisation will depend on whether the Director has received adequate guarantees.

The second paragraph of Art. 33 LOPD establishes how this "comparable level of protection" should be evaluated. Essentially, the level will be decided by the AEPD, taking into account all the circumstances, among others, the type of data, purpose, countries involved, EU reports on the matters, and the level of general, or sectorial, legal protection offered by the third country etc.

The derogations or exceptions to the general rule regarding international data transfer, in line with those contemplated by Art. 26 Data Protection Directive, are introduced in Art. 34 LOPD. There are 11 exceptions, including, notably, when the transfer takes place to a country with which Spain shares a Convention or

---

381 ECJ Case C-101/01 (6.11.2003), *Lindqvist.*

Treaty, that is a member of the EU or that is a country in respect of which the EU has declared an adequate level of protection is guaranteed. Other exceptions include where the data subject has consented or where medical reasons make it necessary, or where there are standard contractual clauses approved by the Commission. It is worth noting that the LOPD uses the term "comparable" instead of adopting the direct translation of the directive's "adequate".

1.3.4.3.11 Codes of conduct (*códigos tipo*)

The LOPD contemplates the possibility for codes of conduct to be drafted, not only by the owners of private filing systems, but also by public ones.

The Regulation, in its Title VII, elaborates on this type of model contract as per Art. 32 LOPD. In legal terms, they are considered to be deontological codes (*códigos deontológicos*), good professional practice codes (*códigos de buenas prácticas*) or codes of conduct (*códigos de conducta*).

These codes, whose central aim is to coordinate and harmonise data processing in line with the LOPD, are voluntary in nature but binding for those who choose to adhere to their principles. That is, they follow self-regulation. The Regulation specifies the minimum content of these codes of conduct as well as additional commitments in its Arts 73 and 74. Importantly, the Regulation also highlights the importance of monitoring and enforcement (Art. 75) and the publicity requirement. The codes need to be registered with the AEPD in accordance with Art. 77 and need to guarantee accessibility, ongoing monitoring, reporting to the AEPD and updating of the codes. The responsibility for these tasks falls on those entities designated by the codes themselves.

1.3.5 France

This section discusses the legal provisions of French data protection laws, with special emphasis on those that can potentially create legal barriers for online sharing of research data in the framework of the Open Research Data Pilot.

In France, the main legal instrument regulating data protection and data sharing is the French Data Protection Act enacted in 1978 (Loi du 6 janvier 1978 relative à l'informatique, aux fichiers et aux libertés modifiée, "FDPA")[382]. The FDPA is said to have originally inspired EU data protection legislation but has also undergone successive amendments. The most relevant is the overhaul undertaken by Act No. 2004-801 of 7 August 2004 (Data Process Act), which transposes the Data Protection Directive into French law and establishes the limits and guarantees of the right to data protection. Interestingly enough, France

[382] The last amendment of the DPA dates from 2014.

was the last EU country to implement the Data Protection Directive. The FDPA sets out to protect "human identity, human rights, privacy, individual or public liberties" (Art. 1), a somewhat mixed bag of what appear to be general and specific concepts.

The FDPA also creates, in its original 1978 incarnation, the National Data Protection Authority, the so-called Commission Nationale de l'Information et des Libertés ("CNIL") in its Art. 11. Its powers were strengthened by means of the 2004 amendment, which allowed the CNIL to "investigate, issue warnings and impose sanctions" as opposed to its mere supervisory nature. The CNIL is an independent administrative authority. It is made up of 17 members who, in turn, elect the Chair. The FDPA, which regulates its composition and responsibilities, keenly highlights the independent nature of the CNIL.

The FDPA, which broadly follows the structure of the Data Protection Directive, contains 13 chapters and 72 articles. In addition, the collection of personal data is also regulated by sectorial regulation, such as the Postal and Electronics Communication Code (Arts L. 34-1 et seq. and Arts R. 10-12 et seq.). Other sectorial regulation chooses to focus on the deontological issues arising from the collection of personal data rather than on the actual medium of collection. As such, there are specific rules on professional secrecy and data protection applicable in the medical area (Arts L. 1110-4, L. 1111-8, L. 1112-3, L. 1121-3, L. 1343-3 and L. 2132-1, Public Health Code)[383].

Further, the French legislator has also enacted Décret n° 2005-1309 du 20 octobre 2005 pris pour l'application de la loi n° 78-17 du 6 janvier 1978 relative à l'informatique, aux fichiers et aux libertés (hereafter, the "Regulation"). The Regulation mostly deals with the functioning of the CNIL.

1.3.5.1 Fundamental legal terms

1.3.5.1.1 Personal data

According to the law, in line with Art. 2(a) Data Protection Directive, personal data means "any information relating to a natural person who is or can be identified, directly or indirectly, by reference to an identification number or to one or more factors specific to them ...".

The CNIL further explains that:

> *to define personal data, account must be taken of all the means available to the "data controller" to determine whether a person is identifiable. Personal data are any anonymous data that can be double-checked to identify a specific individual (e.g. fingerprints, DNA, or information such as "the son of the doctor living at 11 Belleville St. in Montpellier does not perform well at school").*

---

[383] See http://uk.practicallaw.com/6-502-1481.

That is, for the CNIL, the definition of what is comprised by personal data is broad as it includes data as diverse as e-mail addresses, telephone numbers (see CNIL decision n° 2005-019) or biometric characteristics.

It should be noted that French courts have, nonetheless, been divided on the issue of whether IP addresses are personal data[384]. The French Supreme Court (*Court de Cassation*) has yet to provide a clear guideline.

The FDPA does not expressly define the term "information". However, further to the Article 29 Working Party guidelines, French authors believe this reference to "any information" represents a key interpretative concept in the (broad) interpretation of the type of data covered by the law[385].

An identifiable person is one who can be identified "directly or indirectly, in particular by reference to an identification number (e.g. social security number) or one or more factors specific" to their physical, physiological, mental, economic, cultural or social identity (e.g. name and first name, date of birth, biometrics data, fingerprints, DNA[386] etc.). This concept should imply, in line with the guidance provided by the Article 29 Working Party, some degree of certainty as opposed to a "simple hypothetical possibility".

Indeed, when defining the concept of personal data, the FDPA ends the paragraph with the following statement: "in order to determine whether a person is identifiable, all the means that the data controller or any other person uses or may have access to should be taken into consideration" (Art. 2 FDPA).

The FDPA does not expressly define what persons are actually covered by the law and whether these have to be living or not. Art. 2 FDPA simply defines the data subject as an "individual to whom the data covered by the processing relate".

In principle, the individuals protected by the FDPA are only those who are living. This statement derives, indirectly, from Art. 56.3 as well as Art. 40.6 and 7 FDPA. The first article states that "information in relation to deceased persons, including that mentioned on death certificates, may be subjected to data processing unless the person in question expressed their refusal in writing *before their death*" (emphasis added). Similarly, Art. 40 FDPA acknowledges the heirs' rights to demand that controllers "take the death into account and update the data accordingly".

The FDPA is only applicable to individuals (therefore, *a contrario*, not to legal entities).

---

384 For example, the Paris Court of Appeal has decided that an IP address does not qualify as personal data (see CA Paris, 13ème ch., 27 April 2007 no. 338935). No clear decision has yet been taken by the Supreme Court (Cour de Cassation) on IP addresses. The CNIL in a recent decision (see Google decision n° 2013-420, 3 January 2014) decided that an IP address is considered to be personal data.

385 Coulibaly, *La protection des données à caractère personnel dans le domaine de la recherche scientifique,* Droit, University of Grenoble, 2011, p. 53.

386 On their own, some of these data, however, notably DNA, will not be sufficient to identify a person but will require a combination with other items of data, see ibid., p. 22.

1.3.5.1.2 Anonymised data and encoded data

Following the conceptual structure of the Data Protection Directive, the FDPA does not mention anonymised data as such. It does make reference, for example, to the term "undecipherable" in the context of personal data breaches. One therefore needs to look at documents published by the CNIL for some guidance. In its *Good Practices* manual, which contains best-in-class practices to comply with the mandate of the FDPA, the CNIL describes "anonymising" as that which "makes it impossible to establish any connection between personal data and the natural person to whom it relates". The CNIL also offers some descriptions, such as "true anonymisation", which necessarily involves an (irreversible) loss of information (sometimes deletion or blocking suffice to achieve this outcome). In turn, "pseudonymisation" may be defined as the replacement of a name by a pseudonym. In this process, data lose their identifying characteristics (in direct fashion). In this scenario, the data remain linked to the same person across multiple data records and information systems without revealing the individual's identity. It may be performed by or with the possibility of re-identifying names or identities (*reversible* or *irreversible pseudonymisation*).

The CNIL further explains that:

> *anonymisation as a good security practice must be distinguished from the "anonymisation process" within the meaning of the law specifically Art. 8-III, 11-3 and 32-IV. As a general rule, in order for the CNIL to conclude that an "anonymisation process" complies with the law, true anonymisation must be carried out by deleting data or performing a "pseudonymisation"*...[387].

For instance, the use of codes that lead to, or allow, identification should be considered as personal data processing indirectly allowing the identification of the data subject. The CNIL notes that the field of research is particularly impacted by this fact, to the extent that direct identifying data are retained in filing systems that can lead to the identification of the data subject. Indeed, the CNIL has used this reasoning for the existence of biobanks, given that even if no directly identified data are collected or registered, the reference of the patient code can be traced back to the name of the data subject via the sender/healthcare institution that sent the sample to the biobank.

1.3.5.1.3 Special categories of personal data

Art. 8 FDPA contains a specific provision on the processing of sensitive data. Such sensitive data are defined as "personal data that reveals, directly or indirectly, the racial and ethnic origins, the political, philosophical, religious opinions or trade union affiliation of persons, or which concern their health or sexual life".

---

[387] CNIL, *Measures for the Privacy Risk Treatment,* Translation of June 2012 Edition.

The description of specially protected personal data includes the generally accepted terms. Interestingly, a court decision ruled, before the implementation of the Data Protection Directive into French law, that a photograph of a naked person uploaded onto the Internet qualified as sensitive data as it indirectly revealed such person's sex life[388].

1.3.5.1.4 Processing of personal data

The definition of "processing of personal data" in the FDPA follows closely Art. 2(b) Data Protection Directive. According to Art. 2 FDPA, processing of personal data means "any operation or set of operations in relation to such data, whatever the mechanism used, especially the obtaining, recording, organisation, retention, adaptation or alteration, retrieval, consultation, use, disclosure by transmission, dissemination or otherwise making available, alignment or combination, blocking, deletion or destruction".

The FDPA also distinguishes in its Art. 2 between automatic processing of personal data and non-automatic processing of personal data. Both require compliance with the FDPA yet the law does not define them, perhaps because once the processing is deemed "automatic" the actual technique used is not really relevant. In any case, Art. 2 describes an exception, namely, "processing carried out for the exercise of exclusively private activities, where the data controller meets the conditions provided in Art. 5". Further, the FDPA distinguishes between the two where necessary. It makes reference, in different provisions, to situations relevant in cases of automatic processing of personal data (e.g. Art. 22 FDPA, regarding the prior notification obligation) that should be construed as not applying to non-automatic processing.

Another exception, not covered by the FDPA, is that contained in Art. 4 which excludes "cache copies" or temporary copies made "in the context of technical operations of transmission and access provision to a digital network for the purpose of automatic, intermediate and transitory retention of data and with the sole aim of allowing other recipients of the service to benefit from the best access possible to the transmitted information".

1.3.5.1.5 Controller

The figure of the controller (*responsable d'un traitement de données*) has been introduced by the FDPA, in line with Art. 2(d) Data Protection Directive, and is defined in its Art. 3.I. A controller can be "a person, public authority, department or any other organisation who determines the purposes and means of the data processing".

---

[388] See TGI Privas, 3 September 1997, JCP E 1999, no. 21, p. 913.

Art. 5 FDPA limits the mandate under the French FDPA to those controllers that are established, in whatever legal form, on French territory or use means of processing located on French territory (excluding when they do so for mere "transit" reasons).

1.3.5.1.6 Processor

Art. 35 FDPA defines briefly the figure of the data processor (*sous-traitant*), expanding on the definition offered by Art. 2(e) Data Protection Directive, as "any person who processes personal data on behalf of the data controller". The article focuses rather on the obligations of the processor who (i) "may process data only under the data controller's instructions" and (ii) "shall offer adequate guarantees to ensure the implementation of the security and confidentiality measures". These measures are those mentioned in the FDPA which are specified in Art. 34 regarding security requirements. Further, Art. 35 FDPA states that the obligations of the processor in this respect do not exempt the controller "from the obligation to supervise the observance of such measures". Thus, the type of relationship between the controller and the processor calls for a contract that clearly specifies the obligations as per (i) and (ii). The responsibilities of the processor, generally a subcontractor, are limited.

Given that both the controller and processor are defined not by the person themselves but rather by the activities they conduct and the freedom to act, the same person might in some instances act as a controller whereas in others as a processor based on the activity level of instructions they follow. The CNIL is thus "not bound by the qualification chosen by an entity"[389].

1.3.5.1.7 Recipient of processing

The concept of "third party" is not defined as such by the FDPA, unlike in Art. 2(f) Data Protection Directive. It is instead the figure of the "recipient of a processing" that is defined in Art. 3 FDPA. It follows Art. 2(g) Data Protection Directive though it excludes the figure of the "third party" from the definition where the directive included it ("whether a third party or not"). The figure is that of "any authorised person to whom the data are disclosed, other than the data subject, the data controller, the sub-contractor and persons who, due to their functions, are in charge of processing the data". However, Art. 3.II FDPA continues, "the authorities who are legally entitled to ask the data controller to send them the personal data, in the context of a particular mission or that of the exercise of a right to receive such data, shall not be regarded as recipients" (in line with the Data Protection Directive: "authorities which may receive data in the framework of a particular inquiry shall not be regarded as recipients").

---

[389] See http://uk.practicallaw.com/6-502-1481?service=crossborder#a481778.

1.3.5.1.8 Consent of the data subject

The FDPA does not contain any provision on the definition of consent, of its form or content, or of evidence of such consent. Generally, French data protection legislators look at the French Civil Code for a definition of consent. Similarly, we understand that other French legislative instruments also provide a definition[390].

1.3.5.2 Principles of personal data processing: Data quality

In line with the Data Protection Directive, the FDPA provides, in its Art. 6, the principles related to data quality. The guiding principles are data minimisation and purpose specification, implemented by the Data Protection Directive.

1.3.5.2.1 Purpose limitation

According to the FDPA, personal data can only be collected when the purpose of the collection is specified, explicit and legitimate (Art. 6.2 FDPA). This is in line with Art. 6(a)–(c) Data Protection Directive. Art. 6.2 FDPA sets forth the requirement of compatibility of further processing.

1.3.5.2.2 Further processing for historical, statistical or scientific purposes

Regarding compatibility, the only exception to the requirement of compatibility of purposes is for reasons of statistical, scientific and historical purposes. These purposes are thus considered to be compatible with any original use.

In line with Art. 6(1)(b) Data Protection Directive, Art. 6(2) FDPA provides that further processing of personal data for historical, statistical or scientific purposes shall not be regarded as incompatible with the “initial purposes of the data collection, if it is carried out in conformity with the principles and procedures provided for …”and “if it is not used to take decisions with respect to the data subjects”. Of course, the standard principles and procedures of the FDPA should be met (e.g. formalities prior to data processing or obligations of the data controller).

Similarly, the prohibition on collecting especially sensitive data does not apply to processing necessary for the purposes of preventive medicine, medical diagnosis (Art. 6.6 FDPA), statistical processing (Art. 6.7 FDPA) or processing necessary for medical research (Art. 6.8 FDPA).

---

[390] A definition of consent has been added to the Post Offices and Electronic Communications Code in relation to direct marketing by electronic means. It is defined as a freely given manifestation of wishes, specific and informed, by which a person accepts that personal data relating to him will be used for direct prospecting. This definition is similar to the definition of consent found in Directive 95/46/EC.

1.3.5.2.3 Data minimisation

The principle of data minimisation is envisaged in Art. 6 FDPA and deals with the scope of data collection. In line with Art. 6(1)(c) and 6(1)(e) Data Protection Directive, the article requires that:

- personal data shall only be processed where, given the purposes for which they are collected or subsequently processed, they are "adequate", "relevant" and "not excessive" (Art. 6(3) FDPA), and
- personal data shall be retained "in a form that allows the identification of the data subjects for a period no longer than is necessary for the purposes for which they are obtained and processed" (Art. 6(5) FDPA).

Data minimisation requires an ongoing, continuous assessment. Art. 6(4) FDPA states that the data should be "accurate", "complete" and "kept up to date" so that they respond to the true situation of the individual. This requires that controllers adopt "appropriate steps … in order to delete and rectify data that are inaccurate and incomplete with regard to the purposes for which they were obtained and processed". This is in line with Art. 6(d) Data Protection Directive.

1.3.5.2.4 Longer-term storage of personal data for scientific use

Art. 36 FDPA states that exceptions can be made to the aforementioned retention period "only for processing for historical, statistical and scientific purposes". Further, Art. 36 FDPA notes that the conditions of Art. L.212-3 of the Code du Patrimoine (Heritage Code) shall "apply to the determination of the retained data". Paragraph 2 of the same article states that "processing whose purpose is limited to ensuring the long-term conservation of archive documents in the context of Book II of that Code is exempt from the formalities prior to commencing processing provided for in Chapter IV of this Act".

Art. 36 FDPA *in fine* describes a general exception, as opposed to the specific exception described above, whereby processing for purposes that are not historical, statistical or scientific can be carried out with (i) the explicit agreement of the data subject, (ii) the authorisation of the CNIL or (iii) in certain cases regarding processing necessary for medical research, or processing justified by the public interest.

1.3.5.2.5 Legal grounds for lawful processing of personal data

The FDPA follows the Data Protection Directive in its distinction of two blocks of legal grounds for lawful processing of personal data: (i) general rules for general (non-sensitive) categories of personal data (section 1 on "General Provisions",

Arts 6-7 FDPA) and (ii) special stricter provisions with respect to special categories of personal data (section 2 on "Specific Provisions of Certain Categories of Data", Art. 8 FDPA).

1.3.5.2.5.1 Processing of general categories of personal data

Legal grounds for the processing of general categories of personal data are implemented by Art. 7 FDPA, which expressly provides that consent of data subjects is required prior to the collecting and processing of personal data. However, there is no description of how this consent should be given or evidenced[391].

Alternatively to the granting of consent, Art. 7 FDPA provides a list of "conditions" which preclude the requirement of consent. It should be interpreted as an exceptional and closed list and includes (i) "compliance with any legal obligation to which the data controller is subject", (ii) "the protection of the data subject's life", (iii) "the performance of a public service mission entrusted to the data controller of the data recipient", (iv) "the performance of either a contract to which the data subject is a party or steps taken at the request of the data subject prior to entering into a contract" or (v) "the pursuit of the data controller's or the data recipient's legitimate interest, provided this is not incompatible with the interests or the fundamental rights and liberties of the data subject".

This list is in line with those of other Member States, where we encounter exceptions revolving around contractual relationships, health issues or legal obligations.

1.3.5.2.5.2 Processing of special categories of personal data

Art. 8 FDPA opens with an absolute prohibition on the collection and processing of sensitive data. The governing principle is the right to non-disclosure of specially protected personal data.

Section II then goes on to enumerate a series of exceptions to the prior section I. These are (i) "express consent", unless the applicable law recognises the non-waivability of the prohibition, (ii) when the processing is necessary "for the

---

[391] As a basic principle, consent must be obtained in accordance with the principle of transparency. Therefore, pre-ticked boxes cannot constitute a valid consent. In theory, except in specific cases where express consent is required by law, consent can be express, written, oral or implied. However, in practice, a data subject's consent must be in French and given either in writing or by a click-through, if given over the Internet. Obtaining consent from employees is deemed impossible, except in limited cases, as it is considered that it will never be given freely by the employee.

protection of human life, but to which the data subject is unable to give their consent because of a legal incapacity or physical impossibility" or (iii) if the processing

> *is carried out by an association or any other non-profit seeking religious, philosophical, political or trade union body, only for the data corresponding to the object of the association, if it relates to members or close collaborators and the data is not transferred to third parties unless expressly consents to, (iv) made public by the data subject itself, (v) necessary for the establishment, exercise or defence of a legal claim (vi) preventive medicine, (vii) statistics, or (viii) medical research.*

It should be noted that, whereas the FDPA does not treat information relating to offences, convictions and security measures as sensitive personal data, it does place strict controls on its processing. The processing of such data is described in Art. 9 FDPA. For instance, the processing requires prior authorisation by the CNIL unless the controller is a representative of justice (*auxiliaries de justice*). There are also simplified authorisation procedures for merchants or for the French state in particular instances (prevention and investigation of offences etc.).

Finally, Art. 10 FDPA prohibits court decisions on the back of assessments based solely on automatic processing of personal data.

1.3.5.2.6 Transparency of personal data processing

The principle of transparency of personal data processing is elaborated in Chapter V, section 1 of the FDPA, which deals with the obligations of data controllers. This transparency starts at the moment of collection of data for processing which, according to Art. 6(1) FDPA, should be done "fairly" and "lawfully".

In addition, the FDPA contributes to the transparency requirement by establishing a series of formalities that need to be met to make the processing lawful. The general principle is that the data controller must notify the CNIL of the processing of personal data. The formalities make up Chapter IV of the FDPA. Nonetheless, the chapter also details a series of exceptions to this prior notification. These exceptions are dictated either by the law or by the CNIL.

Art. 22 FDPA states that automatic processing of personal data must be notified to the CNIL except when the processing falls under the provisions of Art. 25 (sensitive), Art. 26 (state security and criminal offences processing) and Art. 27 (public processing, census, online services etc.) "as indicated in paragraph 2 of Art. 36 (conservation of archives)".

However, the notification to the CNIL will not take place when (i) the processing is solely for keeping a register for public information, generally openly available for consultation, (ii) processing mentioned in sub-section 3 of section II of Art. 8 FDPA (religious, philosophical, political etc. by an association as regards the data of active members corresponding to the object of the association) or (iii) a personal data protection officer has been appointed (Art. 22 III FDPA). The involvement of this officer replaces the obligation to notify the CNIL given that they are in charge of "ensuring, in an independent manner, compliance with the obligations provided for in this Act". The exception is where a transfer of personal data outside the EU is envisaged[392].

Art. 32 FDPA describes the information that the data controller or their representative needs to provide to the data subject:

a) the identity of the controller and of their representative, if any;

b) the purpose of the processing;

c) whether replies to the questions are compulsory or optional;

d) the possible consequences of the absence of a reply;

e) the recipients or categories of recipients of the data;

f) the rights of individuals in relation to the processing of data;

g) when applicable, the intended transfer of personal data to states outside the EU.

These provisions are almost identical to those of Art. 10 Data Protection Directive.

Art. 32.I FDPA *in fine* specifies that if questionnaires are used to collect the data, the above requirements are applicable too and that 1, 2, 3 and 6 should be directly mentioned in the questionnaire.

Beside the general principles on the collection and processing of data laid down in Art. 6 FDPA, the Act does not expressly describe the manner in which the information of Art. 32 FDPA should be communicated to the data subject.

Sections IV, V and VI of Art. 32 FDPA describe the exceptions to the above information requirement on collection. Section IV explains that:

> *if the personal data obtained are, within a short period of time, to form part of an anonymisation procedure that was recognised beforehand by the CNIL as complying with the provisions of this Act, the information delivered by the data controller to the data subject may be limited to that mentioned in Sub-Section 1 and 2 of Section I.*

A second exception is that of Section V. It states that Section I will not apply "to the data obtained under the conditions provided for in Section III when processing is carried out on behalf of the state and relating to state security, defence, or public safety, to the extent that such limitation is necessary for the observance of the purposes pursued by the processing". Finally, Section VI provides one last exempted scenario: the provisions shall not apply to data processing "in relation to the prevention, investigation or proof of criminal offences and the prosecution of offenders".

---

[392] The figure of the "personal data protection officer" was introduced in French law in 2004.

According to Section III of Art. 32 FDPA, if personal data are obtained other than from the data subject, the data controller or their representative must at the time of recording the personal data or, if disclosure to a third party is planned, no later than the time when the data are first disclosed, provide the data subject with the information enumerated in Section I.

The second paragraph of Section III deals with personal data that were originally collected for other purposes. In this context, the provision explains the preceding paragraph, that is, the general rule for data not obtained from the data subject, in the cases of data retention for historical, statistical and scientific purposes or the re-use of these data for statistical purposes. In order to understand the extent of this exception we should revert to sectorial legislation regarding Book II of the Heritage Code or the Act on obligation, coordination and confidentiality as regards statistics (both duly mentioned in Section III).

The paragraph finishes by stating that "these provisions shall not apply whenever the data subject has already been informed or whenever informing the data subject proves impossible or would involve disproportionate efforts compared with the interest of the procedure". Whether an effort to provide information is disproportionate or not should depend on the criteria of the CNIL given that the FDPA does not provide further guidance.

1.3.5.2.7 Data subject's rights

The FDPA grants data subjects a series of rights and defences in the context of the collection and treatment of their personal data by the controller. Apart from the right to consent and the right to be informed, which have already been described in the previous paragraphs, section 2 of the FDPA is dedicated to a series of specific rights of the data subject in the context of data processing (Rights of Individuals in Respect to the Processing of Personal Data).

Art. 38 FDPA gives the data subject the right to object to automated individual decisions based on the processing of personal data[393]. There must be legitimate grounds, such as those related to a particular situation of the data subject, that have priority over any interest the data controller might have. Data subjects also have the right to object to the processing of their personal data for direct marketing purposes.

Art. 39 FDPA contains the right of access. The data subject is entitled to request and obtain information about the processing of personal data, including confirmation of the processing of personal data and information relating to the purposes, categories, recipients and cross-border transfers (ex EU).

The right of access includes several limitations, including payment for copies or against excessive requests (even if in these cases the burden of proof lies with the data controller). The last paragraph excludes the provisions of the article

---

[393] What the Data Protection Directive defines in its Art. 15 as "automated individual decisions".

altogether in cases where the personal data are retained in a form that clearly excludes all risk of violating the privacy of the data subject and for a period that does not exceed that necessary for the sole purpose of creating statistics, or for scientific or historical research".

Under Art. 41 FDPA, in those cases where the data processing relates to the security of the state, defence or public security the data subject has a right of indirect access. The data subject might then request the CNIL to check the information, therefore making the access indirect. The CNIL not only checks, but can also demand correction if so required. The CNIL can disclose the data to the data subject after prior authorisation of the controller.

According to Art. 40 FDPA the data subject has the right to "rectify, complete, update, block or delete personal data relating to them that are inaccurate, incomplete, equivocal, expired, or whose collection, usage, disclosure or retention is prohibited" (right of rectification).

The data controller must demonstrate, at the request of the data subject and at no cost to the data subject, that they have carried out the rectification activities. In the event of a dispute, again as in the case of the right of access, the burden of proof shall be with the data controller, "except where it is established that the data was disclosed by the data subject or with his consent".

There is no express obligation to inform third parties about rectification and blocking. However, Art. 40, paragraph 5 FDPA deals with the situation where the data that need to be rectified have previously been transmitted to a third party. In this case the data controller must indeed "accomplish the necessary formalities to inform that third party of the operations carried out in conformity with the first paragraph", which deals with the activities involved in the right of rectification.

1.3.5.2.8 Measures to ensure security of processing

Art. 34 FDPA states that the controller "shall take all useful precautions, with regard to the nature of the data and the risks of the processing, to preserve the security of the data and, in particular, prevent their alteration and damage, or access by non-authorised third parties". So the FDPA makes the data controller responsible for the adoption of security measures.

Further, it should be noted that, in 2012, the CNIL published a guide on the identification of risks and security best practices[394]. These measures range from password security management to training users. Failure to implement the required security measures leads to sanctions per the French Criminal Code.

---

[394] See http://www.cil.cnrs.fr/CIL/spip.php?article1748.

1.3.5.2.9 Cross-border data transfer

Chapter XII of the FDPA deals with transfers of personal data to states outside the EU/EEA. Art. 68 FDPA starts with a general prohibition on such transfers where the state "does not provide a sufficient level of protection of individuals privacy, liberties and fundamental rights with regard to the actual or possible processing of their personal data". The term used, at least in the official English translation, is "sufficient" whereas the Data Protection Directive uses the term "adequate".

Art. 68 FDPA explains that, in order to assess the nature of the protection, several issues should be taken into account (nature, characteristics, purpose, duration etc.). However, it does not expressly say who should decide on the circumstances being met. It also does not exclude transfer of sensitive data outside the EU.

Art. 69 FDPA describes the exceptions to the general prohibition. The most obvious one is where the data subject themself has given consent. Further, there are six exceptions set by the law and one additional exception. Data may be transferred to a third country, if the CNIL has recognised the recipient country as providing adequate protection. This last exception should involve the communication to the EU Commission and the other national supervisory authorities.

Finally, it might be worth noting that in Art. 70 FDPA the law now uses the term "adequate" instead of "sufficient", which is in line with the Data Protection Directive. The article describes the procedure for prohibiting transfer of personal data should the EU Commission note that the level of protection of that third country is not "adequate". In these situations, the CNIL is expected to prohibit such transfer.

The CNIL supports the use of BCRs by companies (which allows single decisions per legal group of companies instead of mere individual authorisations) even if cross-border data transfers in this case still require authorisation from the CNIL. The legal entities need merely to present a compliance commitment for their cross-border transfers. Thereafter, controllers should keep an updated list of each transfer, which the CNIL can consult on request.

1.3.6 The United Kingdom

Interestingly, the United Kingdom was one of the first countries to discuss a "right of privacy". The very first draft of a "Right of Privacy Bill" was brought before the House of Commons in 1961[395]. However, those early efforts to codify a right of privacy failed, as did later initiatives. The leading opinion in the UK was for a long time that data protection legislation could potentially hamper innovation in information technology and endanger economic growth.

---

[395] See Panagiotides, *Der Data Protection Act 1984*, Baden-Baden, Nomos, 1998, pp. 58 et seqq.

Data protection was seen as an economic factor and not as a fundamental right of the individual. Indeed it was the success of the Convention of the Council of Europe on data protection that led to a change. Being a member of this convention became increasingly important economically. There was seen to be a risk that the lack of data protection legislation could place the UK increasingly at a disadvantage in relation to other countries[396]. Hence the government changed its opinion and introduced a Bill in July 1983, which became the Data Protection Act 1984.

This Act has since been repealed. Nevertheless, it introduced for the first time a regime for the holding and processing of personal data and laid down data protection principles[397].

1.3.6.1 Aim of data protection legislation

In 1998 the Data Protection Act 1984 was replaced by the Act of 1998 (DPA 1998). The DPA 1998 describes itself as "an Act to make new provision for the regulation of the processing of information relating to individuals, including the obtaining, holding, use or disclosure of such information". In fact the Act implemented the Data Protection Directive into the national legislation of the UK. There is no explicit mention in the Act of a special normative goal, such as the protection of interests of data subjects.

1.3.6.2 Scope of application

The scope of application of the DPA 1998 is defined in its section 5(1). Except as otherwise provided, the Act applies to data controllers in respect of any data if

> *(a) the data controller is established in the United Kingdom and the data are processed in the context of that establishment, or*
>
> *(b) the data controller is established neither in the United Kingdom nor in any other EEA State but uses equipment in the United Kingdom for processing the data otherwise than for the purposes of transit through the United Kingdom.*

This means that UK data protection law applies to all organisations in the UK, as well as non-UK organisations that use equipment in the UK for processing of personal data. Thus, for example, a Chilean organisation that uses a company in the UK for personal data storage will be subject to the provisions of UK data protection law[398].

---

396 See ibid., p. 139.
397 See Carey, *Data Protection*, 4th edition, Oxford, Oxford University Press, 2015, pp. 4 et seq.
398 Ibid., p. 18.

1.3.6.3 Definitions

The most important definitions are found at the beginning of the Act in section 1.

1.3.6.3.1 Data

Unlike the Data Protection Directive and legislation of other European states, the DPA 1998 defines the term "data" separately. "Data" means information which (section 1(1) DPA 1998):

> *(a) is being processed by means of equipment operating automatically in response to instructions given for that purpose,*
>
> *(b) is recorded with the intention that it should be processed by means of such equipment,*
>
> *(c) is recorded as part of a relevant filing system or with the intention that it should form part of a relevant filing system, or*
>
> *(d) does not fall within paragraph (a), (b) or (c) but forms part of an accessible record, or*
>
> *(e) is recorded information held by a public authority and does not fall within any of paragraphs (a) to (d).*

Information that is held by a private sector entity in the form of unstructured bundles kept in boxes is not considered as data[399].

1.3.6.3.2 Personal data

According to section 1(1) DPA 1998 personal data means:

> *data which relate to a living individual who can be identified (a) from those data, or (b) from those data and other information which is in the possession of, or is likely to come into the possession of, the data controller, and includes any expression of opinion about the individual and any indication of the intentions of the data controller or any other person in respect of the individual.*

So whether data constitute personal data depends on the possibility of identifying the living individual behind them. Therefore it is not necessary for the information itself to identify a person. The ability to identify a person can depend partly on the relevant data and partly on other information:

> *Example: An organisation holds data on microfiche. The microfiche records do not identify individuals by name, but bear unique reference numbers which can be matched to a card index system to identify the individuals concerned. The information held on the microfiche records is personal data*[400].

---

399 See *Smith v Lloyds TSB Bank plc* [2005] EWHC 246.

400 Example taken from: ICO, *Key definitions of the Data Protection Act*, available at: https://ico.org.uk/for-organisations/guide-to-data-protection/key-definitions.

However, it is not even necessary that the identifying information is in the possession of the data controller. Sub-subsection (b) also includes information that is likely to come into the possession of the data controller. Thus it is possible that information held by an organisation can amount to personal data even where no individual can currently be identified from it, provided that such identification will be possible when relevant additional information is acquired by the organisation and that such acquisition is likely[401]. In the example above the data on the microfiche could be personal data, even if the card index system to identify the individuals concerned is held by another organisation.

As can be seen from the definition, personal data must relate to a living person. Data of deceased persons and companies do not fall under the definition. Where personal data have been successfully anonymised, the DPA 1998 no longer applies[402].

1.3.6.3.3 Processing

The DPA 1998 regulates the processing of personal data. This central term of the Act is defined in section 1(1) DPA 1998:

> *Processing, in relation to information or data, means obtaining, recording or holding the information or data or carrying out any operation or set of operations on the information or data, including*
>
> *(a) organisation, adaptation or alteration of the information or data,*
>
> *(b) retrieval, consultation or use of the information or data,*
>
> *(c) disclosure of the information or data by transmission, dissemination or otherwise making available, or*
>
> *(d) alignment, combination, blocking, erasure or destruction of the information or data.*

This definition of processing is very wide and it is difficult to think of anything an organisation might do with data that will not be processing[403].

1.3.6.3.4 Data controller

A data controller is the entity that is responsible for complying with data protection law[404]. According to section 1(1) DPA 1998:

---

401 Carey, *Data Protection*, 4th edition, Oxford, Oxford University Press, 2015, p. 22.
402 Ibid., p. 222.
403 ICO, *Key definitions of the Data Protection Act*, available at: https://ico.org.uk/for-organisations/guide-to-data-protection/key-definitions.
404 Carey, *Data Protection*, 4th edition, Oxford, Oxford University Press, 2015, p. 29.

data controller" means a person who (either alone or jointly or in common with other persons) determines the purposes for which and the manner in which any personal data are, or are to be, processed.

The word "person" in the definition means legal person and should not be taken to refer to an individual person in most cases[405].

1.3.6.3.5 Sensitive personal data

Like the directive, the DPA 1998 includes special categories of personal data, so-called sensitive personal data. Section 2 DPA 1998 defines such data:

Sensitive personal data means personal data consisting of information as to

(a) the racial or ethnic origin of the data subject,

(b) his political opinions,

(c) his religious beliefs or other beliefs of a similar nature,

(d) whether he is a member of a trade union,

(e) his physical or mental health or condition,

(f) his sexual life,

(g) the commission or alleged commission by him of any offence, or

(h) any proceedings for any offence committed or alleged to have been committed by him, the disposal of such proceedings or the sentence of any court in such proceedings.

The presumption is that, because information about these matters could be used in a discriminatory way, and is likely to be of a private nature, it needs to be treated with greater care than other personal data[406].

1.3.6.3.6 Data processor

Section 1(1) DPA 1998 again defines the data processor:

Data processor, in relation to personal data, means any person (other than an employee of the data controller) who processes the data on behalf of the data controller.

Data controllers often use third-party companies to process their data, for example in the course of outsourcing activities. As long as the third party merely acts on the instructions of the data controller, it will be a data processor and not have statutory obligations under UK law in respect of the processing[407].

---

405 Ibid., p. 29.

406 ICO, *Key definitions of the Data Protection Act*, available at: https://ico.org.uk/for-organisations/guide-to-data-protection/key-definitions.

407 See Carey, *Data Protection*, 4th edition, Oxford, Oxford University Press, 2015, p. 30.

1.3.6.3.7 Consent

Although the DPA 1998 uses the term "consent" in its provisions, for example it treats the consent of the data subject as a legitimisation for the processing of data, the Act does not define what is meant by consent.

1.3.6.4 Data protection principles

Data protection law requires compliance with a set of rules. Section 4 DPA 1998 refers to the data protection principles. Those data protection principles are set out in Schedule 1 Part I to the DPA. Schedule 1 Part II provides guidance on interpretation of the principles[408]. The following principles are listed in Schedule 1 Part I to the DPA 1998:

1. *Personal data shall be processed fairly and lawfully and, in particular, shall not be processed unless*

   (a) at least one of the conditions in Schedule 2 is met, and

   (b) in the case of sensitive personal data, at least one of the conditions in Schedule 3 is also met.

2. *Personal data shall be obtained only for one or more specified and lawful purposes, and shall not be further processed in any manner incompatible with that purpose or those purposes.*

3. *Personal data shall be adequate, relevant and not excessive in relation to the purpose or purposes for which they are processed.*

4. *Personal data shall be accurate and, where necessary, kept up to date.*

5. *Personal data processed for any purpose or purposes shall not be kept for longer than is necessary for that purpose or those purposes.*

6. *Personal data shall be processed in accordance with the rights of data subjects under this Act.*

7. *Appropriate technical and organisational measures shall be taken against unauthorised or unlawful processing of personal data and against accidental loss or destruction of, or damage to, personal data.*

8. *Personal data shall not be transferred to a country or territory outside the European Economic Area unless that country or territory ensures an adequate level of protection for the rights and freedoms of data subjects in relation to the processing of personal data.*

---

[408] Ibid., p. 55.

Those principles apply to every processing of personal data. Section 4(4) DPA 1998 clarifies that it shall be the duty of a data controller to comply with the data protection principles in relation to all personal data with respect to which they are the data controller.

1.3.6.4.1 Fair and lawful processing

The DPA 1998 requires data controllers to process personal data fairly and lawfully. Fairness generally requires the controller to be transparent – clear and open with individuals about how their information will be used.

In determining for the purposes of the first principle whether personal data are processed fairly, regard is to be had to the method by which they are obtained, including, in particular, whether any person from whom they are obtained is deceived or misled as to the purpose or purposes for which they are to be processed (Schedule 1 Part II (1) (1) to the DPA 1998).

Fairness requires the controller to be open and honest about the identity of the controller; to tell people how personal data are intended to be used; usually to handle their personal data only in ways they would reasonably expect; and above all, not to use their information in ways that unjustifiably have a negative effect on them[409].

What is meant by lawful processing is not defined in the Act. Processing may be unlawful if it involves committing a criminal offence or results in a breach of confidence, an infringement of copyright, a breach of an enforceable contractual agreement, a breach of industry-specific legislation or regulations, or a breach of the Human Rights Act 1998[410].

Personal data must not be processed unless at least one of the conditions in Schedule 2 is met. The relevant conditions are:

1. *The data subject has given his consent to the processing.*
2. *The processing is necessary*

   (a) for the performance of a contract to which the data subject is a party, or

   (b) for the taking of steps at the request of the data subject with a view to entering into a contract.
3. *The processing is necessary for compliance with any legal obligation … .*
4. *The processing is necessary in order to protect the vital interests of the data subject.*

---

[409] ICO, *Processing personal data fairly and lawfully*, available at: https://ico.org.uk/for-organisations/guide-to-data-protection/principle-1-fair-and-lawful.

[410] See ibid.

5. *The processing is necessary*

   (a) for the administration of justice … .

6. *The processing is necessary for the purposes of legitimate interests pursued by the data controller or by the third party or parties to whom the data are disclosed, except where the processing is unwarranted in any particular case by reason of prejudice to the rights and freedoms or legitimate interests of the data subject.*

Schedule 3 to the DPA 1998 contains some special conditions for the processing of sensitive data. Some of them are:

a) The data subject has given their explicit consent to the processing of the personal data.

b) The processing is necessary for the purposes of exercising or performing any right or obligation which is conferred or imposed by law on the data controller in connection with employment.

c) The processing is necessary in order to protect the vital interests of the data subject or another person.

d) The information contained in the personal data has been made public as a result of steps deliberately taken by the data subject.

Besides the requirement of the processing being fair and lawful, data controllers need to be able to satisfy one or more of the conditions for processing[411] listed in Schedule 2 or Schedule 3, respectively.

1.3.6.4.2 Processing for specified purposes

The second principle says that personal data shall be obtained only for one or more specified and lawful purposes, and shall not be further processed in any manner incompatible with that purpose or those purposes.

This principle requires the data controller, on the one hand, to specify the purposes for which the data will be collected and used. On the other hand, it requires the data controller not to process the data in any manner incompatible with that specified purpose.

The purpose or purposes for which personal data are obtained may in particular be specified (a) in a notice given by the data controller to the data subject, or (b) in a notification given to the Commissioner. In determining whether any disclosure of personal data is compatible with the purpose or purposes for which the data were obtained, regard is to be had to the purpose or purposes for which the personal data are intended to be processed by any person to whom they are disclosed (Schedule 1 Part II (5) and (6) to the DPA 1998).

---

[411] Those conditions are described in more detail by Carey, *Data Protection*, 4th edition, Oxford, Oxford University Press, 2015, pp. 79 et seqq.

1.3.6.4.3 Adequacy

The Act says that personal data shall be adequate, relevant and not excessive in relation to the purpose or purposes for which they are processed.

This principle requires data controllers to hold personal data about a data subject that are sufficient for the intended purpose and moreover that the controller does not hold more information than needed for the intended purpose. Especially the latter has to be kept in mind since organisations tend to collect too much information on people rather than too little[412].

1.3.6.4.4 Accuracy

Personal data shall be accurate and, where necessary, kept up to date. This principle is self-explanatory. The data controller has the obligation to ensure the accuracy of the processed personal data and to keep them up to date where necessary.

The DPA 1998 does not explain what is accurate. However, there is at least a definition of what is inaccurate in section 70(2) DPA 1998:

> *For the purposes of this Act data are inaccurate if they are incorrect or misleading as to any matter of fact.*

1.3.6.4.5 Limited retention of personal data

The fifth principle says that personal data processed for any purpose or purposes shall not be kept for longer than is necessary for that purpose or those purposes.

According to this principle, data controllers are required to delete, destruct or anonymise personal data as soon as they are no longer required for the intended purposes. Unfortunately there are no time limits or periods mentioned in the Act to give guidance as to when data are no longer necessary and so it is up to the providers to consider how long it is necessary to keep personal data and review the length of time regularly.

1.3.6.4.6 Rights of the data subject

The rights of data subjects are incorporated in the sixth principle, which simply says that personal data shall be processed in accordance with the rights of data subjects under the DPA 1998.

---

412 Ibid., p. 60.

The rights of the individual are contained in Part II of the DPA 1998. Such rights of the data subject are transposed accurately from the Data Protection Directive into UK law[413]. That is why the rights need not be described in detail but must at least be named[414]. The most important individual rights are:

- the right of access to a copy of the information comprised in their personal data (section 7(1) DPA 1998);
- the right to prevent processing likely to cause damage or distress (section 11(1) DPA 1998);
- the right to prevent processing for purposes of direct marketing (section 11(1) DPA 1998);
- the right to object to decisions being taken by automated means (section 12(1) DPA 1998);
- the right to have inaccurate personal data rectified, blocked, erased or destroyed (section 14(1) DPA 1998);
- the right to claim compensation from the data controller for damages caused by a contravention of any of the requirements of the DPA 1998 (section 13(1) DPA 1998).

1.3.6.4.7 Data security

Appropriate technical and organisational measures shall be taken against unauthorised or unlawful processing of personal data and against accidental loss or destruction of, or damage to, personal data.

Security of personal data processing is of fundamental importance to protect data subjects. The best data protection standards set by law are insufficient when personal data are processed without safeguards against unauthorised processing, accidental loss or damage to the data. That is why data controllers are obliged to have appropriate security to prevent the personal data held being accidentally or deliberately compromised[415]. Data controllers should adopt a risk-based approach to the determination of what type of data security measures to implement[416].

---

[413] Ibid., p. 66.

[414] A detailed description of the rights of data subjects can be found in ibid., pp. 165 et seqq.

[415] ICO, *Information security*, available at: https://ico.org.uk/for-organisations/guide-to-data-protection/principle-7-security.

[416] Carey, *Data Protection*, 4th edition, Oxford, Oxford University Press, 2015, p. 122.

1.3.6.4.8 International data transfers

The last data protection principle is a ban on personal data transfers to third countries outside the EEA. Personal data shall not be transferred to a country or territory outside the EEA unless that country or territory ensures an adequate level of protection for the rights and freedoms of data subjects in relation to the processing of personal data.

The rationale behind the principle is that the protection for individual data subjects will be lost where their data are transferred to countries that are not bound by the Data Protection Directive or which do not have sufficiently restrictive data privacy laws[417].

Nevertheless, there are a number of exceptions to this principle listed in Schedule 4 to the DPA 1998. It does not apply if, inter alia:

- the data subject has given their consent to the transfer;
- the transfer is necessary (a) for the performance of a contract between the data subject and the data controller, or (b) for the taking of steps at the request of the data subject with a view to their entering into a contract with the data controller;
- the transfer is necessary for reasons of substantial public interest;
- the transfer is made on terms which are of a kind approved by the Commissioner as ensuring adequate safeguards for the rights and freedoms of data subjects;
- the transfer has been authorised by the Commissioner as being made in such a manner as to ensure adequate safeguards for the rights and freedoms of data subjects.

Which countries guarantee a sufficient level of data protection is determined by the European Commission (Art. 25(6) Data Protection Directive).

1.3.6.5 Exemptions

There are a number of exemptions to the existing data protection principles. Art. 13 Data Protection Directive gives Member States the opportunity to implement their own exemptions. In the UK the main exemptions can be found in Part IV of the DPA 1998. The exemptions permit non-compliance with some provisions of the DPA 1998. There are exemptions, for example, for national security (section 28 DPA 1998), crime and taxation (section 29 DPA 1998) or health, education

[417] Ibid., p. 67.

and social work (section 30 DPA 1998). The most important exemption for this study is the one for research, history and statistics, which can be found in section 33 DPA 1998.

Section 33(2) DPA 1998 introduces an exemption to the principle of purpose specification:

> *For the purposes of the second data protection principle, the further processing of personal data only for research purposes in compliance with the relevant conditions is not to be regarded as incompatible with the purposes for which they were obtained.*

Section 33(3) DPA 1998 contains an exemption to the principle of limited storage of personal data:

> Personal data which *are* processed only for research purposes in compliance with the relevant conditions may, notwithstanding the fifth data protection principle, be kept indefinitely.

Finally, section 33(4) DPA 1998 contains an exemption from the data subject access provisions for personal data which are processed for research purposes where the processing complies with the relevant conditions and the results of the research or any resulting statistics are not made available in a form which identifies data subjects or any of them.

"The relevant conditions" are defined by section 33(1) DPA 1998. These are:

> (a) *that the data are not processed to support measures or decisions with respect to particular individuals, and*
>
> *(b) that the data are not processed in such a way that substantial damage or substantial distress is, or is likely to be, caused to any data subject.*

To fall under the exemption for research, the relevant conditions have to be met and the processing has to be carried out for research purposes. What is meant by research purposes is not defined. Section 33(1) DPA 1998 just says that research purposes include statistical or historical purposes.

Overall, the ambit of the exemption is relatively narrow[418]. At least it is not possible to legitimise open access online sharing with reference to this clause.

1.3.6.6 Enforcement

In the UK enforcement of data protection rules is mainly the task of the Information Commissioner. Part V of the DPA 1998 sets out the methods by which the Commissioner can seek to ensure that data controllers comply with the

---

[418] Ibid., p. 221.

provisions of the Act. The Commissioner's formal enforcement activities consist mostly of serving notices on data controllers and imposing fines (monetary penalties)[419].

1.3.7 National differences

The Data Protection Directive aimed at a full harmonisation of data protection law in the EU[420] but this goal was not actually fulfilled. In fact, the national rules in this field differ significantly under the regime of the directive[421]. Neither has it been possible to achieve the intended harmonisation through the case law of the ECJ. Although the Court has been able to ensure consistent interpretation of individual terms and provisions of the directive, it has not been able to deal with all of them owing to the significant number of varying provisions. Moreover, the Data Protection Directive explicitly identifies points on which Member States can create special rules or exemptions as compared to the provisions of the directive. In the following, some noteworthy differences will be highlighted.

1.3.7.1 Consent

According to Art. 2(h) Data Protection Directive the data subject's consent

> *shall mean any freely given specific and informed indication of his wishes by which the data subject signifies his agreement to personal data relating to him being processed.*

In practice, the data subject's consent is the most important legitimisation for the processing of personal data. To a large extent it is possible to process personal data based on the consent of the data subject. A particular form of consent is not required by the directive. Consent can, for example, be given verbally or in writing.

One consequence of this uncertainty is that the formal requirements of giving consent vary between the Member States[422]. The French DPA as well as the UK's DPA 1998 do not contain any provision on the definition of consent, of its form or content, or evidence of such consent[423].

In contrast, Spanish and Dutch legislation – closely following the wording of the Data Protection Directive – specify the consent of the data subject as any freely given, unambiguous, specific and informed expression of will whereby data

---

[419] Ibid, p. 234.

[420] See ECJ Case C-101/01 (6.11.2003), *Lindqvist*, para. 96.

[421] Koós, 'Das Vorhaben eines einheitlichen Datenschutzes in Europa', ZD 2014, 9 (12); Pötters, 'Primärrechtliche Vorgaben für eine Reform des Datenschutzrechts', RDV 2015, 10 (11).

[422] See Gundermann, 'Das Datenschutzrecht in Europa kommt in Bewegung', VuR 2011, 74 (76).

[423] See above Sections 1.3.5.1.8 (French law) and 1.3.6.3.7 (UK law).

subjects agree to the processing of personal data relating to them[424]. In Poland, Art. 7.5 of the Act determines that consent for the processing of personal data cannot be implied or deducted from a statement of another meaning[425].

German legislation specifies in Art. 4a BDSG that consent will be effective only when based on the data subject's free decision. Data subjects shall be informed of the purpose of collection, processing or use and, in so far as the circumstances of the individual case dictate or upon request, of the consequences of withholding consent. Additionally written consent is required[426]. According to Art. 4a(1) of the German BDSG, consent must, in principle, meet the requirements of written form, except where, due to exceptional circumstances, a form other than the written form is appropriate. Thus the present German standards on consent are stricter than the provisions of the Data Protection Directive and the legislation of the other Member States. In fact no other EU Member State requires a written form of consent[427].

Withdrawing consent: A right of the data subject to withdraw consent is not explicitly mentioned in the Data Protection Directive but nevertheless, the Article 29 Working Party points out that this right is implicit in the directive[428]. While many jurisdictions are silent on the issue of withdrawing consent, some provide an explicit right of the data subject to withdraw their consent at any time[429] or at least if there is justified reason for it[430].

1.3.7.2 Processing

In most European jurisdictions the definition of processing of personal data follows the wording of the Data Protection Directive[431]. Its Art. 2(b) defines processing as:

> *any operation or set of operations which is performed upon personal data, whether or not by automatic means, such as collection, recording, organisation, storage, adaptation or alteration, retrieval, consultation, use, disclosure by transmission, dissemination or otherwise making available, alignment or combination, blocking, erasure or destruction.*

---

424 See above Sections 1.3.4.2.8 (Spanish law) and 1.3.1.1.8 (Dutch law).

425 See above Section 1.3.3.4.6.

426 See above Section 1.3.2.4.6.

427 Drewes/Siegert, 'Die konkludente Einwilligung in Telefonmarketing und das Ende des Dogmas von der datenschutzrechtlichen Schriftform', RDV 2006, 139.

428 Article 29 Data Protection Working Party, *Opinion 15/2011 on the definition of consent*, p. 33.

429 This is the case in Dutch law, see above Section 1.3.1.1.8.

430 This is the case in Spanish law, see above Section 1.3.4.2.8.

431 See above Sections 1.3.1.1.4 (Dutch law), 1.3.4.2.4 (Spanish law), 1.3.4.2.4 (Polish law), 1.3.5.1.4 (French law) and 1.3.6.3.3 (UK law).

Most Member States follow this wording, but Germany does not do so[432]. Unlike the Data Protection Directive, the German BDSG does not just use the term "processing" of personal data as a relevant act, but distinguishes between collecting, processing and use of personal data. According to Art. 3(4) BDSG, processing just means the storage, modification, transmission, blocking and deletion of personal data. This means that processing is defined more narrowly than in the directive. The other actions falling under the term "processing" in the directive are included in the terms "collecting" and "use" in the BDSG.

This may lead to some confusion, but effectively the provisions of the Data Protection Directive and the BDSG have the same content. Basically any operation which is performed upon personal data constitutes a relevant act according to data protection legislation.

1.3.7.3 Purpose limitation

The principle of purpose limitation is provided for by Art. 6(1)(b) Data Protection Directive:

> *Personal data must be collected for specified, explicit and legitimate purposes and not further processed in a way incompatible with those purposes.*

The Member States analysed in this study have all implemented provisions in their national legislation that are in line with the provision of the directive. However, the interpretation of the principle of purpose limitation varies between the Member States[433]. The Article 29 Working Party states that:

> *Lack of harmonised interpretation has led to divergent applications of the notions of purpose limitation and incompatible processing in the different Member States, especially in comparison to other principles. For example, in some Member States the concepts of purpose limitation and incompatible processing are inherently linked to other concepts such as fairness, transparency or lawfulness. Consequently, while in some cases the outcome of the analysis based on these divergent approaches may ultimately be the same, these divergent approaches may also lead to different views on what data controllers can do with information they have already collected for a particular purpose or set of purposes*[434].

This observation shows that even if there is harmonised terminology, it is still impossible to achieve a real harmonisation between all Member States as long as the terms are interpreted in different ways. Although the ECJ is able to develop a consistent interpretation of individual provisions of European legislative Acts, it is not the right body to ensure a uniform application of national laws. The only way

---

432 See above Section 1.3.2.4.2.

433 Helbing, 'Big Data und der datenschutzrechtliche Grundsatz der Zweckbindung', K&R 2015, 145 (146).

434 Article 29 Data Protection Working Party, *Opinion 3/2013 on purpose limitation*, p. 5.

to achieve this objective would be a single European data protection authority for all Member States, with administrative powers ensuring the proper application of leading data protection principles.

1.3.7.4 Data Protection Control

This leads to another problematic point. The ways in which the Member States have established their data protection authorities vary significantly.

Art. 28(1) Data Protection Directive requires each Member State to

> *provide that one or more public authorities are responsible for monitoring the application within its territory of the provisions adopted by the Member States pursuant to this Directive.*

The competences of the supervisory authorities are set out in Art. 28(3) Data Protection Directive. Each authority shall in particular be endowed with some investigative powers, powers of intervention and powers to engage in legal proceedings. However, the concrete organisation and powers of the authorities are for the Member States to determine.

Hence, the powers of the authorities vary from country to country. The ability to impose fines for breaches of data protection rules, which is generally regarded as the most compelling motivator of compliance activity, has been awarded to authorities by national legislatures in some Member States (e.g. the UK) and not in others (e.g. Ireland)[435].

In addition to the national supervisory authorities, Art. 29 Data Protection Directive sets up the so-called Article 29 Working Party. However the Article 29 Working Party only has advisory status. Its task is to contribute to the uniform application of the national rules adopted pursuant to the Data Protection Directive[436] but it has no powers to force Member States and national authorities to comply with its recommendations.

1.3.7.5 Exemption for scientific research

Art. 6(1)(b) Data Protection Directive specifies that:

> *Further processing of data for historical, statistical or scientific purposes shall not be considered as incompatible provided that Member States provide appropriate safeguards.*

Keeping data for future scientific, historical or statistical use is explicitly exempt from the principle of limited data retention in the Data Protection Directive (Art. 6(1)(e)). Special safeguards laid down by the Member States should accompany such ongoing storage and use.

---

435 Carey, *Data Protection*, 4th edition, Oxford, Oxford University Press, 2015, p. 233.
436 See Recital 65 Data Protection Directive.

All of the countries surveyed in this study have implemented an exemption for scientific use. The wording varies, but all implementations seem to be in line with the Data Protection Directive. A problem that emerges is that it is rather unclear what the term "scientific research" means[437]. Some scholars say that the term should be understood in a very broad way as including all research which is carried out in a scientifically responsible manner[438] but whether market research, direct marketing, work of statistical bureaus and data mining can also be recognised as scientific research and statistics within the data protection framework is rather questionable[439]. In any case, none of the countries analysed provides a satisfactory definition.

Moreover, it is problematic that it is up to the Member States to provide appropriate safeguards for the further use of personal data for scientific research purposes. There is in fact no harmonisation on this issue and there can be substantial differences between the Member States.

1.3.8 Summary

Today's data protection law is one of the greatest achievements of the information society[440] and Europe is an important engine in the area of freedom of information and data protection[441].

The Data Protection Directive of 1995 was a great step towards a consistent European data protection framework. It partially harmonised data protection legislation in the Member States of the EU and took data protection law to the next level. However, the Data Protection Directive has not prevented fragmentation in the way data protection is implemented across the Union[442].

Moreover, things have changed during the last 20 years. Especially the development and growth of the Internet towards big data and mobile applications necessitate changes in the European legislation. From today's perspective, there are considerable differences persisting between national data protection regimes across the EU and points of uncertainty and inefficiency in their application, particularly regarding the online environment[443]. For this reason the European Commission started a reform process not just to push the complete harmonisation of data protection legislation in the Union, but also to adjust the EU legal framework on data protection to the new practical situation.

---

437 See Hatt, *Konfliktfeld Datenschutz und Forschung*, Baden-Baden, Nomos, 2012, pp. 96 et seqq.

438 Holvast, *Wetenschappelijk onderzoek en privacy*, in Prins/Berkvens, *Privacyregulering in theorie en praktijk*, Deventer, Kluwer, 2002, p. 356.

439 But see for the Netherlands, above Section 1.3.1.2.2.

440 Tinnefeld/Buchner/Petri, *Einführung in das Datenschutzrecht*, 5th edition, Munich, Oldenbourg Verlag, 2012, p. XIII.

441 Ibid., p. 40.

442 Recital 9 GDPR.

443 Bygrave, *Data Privacy Law*, Oxford, Oxford University Press, 2014, p. 71.

1.4 The General Data Protection Regulation

As is well known, the EU framework for data protection law is undergoing major reform[444]. The first reform proposals were issued by the European Commission in January 2012[445]. However it took about four years and many proposals for modification before an agreement on a new data protection framework was reached. Finally, on 15 December 2015, the European Parliament, the Council and the Commission reached agreement on the new data protection rules[446]. The core of the reform is the Regulation on the protection of individuals with regard to the processing of personal data and on the free movement of such data[447]. Through the GDPR, the data protection framework will be harmonised to the largest extent possible across the EU. This legal reform was formally adopted by the European Parliament and the Council on 27 April 2016 and was published in the Official Journal on 4 May 2016. The new rules will come into force two years thereafter. The GDPR will replace most of the national data protection rules[448]. Thus the reform has the potential to remove much of the confusion accompanying the current proliferation of different national and European provisions on data protection[449].

We analyse here the ways in which the GDPR will influence the use of research results within the EU. Special focus will be given to making research data open access.

1.4.1 Aim of the regulation

According to Art. 1 GDPR:

> *(1) This Regulation lays down rules relating to the protection of individuals with regard to the processing of personal data and rules relating to the free movement of personal data.*

---

[444] Ibid., p. xxviii.

[445] See Proposal for a Regulation of the European Parliament and of the Council on the protection of the individuals with regard to the processing of personal data and on the free movement of such data (General Data Protection Regulation), COM(2012) 11 final, available at: http://ec.europa.eu/justice/data-protection/document/review2012/com_2012_11_en.pdf.

[446] See Press Release of the European Commission, available at: http://europa.eu/rapid/press-release_IP-15-6321_en.htm.

[447] Regulation 2016/679/EU of the European Parliament and of the Council of 27 April 2016 on the protection of natural persons with regard to the processing of personal data and on the free movement of such data, and repealing Directive 95/46/EC (General Data Protection Regulation).

[448] Pötters, 'Primärrechtliche Vorgaben für eine Reform des Datenschutzrechts', RDV 2015, 10 (12).

[449] Schaar, 'EU-Datenschutz: Schluss mit der Verzögerungstaktik!', ZD 2014, 113 (114).

(2) This Regulation protects fundamental rights and freedoms of natural persons and in particular their right to the protection of personal data.

(3) The free movement of personal data within the Union shall neither be restricted nor prohibited for reasons connected with the protection of individuals with regard to the processing of personal data.

As can be seen from this first article of the GDPR, the new regulation has the same two objectives as the Data Protection Directive. It will protect the fundamental rights and freedoms of natural persons, in particular their right to the protection of personal data, and the free movement of personal data within the EU will not be restricted.

Recital 9 GDPR confirms that the objectives and principles of the Data Protection Directive remain sound, but it has not prevented legal uncertainty, fragmentation in the way data protection is implemented across the Union, and a widespread public perception that there are significant risks for the protection of individuals, associated notably with online activity. Recital 10 GDPR adds that the level of protection of the rights and freedoms of individuals with regard to the processing of such data should be equivalent in all Member States.

Obviously, the new regulation maintains the objectives of the directive but adjusts the provisions to the needs of the online environment and achieves as far as possible full harmonisation of the data protection framework across the EU.

1.4.2 Scope of application

The material scope of application of the GDPR is identical to that of the Data Protection Directive. The rules of the regulation are only applicable to natural persons[450]. Art. 2 GDPR states that:

This Regulation applies to the processing of personal data wholly or partly by automated means, and to the processing other than by automated means of personal data which form part of a filing system or are intended to form part of a filing system.

Regarding the territorial scope, Art. 3(1) GDPR stipulates that:

This Regulation applies to the processing of personal data in the context of the activities of an establishment of a controller or a processor in the Union, regardless of whether the processing takes place in the Union or not.

But moreover, according to Art. 3(2) GDPR:

This Regulation applies to the processing of personal data of data subjects who are in the Union by a controller or processor not established in the Union, where the processing activities are related to:

---

[450] See Recitals 1 et seqq. GDPR.

(a) the offering of goods or services, irrespective of whether a payment of the data subject is required, to such data subjects in the Union; or

(b) the monitoring of their behaviour as far as their behaviour takes place within the European Union.

This provision means a substantial widening of the scope of application of European data protection rules. When the regulation enters into force, European rules will always apply when the controller or processor is located in the Union, but also when personal data of data subjects who are in the Union are processed, irrespective of whether the controller or processor is established in the Union or not, as long as goods or services are offered to data subjects in the Union or their behaviour is monitored. The aim of this provision is to ensure that individuals are not deprived of the protection to which they are entitled under the new regulation[451].

1.4.3 Fundamental legal terms

Definitions for the purposes of the GDPR can be found in its Art. 4.

1.4.3.1 Personal data

According to Art. 4(1) GDPR personal data means:

> *any information relating to an identified or identifiable natural person (data subject); an identifiable person is one who can be identified, directly or indirectly, in particular by reference to an identifier such as a name, an identification number, location data, online identifier or to one or more factors specific to the physical, physiological, genetic, mental, economic, cultural or social identity of that person.*

This definition is almost identical to that of the Data Protection Directive and consists of the key elements “any information”, “relating to”, “identified or identifiable” and “natural person”. The only difference is that the GDPR gives more examples of identification of a person, for example by reference to location data or online identifier. A key element is still the possible identification of a person[452].

The controversial question of whether the data subject must be identifiable by the controller or whether it is sufficient for a third party to be able to link the data in question to a natural person for data to be considered as personal data is regrettably not answered by the GDPR[453].

---

451 See Recital 23 GDPR.

452 See Schneider/Härting, 'Datenschutz in Europa – Plädoyer für einen Neubeginn', CR 2014, 306 (308).

453 See Buchner, 'Grundsätze der Rechtmäßigkeit der Datenverarbeitung unter der DS-GVO', DuD 2016, 155 (156).

According to Recital 26 GDPR, data which have undergone pseudonymisation but which could be attributed to a natural person by the use of additional information should be considered as information on an identifiable natural person. To determine whether a person is identifiable, account should be taken of all the means reasonably likely to be used, such as singling out, either by the controller or by any other person, to identify the individual directly or indirectly. The principles of data protection should not apply to anonymous information, that is information which does not relate to an identified or identifiable natural person or to data rendered anonymous in such a way that the data subject is not or no longer identifiable.

Recital 27 GDPR clarifies that the regulation should not apply to data of deceased persons.

1.4.3.2 Processing

Art. 4(2) GDPR describes "processing" as:

> *any operation or set of operations which is performed upon personal data or sets of personal data, whether or not by automated means, such as collection, recording, organization, structuring, storage, adaptation or alteration, retrieval, consultation, use, disclosure by transmission, dissemination or otherwise making available, alignment or combination, restriction, erasure or destruction.*

This definition is to a large extent inspired by the Data Protection Directive too. Basically any operation with personal data is covered.

1.4.3.3 Controller, processor and third party

The definitions of the terms "controller", "processor" and "third party" do not differ from those of the Data Protection Directive. According to Art. 4(7) GDPR "controller" means:

> *the natural or legal person, public authority, agency or any other body which alone or jointly with others determines the purposes and means of the processing of personal data; where the purposes and means of processing are determined by Union law or Member State law, the controller or the specific criteria for his nomination may be designated by Union law or by Member State law.*

"Processor" (Art. 4(8) GDPR):

> *means a natural or legal person, public authority, agency or any other body which processes personal data on behalf of the controller.*

And "third party" (Art. 4(10) GDPR):

> *means any natural or legal person, public authority, agency or any other body other than the data subject, the controller, the processor and the persons who, under the direct authority of the controller or the processor, are authorised to process the data.*

1.4.3.4 The data subject's consent

The definition of the data subject's consent has undergone a revision. Art. 4(11) GDPR defines it as:

> *any freely given, specific, informed and unambiguous indication of his or her wishes by which the data subject, either by a statement or by a clear affirmative action, signifies agreement to personal data relating to them being processed.*

In particular two important changes have been made. First, the indication of wishes must be not only specific and informed, but also unambiguous[454]. The clarification that consent must in every case be unambiguous is to be welcomed. It may contribute considerably to making the requirement of consent more effective than under the rules of the Data Protection Directive, which seemed to create many uncertainties. Second, consent must be given "either by a statement or by clear affirmative action by the data subject". It seems that the 'opt-in' option will be the general rule from now on. 'Opt-out' versions of consent are not possible under the regime of the GDPR[455]. Recital 32 GDPR confirms this assumption, stating that ticking a box when visiting an Internet website to indicate the data subject's acceptance of proposed processing of personal data could constitute consent. Silence, pre-ticked boxes or inactivity should therefore not constitute consent.

Regarding the right of the data subject to withdraw consent, a specific provision is included in the GDPR. According to Art. 7(3) GDPR:

> *The data subject shall have the right to withdraw his or her consent at any time. The withdrawal of consent shall not affect the lawfulness of processing based on consent before its withdrawal. Prior to giving consent, the data subject shall be informed thereof. It shall be as easy to withdraw consent as to give it.*

This explicit rule on the withdrawal of consent constitutes an essential improvement for data subjects. Under the regime of the GDPR it is clear that consent can be withdrawn at any time and that it must be as easy as to consent to personal data processing.

---

454 The first draft of the GDPR even required an "explicit" consent, see COM(2012) 11 final, available at: http://ec.europa.eu/justice/data-protection/document/review2012/com_2012_11_en.pdf.

455 See Buchner, 'Grundsätze der Rechtmäßigkeit der Datenverarbeitung unter der DS-GVO', DuD 2016, 155 (158).

1.4.4 Processing of personal data

The GDPR lays down in its Art. 5(1) the principles relating to personal data processing. In particular, personal data must be:

(a) *processed lawfully, fairly and in a transparent manner in relation to the data subject ("***lawfulness, fairness and transparency***");*

(b) *collected for specified, explicit and legitimate purposes and not further processed in a way incompatible with those purposes; further processing of personal data for archiving purposes in the public interest, or scientific and historical research purposes or statistical purposes shall, in accordance with Article 89(1), not be considered incompatible with the initial purposes; ("***purpose limitation***");*

(c) *adequate, relevant and limited to what is necessary in relation to the purposes for which they are processed ("***data minimisation***");*

(d) *accurate and, where necessary, kept up to date; every reasonable step must be taken to ensure that personal data that are inaccurate, having regard to the purposes for which they are processed, are erased or rectified without delay ("***accuracy***");*

(e) *kept in a form which permits identification of data subjects for no longer than is necessary for the purposes for which the personal data are processed; personal data may be stored for longer periods insofar as the data will be processed solely for archiving purposes in the public interest, or scientific and historical research purposes or statistical purposes in accordance with Article 89(1) subject to implementation of the appropriate technical and organisational measures required by the Regulation in order to safeguard the rights and freedoms of the data subject ("***storage limitation***").*

As can be seen from these general principles, the European legislator has maintained the key principles such as purpose limitation or data minimisation, although since Art. 8(2) of the EU Charter sets out those principles in the Union's primary law, it would not have been possible to turn away from them anyway. Art. 5(2) GDPR specifies that the controller shall be responsible for and be able to demonstrate compliance with those principles listed in Art. 5(1) GDPR.

1.4.4.1 Lawfulness of processing

Any processing of personal data should be lawful and fair (Recital 39 GDPR). In order for processing to be lawful, personal data should be processed on the basis of the consent of the person concerned or some other legitimate basis, laid down by law (Recital 40 GDPR). Where there is no consent of the data subject or any other justification, the processing of personal data is illegal.

Art. 6 GDPR states more precisely what lawful processing means. According to Art. 6(1) GDPR, processing of personal data shall be lawful only if and to the extent that one of the listed legitimisations applies. Altogether there are just six grounds that are supposed to legitimise all thinkable uses of personal data[456]. These are (a) the consent of the data subject, (b) the processing is necessary for the performance of a contract to which the data subject is party, (c) the processing is necessary for compliance with a legal obligation laid down by Union or Member State law (cf. Art. 6(3) GDPR), (d) the processing is necessary in order to protect the vital interests of the data subject or of another natural person, (e) the processing is necessary for the performance of a task carried out in the public interest, (f) the processing is necessary for the purposes of the legitimate interests pursued by the controller or by a third party.

It is worth noting that where processing is based on consent, the controller must be able to demonstrate that consent was given by the data subject to the processing of their personal data (Art. 7(1) GDPR).

Personal data, which are, by their nature, particularly sensitive in relation to fundamental rights and freedoms, deserve specific protection as the context of their processing may create important risks for the fundamental rights and freedoms (Recital 51 GDPR). Thus Art. 9(1) GDPR clarifies that the processing of personal data revealing racial or ethnic origin, political opinions, religious or philosophical beliefs, trade union membership and the processing of genetic data, biometric data in order to uniquely identify a person, or data concerning health or sex life and sexual orientation shall be prohibited. This processing prohibition is stricter than the general prohibition on the processing of personal data[457].

However, there are some exceptions to this rule. For example, the processing of such sensitive data is allowed if the data subject has given explicit consent to the processing of those data (Art. 9(2)(a) GDPR), or if processing is necessary for archiving purposes in the public interest, scientific and historical research purposes or statistical purposes in accordance with Art. 89(1) based on Union or Member State law, which shall be proportionate to the aim pursued, respect the essence of the right to data protection and provide for suitable and specific measures to safeguard the fundamental rights and the interests of the data subject (Art. 9(2)(j) GDPR).

1.4.4.2 Transparency

The principle of transparency requires that any information addressed to the public or to the data subject be concise, easily accessible and easy to understand, and that clear and plain language and, additionally, where appropriate, visualisation be used[458].

---

456 Roßnagel, 'Was wird aus der Datenschutzgrundverordnung', ZD 2014, 545.
457 Veil, 'DS-GVO: Risikobasierter Ansatz statt rigides Verbotsprinzip', ZD 2015, 347 (349).
458 Recital 58 GDPR.

in Arts 12 et seqq. GDPR the principle of transparency and the duty to inform the data subject are specified. According to Art. 12(1) GDPR:

> *The controller shall take appropriate measures to provide any information referred to in Articles 13 and 14 and any communication under Articles 15 to 22, and 34 relating to the processing of personal data to the data subject in a concise, transparent, intelligible and easily accessible form, using clear and plain language.*

Art. 13 GDPR contains a list of information the controller must provide to the data subject where the personal data are collected from the data subject itself. Such information includes inter alia (a) the identity and the contact details of the controller, (c) the purposes of the processing, (e) the recipients or categories of recipients, 2(a) the period for which the personal data will be stored.

Where the data have not been obtained from the data subject, Art. 14 GDPR requires the controller to provide the data subject with similar information. Art. 14(5)(b) GDPR limits this requirements. The information duties shall not apply insofar as:

> *the provision of such information proves impossible or would involve a disproportionate effort; in particular for processing for archiving purposes in the public interest, or scientific and historical research purposes or statistical purposes subject to the conditions and safeguards referred to in Article 89(1) or in so far as the right referred to in paragraph 1 is likely to render impossible or seriously impair the achievement of the objectives of the archiving purposes in the public interest, or the scientific and historical research purposes or the statistical purposes; in such cases the controller shall take appropriate measures to protect the data subject's rights and freedoms and legitimate interests, including making the information publicly available.*

1.4.4.3 Purpose limitation

Similar to Art. 6(1)(c) Data Protection Directive, Art. 5(1)(b) GDPR outlines the principle of purpose limitation. Personal data may only be collected for specified, explicit and legitimate purposes and not further processed in a way incompatible with those purposes.

This means that after collection, personal data must be used for the intended purpose and not for any other purpose. Processing for purposes other than those for which the personal data were initially collected should be allowed only where the processing is compatible with the purposes for which the personal data were initially collected[459].

---

[459] Recital 50 GDPR.

Recital 50 of the GDPR contains, inter alia, a long sentence on how to ascertain whether a purpose is compatible or not:

> *In order to ascertain whether a purpose of further processing is compatible with the purpose for which the personal data are initially collected, the controller, after having met all the requirements for the lawfulness of the original processing, should take into account, inter alia: any link between those purposes and the purposes of the intended further processing; the context in which the personal data have been collected, in particular the reasonable expectations of data subjects based on their relationship with the controller as to their further use; the nature of the personal data; the consequences of the intended further processing for data subjects; and the existence of appropriate safeguards in both the original and intended further processing operations.*

This shows that it is not possible to give a precise definition of compatible further processing. This question still needs to be assessed on a case-by-case basis.

If the processing of personal data is based on consent, the consent should cover all processing activities carried out for the same purpose or purposes. When the processing has multiple purposes, consent should be given for all of them[460]. Thus the GDPR, just like the Data Protection Directive, requires the processor to inform the data subject in a comprehensive way about the purposes of processing.

1.4.4.4 Further processing for historical, statistical or scientific purposes

The GDPR also applies to the processing of personal data for scientific research purposes. If research is the primary purpose of processing, the legitimate basis for such processing is consent of the data subject. Moreover, at least in some circumstances, it seems to be possible to legitimise data processing with Art. 6(1)(f) GDPR, which allows data processing without consent if processing is necessary for the purposes of the legitimate interests pursued by the controller or by a third party, except where such interests are overridden by the interests or fundamental rights and freedoms of the data subject. It is at least conceivable that research constitutes a legitimate interest. However, determining such legitimate interests requires a careful assessment in the individual case. It should further be noted that this legal basis should not apply to processing by public authorities (Recital 47 GDPR).

The GDPR includes some specific provisions on further processing for scientific purposes. Recital 159 of the GDPR says that the term "scientific research" should be interpreted in a broad manner, including, for example, technological development and demonstration, fundamental research, applied research and privately funded research. This definition is supposed to provide more clarity than the Data Protection Directive does on what should be

[460] Recital 32 GDPR.

understood as scientific research. However, it is still unclear whether, for example, big data analyses carried out by many commercial and non-commercial actors already qualify as scientific research.

Recital 33 of the GDPR acknowledges that:

> *It is often not possible to fully identify the purpose of data processing for scientific research purposes at the time of data collection. Therefore data subjects should be allowed to give their consent to certain areas of scientific research when in keeping with recognised ethical standards for scientific research. Data subjects should have the opportunity to give their consent only to certain areas of research or parts of research projects to the extent allowed by the intended purpose.*

So the GDPR takes account of the specific situation of scientific research and research projects and gives the opportunity to consent to the use of personal data at least to certain areas of research or parts of research projects.

Besides this, Recital 50 of the GDPR says that further processing for archiving purposes in the public interest, for scientific or historical research purposes or statistical purposes should be considered to be compatible lawful processing operations.

Art. 5(1)(b) GDPR clarifies that:

> *further processing of personal data for archiving purposes in the public interest, or* ***scientific and historical research purposes*** *or statistical purposes shall, in accordance with Article 89(1), not be considered incompatible with the initial purposes …*

This means that subsequent processing operations for scientific research purposes shall be considered as compatible with the initial purpose of data collection. Under the regime of the Data Protection Directive, further processing for scientific purposes was not considered to be incompatible with the initial purpose only insofar as Member States provide appropriate safeguards (cf. Art. 6(1)(b) Data Protection Directive). So it was up to the Member States to decide whether further processing for research purposes was compatible or not. Under the GDPR compatibility is the default.

Nevertheless, the processing of personal data for scientific or historical research purposes should be subject to appropriate safeguards of the rights and freedoms of the data subject; those safeguards should ensure that technical and organisational measures are in place in order to ensure, in particular, the principle of data minimisation[461].

This will be assured by Art. 89(1) GDPR, which reads as follows:

> *Processing for archiving purposes in the public interest,* ***scientific or historical research purposes*** *or statistical purposes, shall be subject to appropriate safeguards, in accordance with this Regulation, for the rights and freedoms of the data subject. Those*

[461] Recital 156 GDPR.

safeguards shall ensure that technical and organisational measures are in place in particular in order to ensure respect for the principle of data minimisation. Those measures may include pseudonymisation provided that those purposes can be fulfilled in that manner. Where those purposes can be fulfilled by further processing which does not permit or no longer permits the identification of data subjects, those purposes shall be fulfilled in that manner.

So there is an exception to the general rule of purpose limitation for scientific or historical research purposes. Subject to appropriate safeguards and taking into account the principle of data minimisation, further processing of personal data for scientific or historical research purposes is not considered incompatible with the initial purpose[462].

The technical and organisational measures may include pseudonymisation, as long as the research purposes can be fulfilled in that manner. Pseudonymisation means the processing of personal data in such a manner that the personal data can no longer be attributed to a specific data subject without the use of additional information, provided that such additional information is kept separately and is subject to technical and organisational measures to ensure that the personal data are not attributed to an identified or identifiable natural person (Art. 4(5) GDPR). In the field of research, pseudonymisation is often used to protect the identities of individuals. However, it should be noted that if the purpose of research can be fulfilled without the use of personal data or anonymised data, that purpose must be fulfilled in that manner[463].

This means that not using personal data or anonymised data for research purposes will be the standard. If the use of personal data is necessary for the research, such data must be pseudonymised and only if the purpose of research cannot be fulfilled with pseudonymised data can such data be used. However, even in those cases, appropriate safeguards for the rights and freedoms of the data subject have to be in place.

1.4.4.5 Data minimisation

Art. 5(1)(c) GDPR outlines the principle of data minimisation. Personal data must be

adequate, relevant and limited to what is necessary in relation to the purposes for which they are processed.

---

462 A more in-depth analysis of Art. 89 GDPR and its relevance for the Open Research Data Pilot can be found below in Section 1.5.3.4.

463 See Albrecht, 'Das neue EU-Datenschutzrecht – von der Richtlinie zur Verordnung', CR 2016, 88 (91).

while stating that personal data must be limited to what is necessary in relation to the purposes, the principle of data minimisation seems to be somewhat stricter than in the Data Protection Directive as the latter states in its Art. 6(1)(c) that personal data must be not excessive in relation to the purposes.

The stricter principle of data minimisation requires, in particular, ensuring that the period for which the data are stored is limited to a strict minimum. Personal data should only be processed if the purpose of the processing could not reasonably be fulfilled by other means. In order to ensure that the data are not kept longer than necessary, time limits should be established by the controller for erasure or for a periodic review[464].

Art. 5(1)(d) and (e) GDPR mentions the principles of accuracy and storage limitation. Those principles can be seen as an expression of the principle of data minimisation. Personal data must be accurate, where necessary kept up to date, and kept in a form which permits identification of data subjects for no longer than is necessary for the purposes for which the personal data are processed.

1.4.4.6 Longer-Term storage of personal data for scientific use

Art. 5(1)(e) GDPR contains a provision on longer storage for, inter alia, scientific use:

> *Personal data may be stored for longer periods insofar as the personal data will be processed solely for archiving purposes in the public interest, scientific or historical research purposes or statistical purposes in accordance with Article 89(1) subject to implementation of the appropriate technical and organisational measures required by this Regulation in order to safeguard the rights and freedoms of the data subject.*

So there is an exception to the general rule of data minimisation for scientific or historical research purposes. To exercise this exception, the same safeguards apply as to the exception on purpose limitation for scientific or historical research purposes[465].

1.4.5 Rights of the data subject

The GDPR contains some rights for the data subject. The rights are described in more detail than those in the Data Protection Directive[466] and some of them go beyond the rights of the directive.

Art. 15 GDPR gives the data subject the right of access. He shall have the right to obtain from the controller confirmation as to whether or not personal data concerning them are being processed, and where that is the case, access to

---

464 Recital 39 GDPR.

465 See above Section 1.4.4.4.

466 Roßnagel/Kroschwald, 'Was wird aus der Datenschutzgrundverordnung?', ZD 2014, 495 (498).

the personal data and information such as (a) the purposes of the processing, (b) the categories of personal data concerned, and (c) the recipients or categories of recipients etc.

According to Art. 16 GDPR the data subject shall have the right to obtain from the controller without undue delay the rectification of inaccurate personal data concerning them.

Art. 17 GDPR includes the right to erasure, also described as the right to be forgotten. The data subject shall have the right to obtain from the controller the erasure of personal data concerning them without undue delay and the controller shall have the obligation to erase personal data without undue delay where one of the named grounds applies, for example (a) the personal data are no longer necessary in relation to the purposes for which they were collected, (b) the data subject withdraws consent on which the processing is based, and where there is no other legal ground for the processing, and (d) the personal data have been unlawfully processed etc. Where the controller has made the personal data public and is obliged to erase the personal data, the controller shall take reasonable steps to inform controllers which are processing the personal data that the data subject has requested the erasure by such controllers of any links to, or copy or replication of, those personal data.

The right to erasure shall not apply to the extent that processing is necessary for archiving purposes in the public interest, *scientific or historical research purposes* or statistical purposes in accordance with Art. 89(1) in so far as the right to erasure is likely to render impossible or seriously impair the achievement of the objectives of that processing (Art. 17(3)(d) GDPR).

Completely new is the right to data portability, which is found in Art. 20 GDPR. The data subject shall have the right to receive personal data concerning them, which they have provided to a controller, in a structured, commonly used and machine-readable format and shall have the right to transmit those data to another controller without hindrance from the controller to whom the personal data have been provided.

The right to data portability is especially interesting for users of so-called social networks, other user-generated content and cloud computing services[467]. Individuals could have easier access to their own data and be able to switch electronically processed personal data from one service to another more easily[468] by being given the right to obtain a copy of their data from their service provider[469].

---

467 See ibid.

468 EU Focus 2012, 293, p. 2; likewise Kuschewsky, 'Sweeping reform for EU data protection', Euro. Law. 2012, 112 (113).

469 Kuner, 'The European Commission's Proposed Data Regulation: A Copernican Revolution in European Data Protection Law', Privacy & Security Law Report, 6 February 2012, 5 (6).

According to Art. 21 GDPR the data subject shall have the right to object, on grounds relating to their particular situation, at any time to processing of personal data concerning them in some cases. Concerning the processing of personal data for research purposes, Art. 21(6) GDPR clarifies that the data subject shall have the right to object to processing of personal data concerning them unless the processing is necessary for the performance of a task carried out for reasons of public interest.

1.4.6 Measures to ensure security of processing

Art. 24(1) GDPR requires the controller to implement appropriate technical and organisational measures to ensure and to be able to demonstrate that processing is performed in accordance with the regulation[470].

Art. 25 GDPR contains a new provision on data protection by design and by default:

> *(1) Taking into account the state of the art, the cost of implementation and the nature, scope, context and purposes of processing as well as the risks of varying likelihood and severity for rights and freedoms of natural persons posed by the processing, the controller shall, both at the time of the determination of the means for processing and at the time of the processing itself, implement appropriate technical and organisational measures, such as pseudonymisation, which are designed to implement data-protection principles, such as data minimisation, in an effective manner and to integrate the necessary safeguards into the processing in order to meet the requirements of this Regulation and protect the rights of data subjects.*

Thus the GDPR provides a detailed paragraph on the duty of the controller to implement appropriate technical and organisational measures to fully comply with the GDPR. Moreover:

> *(2) The controller shall implement appropriate technical and organisational measures for ensuring that, by default, only personal data which are necessary for each specific purpose of the processing are processed. That obligation applies to the amount of personal data collected, the extent of their processing, the period of their storage and their accessibility. In particular, such measures shall ensure that by default personal data are not made accessible without the individual's intervention to an indefinite number of natural persons.*

This provision makes it necessary to ensure by default, i.e. as the technical standard, that the use of personal data is limited to the minimum. In fact it requires the controller to consider the principles of data protection at the time of creating new products and services[471].

---

[470] See also Recital 78 GDPR.

[471] Albrecht, 'Das neue EU-Datenschutzrecht – von der Richtlinie zur Verordnung', CR 2016, 88 (91).

According to Art. 30 GDPR, each controller must maintain a record of processing activities for which it is responsible. Art. 32 GDPR clarifies that the controller and the processor shall implement appropriate technical and organisational measures to ensure a level of security appropriate to the risk to the rights and freedoms of the data subjects.

1.4.7 Trans-border data flows

When drafting the GDPR, the intention was generally to retain the rules of the Data Protection Directive on the transfer of personal data to third countries outside the EU[472].

Art. 44 GDPR lays down the principle regarding the transfer of personal data to third countries or international organisations:

> *Any transfer of personal data which are undergoing processing or are intended for processing after transfer to a third country or to an international organisation shall take place only if, subject to the other provisions of this Regulation, the conditions laid down in this Chapter are complied with by the controller and processor, including for onward transfers of personal data from the third country or an international organisation to another third country or to another international organisation. All provisions in this Chapter shall be applied in order to ensure that the level of protection of natural persons guaranteed by this Regulation is not undermined.*

This provision makes clear that in cases of personal data transferred to third countries or international organisations, the level of data protection given by the GDPR has to be guaranteed.

Whether an adequate level of protection is ensured in a third country, a territory or one or more specified sectors within that third country, or an international organisation can be decided by an adequacy decision of the Commission (Art. 45(1) GDPR). Recital 81 GDPR clarifies that in the event of such an adequacy decision the third country should offer guarantees ensuring an adequate level of protection *essentially equivalent* to that ensured within the Union. This clarification was included into the draft of the GDPR after the ECJ judgment in the *Schrems v Ireland* case in which it was held that an adequate level of protection requires a level of protection of fundamental rights and freedoms that is *essentially equivalent* to that guaranteed within the EU[473]. Art. 97(2)(a) GDPR obliges the Commission to examine the application and functioning of its adequacy decisions.

---

[472] See ibid., p. 94.

[473] ECJ Case C-362/14 (6.11.2015), *Schrems v Data Protection Commissioner*, paras 73 et seq.

In the absence of an adequacy decision, the controller or processor should take measures to compensate for the lack of data protection in a third country by way of appropriate safeguards for the data subject[474]. A controller or processor may transfer personal data to a third country or an international organisation only if the controller or processor has provided appropriate safeguards, and on condition that enforceable data subject rights and effective legal remedies for data subjects are available (Art. 46(1) GDPR).

According to Art. 46(2) GDPR the appropriate safeguards may be provided for by (a) a legally binding and enforceable instrument between public authorities or bodies, (b) binding corporate rules, (c, d) standard data protection clauses adopted by the Commission or a supervisory authority, (e) an approved code of conduct, or (f) an approved certification mechanism.

In the absence of an adequacy decision, or of appropriate safeguards, a transfer or a set of transfers of personal data to a third country or an international organisation shall take place only in very limited cases, for example when the data subject has explicitly consented to the proposed transfer, the transfer is necessary for the performance of a contract between the data subject and the controller, or the transfer is necessary for important reasons of public interest (see Art. 49 GDPR).

Art. 48 clarifies that a transfer or disclosure of personal data must always be authorised by EU law. Any judgment of a court or decision of an administrative authority of a third country requiring a controller or processor to transfer or disclose personal data may only be recognised or enforceable in any manner if based on an international agreement in force between the requesting third country and the Union.

1.4.8 Data protection control

One problem with the Data Protection Directive has been its lack of enforceability. Supervisory authorities have often been toothless tigers[475].

Due to the varying implementation of the directive in the different Member States, controllers have been able to choose the jurisdiction with less strict rules on data protection and the least active data protection authorities in order to avoid expenses of data protection[476]. It is not a coincidence that companies like Google or Facebook have their European headquarters in Ireland[477]. In order to avoid

---

474 Recital 108 GDPR.

475 Koós, 'Das Vorhaben eines einheitlichen Datenschutzes in Europa', ZD 2014, 9 (13).

476 See e.g. ECJ Case C-362/14 (6.11.2015), *Schrems v Data Protection Commissioner.*

477 Pötters, 'Primärrechtliche Vorgaben für eine Reform des Datenschutzrechts', RDV 2015, 10 (12).

such "forum shopping" and to establish a so-called "level playing field" it was necessary not just to establish a single legal framework but also a uniform interpretation and enforcement of the legal framework[478].

Art. 51(1) GDPR requires each Member State to provide for one or more independent public authorities to be responsible for monitoring the application of the GDPR. Each supervisory authority shall contribute to the consistent application of the GDPR throughout the Union (Art. 51(2) GDPR). As in the Data Protection Directive, each supervisory authority shall act with complete independence in performing its tasks and exercising its powers (Art. 52(1) GDPR).

The tasks of the authorities are outlined in Art. 57(1) GDPR. Each supervisory authority shall on its territory inter alia (a) monitor and enforce the application of the GDPR, (b) promote public awareness and understanding of the risks in relation to processing, (c) advise the national parliament and government or (d) promote the awareness of controllers and processors of their obligations. Art. 58 GDPR provides the supervisory authorities with investigative, corrective, authorisation and advisory powers.

A novelty that is important for achieving the uniform application of the GDPR are the detailed provisions on cooperation and consistency in Chapter VII of the GDPR. All concerned supervisory authorities shall cooperate in relevant cases in order to reach consensus. In addition, and in order to contribute to the consistent application of the GDPR throughout the Union, the supervisory authorities shall cooperate with each other and, where relevant, with the Commission, through the consistency mechanism (Art. 63 GDPR). This duty of cooperation is to be welcomed[479].

The consistency mechanism enables the European Data Protection Board (the "Board") to adopt *binding* decisions on the correct and consistent application of the GDPR (Art. 65 GDPR). Where the Board is unable to adopt a decision by a two-thirds majority of the members of the Board, it is able to decide by a simple majority of its members (Art. 65(3) GDPR).

The Board is established by Art. 68 GDPR and constitutes a body of the Union and shall have legal personality (Art. 68(1) GDPR). The Board shall be composed of the head of one supervisory authority of each Member State and of the European Data Protection Supervisor, or their respective representatives (Art. 68(3) GDPR). The Board shall act independently when performing its tasks or exercising its powers (Art. 69(1) GDPR).

---

[478] Albrecht, 'Das neue EU-Datenschutzrecht – von der Richtlinie zur Verordnung', CR 2016, 88 (96); see also Recital 13 GDPR.

[479] Kirschner, 'Datenschutzgrundverordnung – ein kritischer Ausblick', ZIR 2015, 6 (7).

According to Art. 70(1) GDPR, the Board shall ensure the consistent application of the GDPR and, inter alia, (a) monitor and ensure the correct application of the regulation, (b) advise the Commission on any issue related to the protection of personal data, (d) issue guidelines, recommendations, and best practices, or (t) issue binding decisions pursuant to Art. 65.

The Board is one of the most important innovations of the GDPR and is absolutely necessary to achieve a uniform application of the GDPR. It should replace the Working Party on the Protection of Individuals with Regard to the Processing of Personal Data established by the Data Protection Directive[480]. Compared to the Article 29 Working Party the Board has many more powers, has legal personality and issues binding decisions. The Article 29 Working Party has had merely advisory status.

1.4.9 Room for manoeuvre for Member States

The GDPR is more detailed and stringent than the Data Protection Directive in many respects. As a regulation it obviously aims at a much higher degree of harmonisation of national regimes than is possible under the current directive[481].

As Art. 288(2) TFEU states, a regulation shall have general application and shall be binding in its entirety and directly applicable in all Member States. This makes clear that the choice of the Commission to implement a regulation on the issue of data protection instead of a directive aims at achieving the greatest possible harmonisation between the different Member States.

It is quite understandable that a higher level of harmonisation is supposed to be realised because even though the Data Protection Directive aimed at a full harmonisation of data protection law in the Union[482], the national rules in this field differ significantly under the regime of the directive[483].

The GDPR leaves the Member States very limited room to create special rules[484] but nevertheless takes into account some areas in which national rules are still required. Art. 85, for example, requires the Member States by law to reconcile the right to the protection of personal data with the right to freedom of expression and information. The reason for this provision is that there are still no EU-wide minimum standards in the area of media freedom[485].

---

480 Recital 139 GDPR.

481 Bygrave, *Data Privacy Law*, Oxford, Oxford University Press, 2014, p. 71.

482 See ECJ Case C-101/01 (6.11.2003), *Lindqvist*, para. 96.

483 Koós, 'Das Vorhaben eines einheitlichen Datenschutzes in Europa', ZD 2014, 9 (12); Pötters, 'Primärrechtliche Vorgaben für eine Reform des Datenschutzrechts', RDV 2015, 10 (11).

484 Roßnagel/Kroschwald, 'Was wird aus der Datenschutzgrundverordnung?', ZD 2014, 495 (499); Pötters, 'Primärrechtliche Vorgaben für eine Reform des Datenschutzrechts', RDV 2015, 10 (11).

485 See Albrecht, 'Das neue EU-Datenschutzrecht – von der Richtlinie zur Verordnung', CR 2016, 88 (97).

Further national legislation can be implemented in the areas of personal data processing in the context of employment (Art. 88 GDPR), obligations of professional secrecy (Art. 90 GDPR) and data protection rules of churches (Art. 91 GDPR).

The most important national rules in the area of scientific research which need to be implemented are the safeguards according to Art. 89(2) GDPR.

> *Where personal data are processed for scientific or historical research purposes or statistical purposes, Union or Member State law may provide for derogations from the rights referred to in Articles 15, 16, 18 and 21 subject to the conditions and safeguards referred to in Article 89(1) in so far as such rights are likely to render impossible or seriously impair the achievement of the specific purposes, and such derogations are necessary for the fulfilment of those purposes.*

So there can be derogations from the data subject's rights of the named Arts 15 (right of access), 16 (right to rectification), 18 (right to restriction of processing) and 21 (right to object) laid down in national legislation. Such derogations could have some influence on scientific activities but it is not yet clear how national legislators will make use of this provision.

First drafts for implementing the GDPR have already been disclosed in some Member States but the implementation is still an ongoing process and it is rather unclear what the final provisions will look like. In Germany, for example, three legislative drafts of an implementation Act have already been published and discussed. The last draft limits the rights of data subjects in Arts 15, 16, 18 and 21 GDPR in so far as such rights are likely to render impossible or seriously impair the achievement of research or statistical purposes and such limitation is necessary for the fulfilment of research or statistical purposes[486]. This wording would be an almost literal transposition of the text of Art. 89(2) GDPR. As yet, however, no agreement on a final version has been reached.

It can be anticipated that the Member States will try to make as much use as possible of the provisions, leaving them room to create special rules, but nevertheless the regulation aims at achieving a much higher degree of harmonisation than the directive. Regardless of the final shape of particular implementation Acts in the Member States, those states shall in any case have to take into account the principles laid down in Art. 89(1), especially the principle of data minimisation.

---

[486] See Art. 27(2) of the draft, available at: http://dip21.bundestag.de/dip21/btd/18/113/1811325.pdf.

1.5 Data protection law and the Open Research Data Pilot

Within Horizon 2020 the European Commission is running the Open Research Data Pilot, which aims to improve and maximise access to and re-use of research data generated by projects. To achieve those goals, projects participating in the Pilot shall open up their research data on an open access basis.

The Open Research Data Pilot applies to two types of data[487]:

- data, including associated metadata, needed to validate the results presented in scientific publications as soon as possible;
- other data, including associated metadata, as specified and within the deadlines laid down in a data management plan.

Projects participating in the Pilot are

- required to deposit the research data, preferably in a research data repository, and
- as far as possible, take measures to enable third parties to access, mine, exploit, reproduce and disseminate this research data.

OpenAIRE provides a repository called Zenodo that can be used for depositing data.

The Pilot comprises various selected areas of Horizon 2020 ("core areas"). For the 2014-2015 Work Programme, the areas of Horizon 2020 that participated in the Open Research Data Pilot were:

- Future and Emerging Technologies
- Research infrastructures – part e-Infrastructures
- Leadership in enabling and industrial technologies – Information and Communication Technologies
- Societal Challenge: Secure, Clean and Efficient Energy – part Smart cities and communities
- Societal Challenge: Climate Action, Environment, Resource Efficiency and Raw materials – with the exemption of raw materials topics

---

[487] See for a description of the Pilot: European Commission, Fact sheet: Open Access in Horizon 2020; available at: https://ec.europa.eu/programmes/horizon2020/sites/horizon2020/files/FactSheet_Open_Access.pdf.

- Societal Challenge: Europe in a changing world – inclusive, innovative and reflective Societies
- Science with and for Society

For the 2016 Work Programme, the core areas have been updated and slightly expanded based on feedback from the thematic directorates and units[488]. In addition to the above listed areas, the following are also supposed to participate in the Open Research Data Pilot:

- Research infrastructures – all parts and not just the part on e-Infrastructures
- Nanotechnologies, Advanced Materials, Advanced Manufacturing and Processing, and Biotechnology: "nanosafety" and "modelling" topics
- Societal Challenge: Food security, sustainable agriculture and forestry, marine and maritime and inland water research and the bio economy – selected topics in the calls H2020-SFS-2016/2017, H2020-BG-2016/2017, H2020-RUR-2016/2017 and H2020-BB-2016/2017, as specified in the work programme

For the 2017 Work Programme, the area of application of the Open Research Data Pilot has been extended again. All projects covered by this Work Programme onwards will, by default, be part of the Open Research Data Pilot. This means that all projects, and not just those of the core areas, starting as of now are by default participating in the Pilot[489].

Projects that started earlier and not stemming from one of the defined core areas and thus not covered by the scope of the Pilot can participate on an individual and voluntary project-by-project, opt-in basis. Projects may also decide not to participate and opt out of the Pilot at any stage of the project lifecycle, for a series of eligible reasons that include conflict with obligation to protect results, with confidentiality obligations, with security obligations or with rules on the protection of personal data.

Alternatively, during the lifetime of a project, a partial (e.g. for selected datasets) or even complete (i.e. for all datasets) opt-out remains possible for any of the reasons above via the data management plan (DMP). In this case, the project participates in the Pilot, but does not open up some of/any of its data for reasons explained in its DMP[490].

---

488 See European Commission, Open Research Data – Explanatory note to the 2015 dataset, p. 5.

489 See https://www.openaire.eu/opendatapilot.

490 European Commission, Guidelines on Open Access to Scientific Publications and Research Data in Horizon 2020, Version 2.1, 15 February 2016, p. 9, available at: http://ec.europa.eu/research /participants/data/ref/h2020/grants_manual/hi/oa_pilot/h2020-hi-oa-pilot-guide_en.pdf.

OpenAIRE provides researcher support and services for the Open Research Data Pilot. Legal barriers to data sharing in the context of the Open Research Data Pilot are analysed here. In the following part of the study, the focus is on the practical implications of European data protection legislation for running the Open Research Data Pilot.

The aim is to identify problem areas where data protection law conflicts with the open access obligation of the Open Research Data Pilot. The results are intended to give guidance to projects participating in the Pilot on the question of whether they should opt out of the Pilot for data protection reasons.

1.5.1 Other funders' open data policies

The European Commission's Open Research Data Pilot (now policy) is not the first such policy of its kind. Many major funders now have data-sharing policies in place, although all have been developed relatively recently. In 2004, 34 countries signed the OECD Declaration on Access to Data from Public Funding, which proposed greater sharing of publicly funded research data based on its recognition that "open access to, and unrestricted use of, data promotes scientific progress and … maximize[s] the value derived from public investments in data collection efforts"[491]. In 2007 the OECD published further Principles and Guidelines to support policy development and foster good practice in this area, which would be a crucial driver for future policies[492].

In the UK some research councils such as the Natural Environment Research Council (NERC), the Economic and Social Research Council (ESRC) and the Arts and Humanities Research Council (AHRC) have had in place some requirements for access to research data since the late 1990s. Since 2010/2011 there has been a drive to harmonise these policies, made concrete in the Research Councils UK (RCUK) Common Principles on Data Policy released in April 2011[493]. In 2016 the Higher Education Funding Council for England (HEFCE), RCUK, Universities UK and the Wellcome Trust collectively signed a Concordat on Open Research Data, which aimed to further foster open research data.

In the US the National Science Foundation's (NSF) Data Sharing Policy[494] has since 2011 required that grant proposals include a two-page DMP detailing how all data resulting from the research will be managed and deposited in a repository.

---

491 OECD, Declaration on Access to Research Data from Public Funding, 30 January 2004, available at: http://acts.oecd.org/Instruments/ShowInstrumentView.aspx?InstrumentID=157.

492 OECD, Principles and Guidelines for Access to Research Data from Public Funding, available at: https://www.oecd.org/sti/sci-tech/38500813.pdf.

493 Jones, 'Developments in Research Funder Data Policy', Int. J. Digit. Curation 2012, 114 (115).

494 The data sharing policy is available at: http://www.nsf.gov/pubs/policydocs/pappguide/nsf11001/aag_6.jsp#VID4.

The Data Sharing Policy of the National Institutes of Health, meanwhile, expects researchers whose grants would exceed $500,000 to include a data-sharing plan in grant proposals.

In Germany, the Deutsche Forschungsgemeinschaft (DFG – the main German research funder) has Guidelines on the Handling of Research Data[495]. These guidelines also point towards a set of Principles for the Handling of Research Data[496], adopted by the Alliance of German Science Organisations on 24 June 2010, and developed in partnership between a number of high-profile German research organisations.

Open data policies continue to take root, but nonetheless there is much work to do. A recent study by SPARC Europe and the Digital Curation Centre advises that many EU countries as yet have no such policy in place.

1.5.2 Experiences of the Commission with the Pilot

In 2016 the European Commission opened up a dataset on the practical experiences with the Open Research Data Pilot[497]. The dataset encompasses all proposals and finalised grant agreements as of July 2015.

At this time, 65.4% of projects in the core areas participate in the Pilot (sample size: 431 signed grant agreements). The average opt-out rate in signed grant agreements is 34.6%. The most important reasons for opt-outs at proposal stage (sample size 1382 opted-out proposals) are (i) IPR (intellectual property rights) concerns (37%), (ii) projects which do not expect to generate data (18%); or (iii) privacy concerns (18%). Outside the core areas, 11.9% of projects make use of the voluntary opt-in possibility (sample size 3268 signed grant agreements)[498].

---

[495] The guidelines are available at: http://www.dfg.de/en/research_funding/proposal_review_decision/applicants/submitting_proposal/research_data.

[496] The principles are available at: http://www.allianzinitiative.de/en/core-activities/research-data/principles.html.

[497] European Commission, Open Research Data – the uptake of the Pilot in the first calls of Horizon 2020, available at: https://data.europa.eu/euodp/data/dataset/open-research-data-the-uptake-of-the-pilot-in-the-first-calls-of-horizon-2020.

[498] See also to the following: European Commission, Open Research Data – Explanatory note to the 2015 dataset, p. 2 et. seqq.

The following graphic illustrates the opt-out reasons:

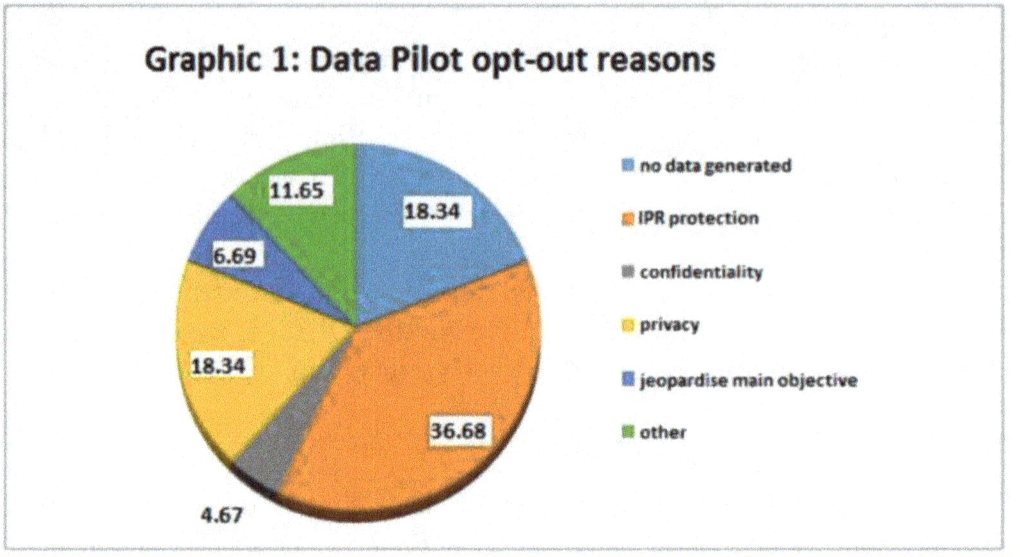

(Source: European Commission, Open Research Data – Explanatory note to the 2015 dataset, p. 3)

Information on why projects choose not to participate in the Open Research Data Pilot is only systematically measured at the proposal stage and not when opting out at another stage of the project lifecycle. As part of the submission process, project applicants are asked the relevant question whether they want to opt out and for what reason. A sample of 1382 proposals has therefore been analysed in this regard by the Commission.

The Commission does not collect detailed information on reasons for opting out. Applicants must merely choose a reason for the opt-out (e.g. "IPR protection", "confidentiality" or "privacy") from a drop-down list. This means that the projects do not have to describe, for example, the relevant IPR when choosing the reason "IPR protection", the grounds for secrecy when choosing the reason "confidentiality" or the data protection issues involved when choosing the reason "privacy". Therefore, it becomes very difficult to analyse in more depth applicants' reasons for opting out.

Moreover, the European Commission does not verify the indicated opt-out reasons. It is the sole responsibility of the projects to determine whether there are concerns about participating in the Open Research Data Pilot and which opt-out reason they choose to indicate during the application process. Hence it cannot be ruled out that applicants choose to opt out for a reason that is actually not relevant for their project. It is, for example, perhaps questionable that 18% of the projects in the core areas do not expect to generate data that could be made open within the Pilot.

Despite these shortcomings, the dataset at least gives an impression of the opt-out reasons projects consider to be relevant.

The protection of results is stated as the most important reason for proposals to opt out. 36.7% of the opted-out project proposals did so for reasons of IPR protection and another 4.7% for confidentially reasons. The second most revalent reasons for opting out are "no data generated" and privacy concerns, with each factor indicated by 18.3% of those opting out. This number of opt-outs for privacy issues was somewhat surprising, with some of the current authors expecting the number to be higher. However, it is at least thinkable that projects in which data protection issues exist opted out for another reason that is also relevant to them, such as IPR protection.

Within this legal study the intention was to identify concrete problem areas where data protection law conflicts with the open access obligations of the Open Research Data Pilot. To analyse those areas, practical examples from those involved in the Pilot should have been identified and examined in detail. Such analysis would have provided a great opportunity to make this study much more practical and to draft recommendations relevant to practice.

However, as just mentioned, it proved impossible to obtain detailed descriptions of data protection issues which led to the decision to opt out of the Open Research Data Pilot. In order to identify at least research areas in which opting out of the Pilot is more common than in others, we had a closer look at the dataset published by the Commission.

The outcome was surprising. As the dataset shows, there are actually no areas with an increased likelihood of opting out for privacy reasons.

There were 7869 relevant proposals in the core areas that were handed in to the Commission. Of this sample, 3% opted out of the Open Research Data Pilot for data protection reasons. The opt-out rates vary between 0% and 13% but it should be noted that the highest percentages are observed in calls with fewer proposals:

CALL	Number of proposals opting out for data protection reasons	Percentage
FETOPEN-2015-CSA	2 out of 15 proposals	13%
EUB-2015	5 out of 42 proposals	12%
GERI-2014-1	5 out of 47 proposals	11%

And even in those calls the most proposals did not opt out of the Pilot at all:

CALL	Number of proposals opting out for all reasons	Percentage
FETOPEN-2015-CSA	5 out of 15 proposals	33%
EUB-2015	10 out of 42 proposals	24%
GERI-2014-1	15 out of 47 proposals	32%

Moreover, the covered topics of the calls are diverse:

CALL	Topic
FETOPEN-2015-CSA	Cooperation in advanced cyber infrastructure
EUB-2015	Support of novel ideas for radical new technologies
GERI-2014-1	Promoting gender equality in research and innovation

As a result it must be said that the opt-out rate for data protection reasons is relatively low (18% of the opt-outs; 3% of the overall proposals). Furthermore the opt-outs for data protection reasons do not seem to follow a specific trend. There are no calls or specific topics with substantially higher numbers or percentages of privacy opt-outs identifiable.

There are of course calls with no opt-outs for privacy reasons, but in most of the calls at least some project proposals decided not to participate in the Pilot for such reasons. However, in relation to the total number of proposals, the privacy opt-outs are always in the minority.

This result does not allow identification of areas within Horizon 2020 that may conflict with data protection legislation more often than others.

Those findings, difficulties in obtaining detailed descriptions of practically relevant data protection issues for the Open Research Data Pilot, and the inconclusive statistical data of the Commission's dataset make it difficult to identify concrete problem areas where data protection law conflicts with the open access obligation of the Open Research Data Pilot.

1.5.3 Open Access use of research data

These factors make it necessary to follow a more theoretical approach. Through the Open Research Data Pilot, the European Commission is promoting open access to research data. The Commission expects that in today's "information economy", where knowledge is a source of competitive advantage, open access can potentially realise a variety of benefits and open access can also increase openness and transparency and thereby contribute to better policymaking and ultimately benefit society and citizens[499].

In the European Commission's view, there should be no need to pay for information funded from the public purse each time it is accessed or used. Moreover, it should benefit European businesses and the public to the full. This means making publicly funded scientific information available online, at no extra cost, to European researchers, innovative industries and the public, while ensuring that it is preserved in the long term[500]. The Open Research Data Pilot is designed to improve and maximise access to and re-use of research data generated by projects[501].

1.5.3.1 Open Access in Horizon 2020

Having such positive effects in mind, the question arises as to what is meant by open access. The idea of open access was developed within the academic environment. The idea on which open access relies is that the knowledge produced by academic and scientific institutions has to be accessible by the academic community and society at large without economic, legal or technological restrictions[502]. The three essential characteristics of open access are: free accessibility, further distribution, and proper archiving[503].

A series of declarations on open access in 2002 and 2003 helped push the debate. Following 2002's Budapest Open Access Initiative[504] and 2003's Bethesda Statement on Open Access Publishing[505], German and international research organisations signed the Berlin Declaration on Open Access to Knowledge in the Sciences and Humanities in October 2003[506]. According to this declaration, open access contributions must satisfy two conditions:

> *1. The author(s) and right holder(s) of such contributions grant(s) to all users a free, irrevocable, worldwide, right of access to, and a license to copy, use, distribute, transmit and display the work publicly and to make and distribute derivative works, in any digital medium for any responsible purpose, subject to proper attribution of authorship*

---

499 European Commission, Fact sheet: Open Access in Horizon 2020, p. 2.

500 European Commission, Guidelines on Open Access to Scientific Publications and Research Data in Horizon 2020, Version 2.1, 15 February 2016, p. 4.

501 Ibid., p. 7.

502 See Guibault/Wiebe (eds.), *Safe to be open*, Göttingen, Göttingen University Press, 2013, p. 143.

503 Open Society Institute, *Open Access Publishing and Scholarly Societies – A Guide*, New York, OSI, 2005, p. 6.

504 See http://www.budapestopenaccessinitiative.org/read.

505 See https://dash.harvard.edu/handle/1/4725199.

506 The text is available at: https://openaccess.mpg.de/67605/berlin_declaration_engl.pdf.

(community standards, will continue to provide the mechanism for enforcement of proper attribution and responsible use of the published work, as they do now), as well as the right to make small numbers of printed copies for their personal use.

2. A complete version of the work and all supplemental materials, including a copy of the permission as stated above, in an appropriate standard electronic format is deposited (and thus published) in at least one online repository using suitable technical standards (such as the Open Archive definitions) that is supported and maintained by an academic institution, scholarly society, government agency, or other well established organisation that seeks to enable open access, unrestricted distribution, interoperability, and long-term archiving.

To date, the Berlin Declaration has been signed by more than 550 organisations worldwide[507].

The European Commission defines open access within Horizon 2020, simplified as the practice of providing online access to scientific information that is free of charge to the end-user[508]. In addition to that, in its guidelines the Commission explicitly makes reference to the Berlin Declaration and clarifies that the scientific information shall also be re-usable[509].

According to the European Commission, open access to research data refers to the right to access and re-use digital research data under the terms and conditions set out in the grant agreement[510]. The grant agreements of projects taking part in the Pilot oblige projects to meet the following requirements[511]:

- Step 1 – they must deposit the research data, preferably in research data repositories. These are online research data archives, which may be subject based/thematic, institutional or centralised.
- Step 2 – as far as possible, projects must then take measures to enable third parties to access, mine, exploit, reproduce and disseminate (free of charge for any user) this research data. One straightforward and effective way of doing this is to attach Creative Commons Licences (CC BY or CC0 tool) to the data deposited.

The term "research data" refers to information, in particular facts or numbers, collected to be examined and considered as a basis for reasoning, discussion or calculation. In a research context, examples of data include statistics, results of

---

507 See https://openaccess.mpg.de/3883/Signatories.

508 See European Commission, Fact sheet: Open Access in Horizon 2020, available at: https://ec.europa.eu/programmes/horizon2020/sites/horizon2020/files/FactSheet_Open_Access.pdf.

509 European Commission, Guidelines on Open Access to Scientific Publications and Research Data in Horizon 2020, Version 2.1, 15 February 2016, p. 2.

510 Ibid, p. 3.

511 Ibid, pp. 9 et seq.

experiments, measurements, observations resulting from fieldwork, survey results, interview recordings and images. The focus is on research data that are available in digital form[512].

As can be seen, the European Commission defines the scope of research data and actions required from their owners within the Open Research Data Pilot in a broad way. The same is true of the operations that further users of the research data can perform with them. These definitions meet the requirements of the open access definition of, for example, the Berlin Declaration.

In the context of this study, it is important to underscore that, according to the Guidelines on Data Management in Horizon 2020, one of the characteristics of the scientific research data shared within the Open Research Data Pilot is that it "should be easily useable *beyond the original purpose for which it was collected*"[513].

1.5.3.1.1 Open access vs. data protection law

The open access requirement of the Open Research Data Pilot is thus to be understood in such a way that all research data needed to validate the results presented in scientific publications or specified in a DMP shall as far as possible be publicly available and re-usable online without any restrictions.

1.5.3.1.2 Research data as personal data

The very first question on whether such an open access obligation can conflict with data protection rules is whether the research data that shall be opened up constitute personal data.

"Personal data" means any information relating to an identified or identifiable natural person[514]. The key element of the evaluation is the possible identification of a person. Identifiers could be, in particular, names, identification numbers, location data, online identifiers or one or more factors specific to the physical, physiological, genetic, mental, economic, cultural or social identity of that person (Art. 4(1) GDPR).

Even data which have undergone pseudonymisation should be considered as information on an identifiable natural person. To determine whether a person is identifiable, account should be taken of all the means reasonably likely to be used, either by the controller or by any other person, to identify the individual directly or indirectly. However, data protection legislation should not apply to anonymous information, that is information which does not relate to an identified or

---

512 European Commission, Open Research Data – Explanatory note to the 2015 dataset, p. 1, available at: https://data.europa.eu/euodp/data/dataset/open-research-data-the-uptake-of-the-pilot-in-the-first-calls-of-horizon-2020.

513 Guidelines on Data Management in Horizon 2020. Version 2.1, 15 February 2016, Annex 2, para. 4, available at: http://ec.europa.eu/research/participants/data/ref/h2020/grants_manual/hi/oa_pilot/h2020-hi-oa-data-mgt_en.pdf.

514 Art. 4(1) GDPR; Art. 2(a) Data Protection Directive.

identifiable natural person or to data rendered anonymous in such a way that the data subject is not or no longer identifiable (Recital 26 GDPR; see also Recital 26 Data Protection Directive).

For the Open Research Data Pilot, the term "research data" is defined extremely broadly by the Commission and the funded fields of research are diverse. Thus it is not possible to determine in a general way whether such research data include personal data or not. There must be a case-by-case evaluation of whether the research data concerned fall under the definition of personal data. Research data often do not contain identifying data, but may still, alone or in combination with other available data, allow a particular person to be identified.

What can be said is that a careful evaluation is necessary in cases where the research in any way involves natural persons. Especially in the fields of medicine, biotechnology and social sciences, research data often contain information traceable to individuals that can qualify as personal data but it depends on the individual case. For example, it is very likely that research data from a project analysing biological traits of humans will include personal data; for research on biological traits of animals or plants it is rather unlikely.

If the research data in question do not include personal data, data protection law is not applicable and the open access use of the data is not restricted by such rules.

1.5.3.2 Processing of research data

On the other hand, if personal data are concerned, data protection rules must be taken into account. Such rules always apply whenever personal data are processed. Processing here includes practically any operation in connection with personal data – including collection, recording, organisation, structuring, storage, adaptation or alteration, retrieval, consultation, use, disclosure by transmission, dissemination or otherwise making available, alignment or combination, restriction, erasure or destruction[515]. The term "processing" is all embracing and includes the whole process that the data undergo from the moment of collection to the moment of destruction[516]. Any operation with personal data not qualifying as processing is almost unthinkable[517].

Within the Open Research Data Pilot of Horizon 2020, research data shall be deposited in a research data repository. This means that the data must be uploaded to an online research data archive. Furthermore, third parties shall be enabled to access, mine, exploit, reproduce and disseminate these research data.

---

515 See Art. 4(2) GDPR; Art. 2(b) Data Protection Directive.

516 Explanatory Memorandum DDPA, pp. 51 et seq.

517 Kuner, *European Data Protection Law: Corporate Compliance and Regulation*, Oxford, Oxford University Press, 2007, p. 75.

It is clear that such actions, the uploading of data to a research data repository as well as the re-use of the data, qualify as processing within the meaning of the relevant legal instruments.

1.5.3.3 Consequences

The consequence is that the data protection rules apply to the use of research data, including personal data within the Open Research Data Pilot. The basic rule is that personal data may not be processed unless the data subject has consented to the processing or another legal provision permits the processing[518]. The processing of personal data always requires a justification.

The most important data protection principles are fair and lawful processing, purpose limitation and data minimisation.

Fair and lawful processing: The principle of fair and lawful processing[519] basically requires data controllers to comply with all relevant data protection rules, especially those of the GDPR and the Data Protection Directive. This obligation is rather logical, but the requirement of fair and lawful processing illustrates once again the importance the legislator attaches to data protection.

Principle of purpose limitation: The principle of purpose limitation stipulates that personal data should be collected for specified, legitimate purposes and not further processed in a way incompatible with those purposes[520]. This means that after the collection, the personal data must be used for the intended purpose and not for any other purpose. Regarding the definition of the purpose for processing it is important to note that the purpose needs to be defined as precisely as possible. The data subject must be able to understand for what purposes their data are intended to be used. Hence it is not sufficient, for example, to simply name "scientific research" as the purpose of processing. The term "scientific research" is far too vague to give the data subject an idea of what is done with their personal data. It seems to be necessary at least to define within which project or study the personal data are processed, for what reasons and by whom.

Principle of data minimisation: The principle of data minimisation says that personal data must be adequate, relevant and limited to what is necessary in relation to the purposes for which they are processed[521]. This rule clarifies that the processing of personal data should be limited to the minimum amount necessary[522]. Personal data should only be processed if the purpose of the processing could not reasonably be fulfilled by other means.

---

518 See Art. 8(2) EU Charter.

519 See Art. 6 GDPR; Art. 6(1)(a) Data Protection Directive.

520 See Art. 6(1)(c) Data Protection Directive; Art. 5(1)(b) GDPR.

521 Art. 5(1)(c) GDPR; see also Art. 6(1)(c) Data Protection Directive.

522 Kuner, *European Data Protection Law: Corporate Compliance and Regulation*, Oxford, Oxford University Press, 2007, p. 74.

The Open Research Data Pilot: within the Open Research Data Pilot in Horizon 2020, research data shall be deposited in an open research data repository. The Pilot is designed to improve and maximise access to and re-use of research data generated by projects[523]. Third parties shall be enabled to access, mine, exploit, reproduce and disseminate this research data without any restrictions. The general public shall be able to use the deposited data easily beyond the original purpose for which they were collected[524]. The research data shall be available to the public in a permanent way, without any time-limit[525].

In short, the research data in the Open Research Data Pilot shall be

- available to the public without a time-limit, and
- usable beyond the original purpose for which they were collected.

These extensive permissions are clearly at odds with the fundamental data protection principles of purpose limitation and data minimisation, as (1) all data falling under the Pilot shall be made openly available and not just the minimum amount necessary to perform a task, and (2) the use of the data is not limited to specific purposes and not even by time. This means that personal data, in principle, cannot be made available on an open access basis as is required by the Open Research Data Pilot due to conflicts with principle rules on the protection of personal data.

1.5.3.4 Research exemption

However, since the European legislative Acts contain some special provisions on the use of personal data for scientific purposes, one could think about legitimising the further use of research data within the Pilot through such exemptions. Indeed there are exemptions on the principles of purpose limitation and data minimisation incorporated in the Data Protection Directive as well as in the GDPR.

According to Art. 6(1)(b) Data Protection Directive and Art. 5(1)(b) GDPR the further processing of personal data for scientific purposes shall not be considered as incompatible with the initial purposes for which the data have been collected, provided that appropriate safeguards are in place.

Under the regime of the Data Protection Directive, keeping data for future scientific use is exempt from the principle of limited data retention (Art. 6(1)(e) of the directive). Art. 5(1)(e) GDPR contains a provision on longer storage for

---

523 European Commission, Guidelines on Open Access to Scientific Publications and Research Data in Horizon 2020, Version 2.1, 15 February 2016, p. 7.

524 Guidelines on Data Management in Horizon 2020. Version 2.1, 15 February 2016, Annex 2, para. 4, available at: http://ec.europa.eu/research/participants/data/ref/h2020/grants_manual/hi/oa_pilot/h2020-hi-oa-data-mgt_en.pdf.

525 The Commission recommends the use of CC licences. Those licences grant permanent rights to the public. See European Commission, Guidelines on Open Access to Scientific Publications and Research Data in Horizon 2020, Version 2.1, 15 February 2016, p. 9 et seq.

scientific use too. Personal data may be stored for longer periods insofar as the personal data will be processed solely for scientific research purposes, subject to implementation of the appropriate technical and organisational measures in order to safeguard the rights and freedoms of the data subject.

It is up to the Member States to provide such appropriate safeguards for the further use of personal data for scientific purposes, which means that the provisions on this issue may vary between the Member States.

Art. 89(1) GDPR now clarifies that the safeguards shall ensure that technical and organisational measures are in place in particular in order to ensure respect for the principle of data minimisation. These measures may include pseudonymisation provided that those purposes can be fulfilled in that manner. Where those purposes can be fulfilled by further processing which does not permit, or no longer permits, the identification of data subjects, those purposes shall be fulfilled in that manner.

This provision clarifies that the exemptions for research purposes are limited in that they are applicable only if the purpose of the research cannot be fulfilled without using personal data or with the use of anonymised data[526]. In this way, the exemptions for research purposes are not absolute. They do not generally authorise further processing or longer storage of data for scientific purposes in all cases. The principles of purpose limitation and data minimisation remain in place when the purpose of research does not require an exemption.

The exceptions for research purposes, on the other hand, ensure that the strong data protection principles remain valid for the initial data collection. For example, if a company collects data of its clients for business purposes, based on their consent, the company is only allowed to process the data for those purposes. The company is not allowed to open up the data to the general public or upload them to an open repository.

If the initial purpose of data collection is a scientific use, the data subject shall have the opportunity to consent to the use of personal data, at least to certain areas of research or parts of research projects (Recital 33 GDPR). So the data subject is enabled to give a broader consent if the purpose of data collection is research. Nevertheless, the purpose of processing has to be specified, although it is sufficient to specify certain areas of research or parts of research projects. It should be noted that consenting to all research-related purposes is not possible. One of the consequences is that a data subject is not able to consent to the opening up of data to the general public or to the uploading of their personal data to an open data repository.

As regards the service of the Open Research Data Pilot, this means that deposit of personal data in an open research data repository cannot be legitimised by a scientific research exemption. The data in the Open Research Data Pilot

---

[526] Albrecht, 'The EU's New Data Protection Law – How A Directive Evolved Into A Regulation', CRi 2016, 33 (36).

should, as far as possible, be publicly available and re-usable online without any restrictions and without a time limit. But for the scientific research exemptions on further processing and longer storage of personal data to apply, the intended use has to be bound to a specific research purpose and appropriate safeguards have to be in place, in particular to ensure respect for the principle of data minimisation. Within the Pilot, this is not the case. Deposit of research data in an open access repository is not connected to a specific research project and not even to a scientific purpose at all. It rather makes the data available for any purposes, scientific or not. Furthermore, appropriate safeguards to ensure leading data protection principles are not in place. Indeed no such safeguards at all are intended.

Under these circumstances, the deposit and making available of research data which include personal data in an open access repository, and thus the participation in the Open Research Data Pilot, cannot be legitimised through the research exemptions existing in European data protection legislation.

1.5.3.5 Consent/Licences

Another way to guarantee compliance with data protection rules while participating in the Pilot could be to obtain consent of the data subjects to process and re-use their personal data within the Pilot. The data subject's consent is the most important legitimisation for the processing of their personal data.

(I) According to Art. 2(h) Data Protection Directive to have legal effect, the consent of the data subject to processing their personal data must be freely given, specific and informed. Art. 4(11) GDPR adds the criterion that to be valid the consent additionally has to be unambiguous.

To have legal effect, the definition(s) require(s) consent to be, inter alia, specific and informed. According to the Article 29 Working Party[527], "specific" consent must relate to a well-defined, concrete situation in which the processing is envisaged; "informed" consent means consent by the data subject based upon an appreciation and understanding of the facts and implications of an action. The individual concerned must be given, in a clear and understandable manner, accurate and full information about all relevant issues, such as the nature of the data processed, purposes of the processing, the recipients of possible transfers, and the rights of the data subject.

As this statement clarifies, to guarantee informed consent, the purpose for processing must be defined. It is necessary to give the data subject all the information needed to understand the scope of their decision[528]. The purposes of

---

[527] Article 29 Data Protection Working Party, Working Document on the processing of personal data relating to health in electronic health records (EHR), adopted on 15 February 2007, p. 9.

[528] See Rogosch, *Die Einwilligung im Datenschutzrecht*, Baden-Baden, Nomos, 2013, p. 69; Holznagel/Sonntag, in Roßnagel, *Handbuch Datenschutzrecht*, Munich, C.H. Beck, 2003, chapter 4.8 para. 48.

use of the data must be described in as much detail as possible to legitimise all intended uses of the personal data. The expression of will of the data subject must relate to a particular processing of personal data. It should be clear which processing, of which personal data, for what purpose will take place, and, if the data will be transferred to third parties, to which third parties[529].

However, within the Open Research Data Pilot, the purposes of the further use of the data are unclear. Research data are to be made publicly available on an open access basis. Any uses – and not just specific ones – of the deposited data shall be allowed. The data shall be deposited in an open research data repository where data will potentially be transferred to any third parties which retrieve them. But if the future use of data, as well as the recipients, are not yet known, it is simply impossible to clearly inform the data subject about the uses and recipients in a declaration of consent and to fulfil the requirement of specific and informed consent.

Certainly, one could think of simply informing the data subject that their personal data within the Pilot is free for any uses by any third parties and ask them to consent to such open access use of their personal data, but there would always be a risk that one or more data subjects would subsequently withdraw their consent[530].

As soon as the data subject withdraws their consent, their personal data shall be erased and no longer processed[531]. Where the controller has made the personal data public and is obliged to erase the personal data, for example because the data subject withdraws their consent, the controller, taking account of available technology and the cost of implementation, shall take reasonable steps, including technical measures, to inform controllers which are processing the personal data that the data subject has requested the erasure by such controllers of any links to, or copy or replication of, those personal data (Art. 17(2) GDPR).

Within the Open Research Data Pilot, the data concerned are uploaded to an open research data repository. There are no restrictions, and hence no control, over who downloads and further uses the data. But under such circumstances it is hardly possible to comply with the obligations of Art. 17(2) GDPR.

In fact, if data are distributed via open access it is impossible to ensure that the data are deleted or removed at a later time, which would mean that the withdrawal of consent is practically ineffective.

---

529 Explanatory Memorandum DDPA, pp. 65 et seq.

530 The right of withdrawing consent is implicit in the Data Protection Directive, see above Section 1.2.3.7; under the regime of the GDPR such right is explicitly included in Art. 4(11); see also above Section 1.4.3.4.

531 See Recital 65 GDPR.

To enable the controller to effectively comply with the obligations created by a potential withdrawal, they need to implement measures to make any future withdrawal technically possible. But in an open access environment such as an open repository, it is not desirable, if not impossible, to implement technical measures to ensure that data are deleted or removed after a withdrawal.

Furthermore, even in such cases, when the data subject consents to an open access use of their data, the further uses of the data as well as the recipients are not known. No one, neither the controller nor the data subject, nor a third party, knows in what ways the deposited data will be used and by whom in the future. All uses are conceivable, but then the data subject cannot be informed about the uses and recipients; no one knows yet.

Under these circumstances, the consent of the data subject can be neither specific nor informed. A specific and informed consent always requires a clear and precise definition of the purposes of processing as well as the recipients.

Although it is possible to enable the transfer of personal data in an individual case by consent, it is impossible to legitimise any known and unknown uses by consent of the data subject. Therefore a general agreement of the data subject to the collection of their personal data and to subsequent transfers of these past and future data does not constitute valid consent[532]. This also means that it is not possible to legitimise the use of personal data in the Open Research Data Pilot by consent.

(II) The European Commission suggests that projects taking part in the Open Research Data Pilot enable third parties to access, mine, exploit, reproduce and disseminate (free of charge for any user) the deposited research data via the use of free licences such as Creative Commons Licences (CC BY or CC-0)[533].

We therefore feel bound to issue a warning and clarify that open access licences such as Creative Commons licences do not cover personal rights. These licences are intended to license IPR, such as copyright, and do not include consent to process personal data. To cover data protection rights in such licences would also not be possible, since – as just stated – a general agreement of the data subject to any known and unknown uses is impossible. So opening up research data under for example a Creative Commons licence does not have any legal effect on data protection rules.

---

532 See for health data, Article 29 Data Protection Working Party, *Working Document on the processing of personal data relating to health in electronic health records (EHR)*, adopted on 15 February 2007, p. 9; see also Explanatory Memorandum DDPA, pp. 65 et seq.

533 See European Commission, Guidelines on Open Access to Scientific Publications and Research Data in Horizon 2020, Version 2.1, 15 February 2016, p. 9 et seq.

The best way to fulfil the requirements of the Open Research Data Pilot and avoid conflicts with data protection rules is to exclude the application of such rules. This is possible through anonymisation of personal data.

Data protection law deals with personal data. The key element of the evaluation of whether data are personal is the possible identification of a person. Data protection rules apply to any information concerning an identified or identifiable person[534]. On the other hand, data protection law should not apply to anonymous information, namely information which does not relate to an identified or identifiable natural person or to personal data rendered anonymous in such a manner that the data subject is not, or no longer, identifiable[535]. To determine whether a person is identifiable, account should be taken of "all the means reasonably likely to be used" for the identification process.

This definition of anonymous data sounds logical but in practice the evaluation of whether data are effectively anonymised can give rise to some issues.

First, there is the controversial issue of whether personal data require the data subject to be identifiable for the controller or whether it is sufficient if a third party is able to link the data in question to a natural person. The answer to this question could also have consequences for the definition of anonymised data. However, the wording of Recital 26 GDPR must be understood in the sense that at least anonymisation requires that the data subject is not identifiable at all. Therefore the Article 29 Working Party said that effective anonymisation should prevent all parties from singling out an individual in a dataset, from linking two records within a dataset (or between two separate datasets) and from inferring any information in such dataset[536].

When considering "all the means likely reasonably to be used" the following factors should be taken into account: the cost of conducting identification, the intended purpose, the way the processing is structured, the advantage expected by the controller, the interests at stake for the individuals, the risk of organisational dysfunctions (e.g. breaches of confidentiality duties) and technical failures. At the same time, this test is dynamic. It is sensible to apply it in the light of the state of the art of technologies at the time of processing and during the period of data processing[537].

The latter implies that "personal data" itself is a dynamic concept. Re-identification risks can change over time, given the progress of information technologies. With the availability of new techniques, an effort that used to be "unreasonable" may no longer be recognised as such. Therefore, data that are

---

534 Art. 4(1) GDPR; Art. 2(a) Data Protection Directive.

535 Recital 26 GDPR; Recital 26 Data Protection Directive.

536 Article 29 Data Protection Working Party, *Opinion 5/2014 on anonymisation techniques*, p. 9.

537 Article 29 Data Protection Working Party, *Opinion 4/2007 on the concept of personal data*, p. 15.

considered anonymous data may be qualified as personal data in the future[538]. In the case of longer storage of anonymised data the risks of re-identification should be taken into account and regularly assessed.

Especially in the context of sharing data under free licences on an open access basis, as the Commission suggests for the Open Research Data Pilot, the likelihood that any other person will have the means and will use those means to re-identify the data subjects increases very significantly[539].

When anonymised data can no longer qualify as such in the light of emergent means of re-identification, non-compliance with data protection rules constitutes an unlawful act. Under such circumstances, the controller would have the obligation to remove or delete the data but having shared data under an open access licence the controller loses control over who can access and re-use the data. In an open access environment it is impossible to ensure that data are deleted or removed after they have been made available.

Therefore, we can recommend opening up only data that are unidentifiable and non-personal, i.e., data that are, where needed, anonymised or aggregated in such a way that there is no remaining possibility to identify the data subjects. The creation of such truly anonymous datasets from a rich set of personal data, while preserving much of the underlying information, is not a simple task[540]. Effective anonymisation also depends on the type of personal data. Scholars note, for example, that anonymisation of human genetic information, due to its uniquely identifiable nature, can hardly guarantee absolute confidentiality to data subjects or their genetically related family members. As long as a reference sample is available, it is possible to re-identify genotyped data subjects and data subjects in pooled mixtures of DNA. New sequencing technology also challenges such standard data protection techniques as encryption[541].

Such data, where it cannot be ruled out that they become personal data (again) in the future, should not be opened up for re-use under an open licence without any technical and legal restrictions on re-use. Additionally, periodical assessments of re-identification risks should be carried out. The data should not be made available in a downloadable form or only via a customised API and subject to certain restrictions and security measures which allow the controller to comply with their future data protection obligations. But such restrictions would of course conflict with the open access obligation of the Open Research Data Pilot.

---

538 See Explanatory Memorandum DDPA, p. 49.

539 Article 29 Data Protection Working Party, *Opinion 6/2013 on open data and public sector information ('PSI') reuse*, p. 13.

540 Article 29 Data Protection Working Party, *Opinion 5/2014 on anonymisation techniques*, p. 5.

541 Kaye, 'The Tension Between Data Sharing and the Protection of Privacy in Genomics Research', Annu. Rev. Genomics Hum. Genet. 2012, 415 (423), text available at: http://www.annualreviews.org/doi/pdf/10.1146/annurev-genom-082410-101454.

Having these issues in mind, controllers should carry out a thorough data protection impact assessment. The assessment must evaluate very carefully whether effective anonymisation of research data potentially falling under the Open Research Data Pilot in Horizon 2020 is possible. If this is the case, anonymisation is the best solution to exclude data protection risks and to comply with both data protection legislation and the requirements of the Open Research Data Pilot at the same time. In order to assist projects in anonymising their research data where necessary, OpenAIRE is currently developing AMNESIA, a tool which will allow data curators to parameterise and apply different anonymisation techniques to their data[542].

1.5.3.7 Conclusion for the Pilot

If the research data of a project that falls within the Pilot include personal data – which comprise any information relating to an identified or identifiable natural person[543] – data protection legislation is applicable. The actions carried out on the data within the Pilot constitute processing within the meaning of data protection law[544]. The consequence is that the open access use of research data, including personal data, is at odds with fundamental data protection principles such as purpose limitation and data minimisation[545].

Such extensive use of personal data cannot be legitimised by the scientific research exemptions of the Data Protection Directive or the GDPR, first, because the use of data within the Open Research Data Pilot is not limited to scientific purposes and secondly, because even under a scientific research exemption the principle of data minimisation is still applicable and must be ensured by appropriate safeguards (cf. Art. 89(1) GDPR)[546].

Furthermore, the open access use of personal data cannot be legitimised by the consent of the data subject since to have legal effect, consent must be, inter alia, specific and informed, which means that the data subject must be informed about the use of their data and the recipients. But within an open access environment the further uses of the data as well as the recipients are unknown so consent cannot be informed and specific and is therefore invalid[547].

The only effective way to guarantee compliance with data protection rules as well as the requirements of the Open Research Data Pilot is to effectively anonymise the data to be opened up[548].

---

[542] See https://www.openaire.eu/anonymizing-your-data.

[543] Art. 4(1) GDPR; Art. 2(a) Data Protection Directive.

[544] See above Section 1.5.3.2.

[545] See above Section 1.5.3.3.

[546] See above Section 1.5.3.4.

[547] See above Section 1.5.3.5.

[548] See above Section 1.5.3.6.

1.5.4 Repository data protection issue use – case studies

Repositories are not only places of deposit for datasets, but also data management infrastructure more generally. To illustrate the different repository use forms, some general examples of the use of data in a research data repository will be described and analysed from a data protection point of view.

1.5.4.1 Example 1

Picture a researcher who is participating in a project which is part of the Open Research Data Pilot. During research many pictures of persons were taken in order to analyse their physical development. Those pictures are uploaded to an institutional research data repository. Access is restricted to the researcher. The researcher revises, processes and consolidates the data by using the data management tools of the repository.

1.5.4.1.1 Personal data

Personal data comprises any information relating to an identified or identifiable natural person[549]. Pictures of persons allow the identification of the persons depicted and therefore are personal data. This is true at least if the face is visible, but also if the person can be identified by other identifiers such as skin colour, tattoo or deformity.

1.5.4.1.2 Processing

Processing of personal data includes any operation or set of operations which is performed on personal data or on sets of personal data[550]. In our example, the pictures are taken, uploaded to the repository and later analysed and edited by the researcher. By those actions the data are processed within the meaning of data protection law. The researcher, as the person who determines the purposes and means of the processing of the personal data, thus acts as the controller[551]. They are responsible for compliance with data protection rules.

1.5.4.1.3 Consequences

In the case of such personal data processing, the data protection rules are applicable. Generally, personal data may not be processed unless the data subject has consented to the processing or another legal provision permits the processing[552].

---

549 Art. 4(1) GDPR; Art. 2(a) Data Protection Directive.

550 See Art. 4(2) GDPR; Art. 2 (b) Data Protection Directive.

551 Art. 2(d) Data Protection Directive; Art. 4(7) GDPR.

552 Art. 6 GDPR; Art. 7 Data Protection Directive; Art. 8(2) EU Charter.

In this example there is no legal provision existing that could legitimise the processing (taking, uploading, editing) of the personal data in question (the pictures).

A scientific research exception cannot legitimise the processing of the personal data since such an exception can only legitimise a longer storage period[553] or a further processing for another scientific purpose[554]. It does not allow the collection of the data. Therefore it is necessary that the researcher obtains consent from all the data subjects for the processing of their personal data.

One could also think about the question of whether the institutional research data repository is processing personal data since the data are uploaded to it. But the situation should be interpreted as the repository processing the personal data on behalf of the controller and not having any power of disposition concerning the data. But then the repository acts as a processor[555]. Unlike the controller, the processor does not decide on the purpose, content or use of the processing. They are not responsible for compliance with data protection rules; only the researcher as controller is so responsible.

1.5.4.2 Example 2

A second researcher is part of a project participating in the Open Research Data Pilot. The project's subject is brain research. As part of the research a large amount of raw data are produced. The data consist of information on how the brain waves of diverse test persons react to changes in their environment.

The results of research will be published in a scientific journal. During the peer-review process the mentioned raw data are uploaded to a research data repository by the researcher. Access to the record is restricted to the publisher and reviewers through dedicated links.

After review the raw data are submitted in embargoed state for open access release at the same time as the paper is published in the journal.

1.5.4.2.1 Personal data

Personal data comprise any information relating to an identified or identifiable natural person[556]. In this example, the research data consist of information on how the brain waves of diverse test persons react in certain circumstances. The individual data sets are assigned to different test persons. Hence such data must be regarded as personal data within the meaning of data protection law.

---

[553] See Art. 6(1)(e) Data Protection Directive); Art. 5(1)(e) GDPR.
[554] See Art. 6(1)(b) Data Protection Directive; Art. 5(1)(b) GDPR.
[555] Art. 2(e) Data Protection Directive; Art. 4(8) GDPR.
[556] Art. 4(1) GDPR; Art. 2(a) Data Protection Directive.

1.5.4.2.2 Processing

Processing of personal data includes any operation or set of operations which is performed on personal data or on sets of personal data[557]. In example 2 the personal data are collected, analysed, uploaded to a research data repository and made available to the publisher and reviewers through dedicated links and later to the general public. By all of those actions the data are processed within the meaning of data protection law.

1.5.4.2.3 Consequences

In the case of personal data processing, the controller has to comply with data protection rules. The controller is the one who determines the purposes and means of the processing of personal data[558]. In example 2 this is the researcher who collects, analyses and uploads the data and afterwards makes them available. The research data repository is not a controller, since it is merely processing the data on behalf of the controller and thereby acts as a processor[559].

However, things are different as regards the publisher and reviewers. According to the European legislative acts, processing includes retrieval and consultation of personal data[560]. The publisher and the reviewers are able to retrieve the data via dedicated links and thereby consult the data so they are data controllers too.

The data controllers must comply with the applicable data protection rules. In particular, they need a legal ground for processing[561]. In example 2 there is no legal provision existing that could legitimise the processing (collection, analysis, uploading, making available, consultation).

A scientific research exception cannot legitimise the processing. Such an exemption could just legitimise a longer storage period[562] or a further processing for another scientific purpose[563] but not the initial data collection, the use within a journal publishing process or the free use of the data. That is why controllers need to obtain consent of all the data subjects for the processing of their personal data.

Obtaining consent of the data subjects for collection, analysis, uploading to the repository and making available to the publisher and reviewers, as well as retrieval and consultation through the latter, is relatively unproblematic. This

---

557 See Art. 4(2) GDPR; Art. 2(b) Data Protection Directive.

558 Art. 2(d) Data Protection Directive; Art. 4(7) GDPR.

559 Art. 2(e) Data Protection Directive; Art. 4(8) GDPR.

560 See Art. 4(2) GDPR; Art. 2(b) Data Protection Directive.

561 See Art. 6 GDPR; Art. 7 Data Protection Directive; Art. 8(2) EU Charter.

562 See Art. 6(1)(e) Data Protection Directive); Art. 5(1)(e) GDPR.

563 See Art. 6(1)(b) Data Protection Directive; Art. 5(1)(b) GDPR.

processing constitutes concrete actions that can be described in a declaration of consent and understood by the data subjects. According to those actions, valid consent seems possible.

However, after an embargo period, the data are supposed to be released to the general public on an open access basis. However, as described above[564], it is not possible for data subjects to consent to further, as yet unknown uses of their personal data by unknown third parties. Such consent is not specific nor informed and is thereby invalid. Hence it is not possible to legitimise the open access release of the data in example 2. Such release should be avoided.

1.5.4.3 Example 3

Picture a researcher who is engaged in a project which is participating in the Open Research Data Pilot. The project's subject is a social and medical research study on drug patients. The results of the research are presented in an article in a scientific journal. The results are based on surveys and medical examinations of drug patients. The data are summarised in a table. The table contains the fields name, sex, age, consumption habits and disease. The researcher uploads the table to a research data repository and refers to it in the journal article through a DOI[565]. Via the DOI third parties are able to get full access to the table and to mine, exploit, reproduce and disseminate it.

1.5.4.3.1 Personal data

Personal data comprise any information relating to an identified or identifiable natural person[566]. In example 3, the research data consist of information taken from surveys and medical examinations of drug patients. The data are summarised in a table containing information on name, sex, age, consumption habits and disease. All characteristics (sex, age, consumption habits and disease) are assigned to a person's name. Such data must clearly be regarded as personal data within the meaning of data protection law.

Furthermore, European data protection law provides for special categories of personal data. These are personal data revealing racial or ethnic origin, political opinions, religious or philosophical beliefs, trade union membership, and the processing of genetic data, biometric data in order to uniquely identify a person or data concerning health or sex life and sexual orientation[567]. In example 3 the research data include information on consumption habits and disease. Those information fall under the definition of special categories of personal data.

---

564 See above Section 1.5.3.5.

565 Digital Object Identifier.

566 Art. 4(1) GDPR; Art. 2(a) Data Protection Directive.

567 See Art. 9(1) GDPR; Art. 8(1) Data Protection Directive.

1.5.4.3.2 Processing

Processing of personal data includes any operation or set of operations which is performed on personal data or on sets of personal data[568].

In example 3 the personal data are collected, summarised in a table, uploaded to a research data repository and made openly available via a DOI. By those actions the data are processed within the meaning of data protection law.

1.5.4.3.3 Consequences

The researcher, as the one who collects, summarises, uploads the data and makes them accessible via a DOI, thereby determines the purposes and means of the processing of personal data and acts as the controller[569]. The research data repository again just processes the data on behalf of the controller and thereby act as a processor[570].

The personal data processing is lawful only if and to the extent that a legitimisation applies[571]. An even stricter prohibition on processing exists in relation to the processing of special categories of personal data[572].

A legal provision legitimising the actions of the controller in example 3 is not applicable. A scientific research exemption does not help. Such exemption could only legitimise a longer storage period[573] or further processing for another scientific purpose[574], but not the initial data collection or free use of the data.

Consent of the data subjects is the only way to legitimise the data processing described in this example. It is important to note that as regards the processing of special categories of personal data, consent not only has to be freely given, specific, informed and unambiguous, but must also explicitly cover the sensitive kind of data[575].

Obtaining explicit consent of the data subjects for collection and summarising of the data should be possible. Those actions are concrete and describable for example in a declaration of consent. Valid consent seems possible.

However, the data are to be released to the general public. The controller refers to the table containing the research data in aggregated form in their publication through a DOI. Via the DOI third parties are able to get full access to the table and to mine, exploit, reproduce and disseminate it. However, again, it is

568 See Art. 4(2) GDPR; Art. 2(b) Data Protection Directive.
569 Art. 2(d) Data Protection Directive; Art. 4(7) GDPR.
570 Art. 2(e) Data Protection Directive; Art. 4(8) GDPR.
571 See Art. 6 GDPR; Art. 7 Data Protection Directive; Art. 8(2) EU Charter.
572 See Art. 9(1) GDPR; Art. 8(1) Data Protection Directive.
573 See Art. 6(1)(e) Data Protection Directive; Art. 5(1)(e) GDPR.
574 See Art. 6(1)(b) Data Protection Directive; Art. 5(1)(b) GDPR.
575 Art. 9(2)(a) GDPR; Art. 8(2)(a) Data Protection Directive.

impossible for data subjects to consent to all further known or unknown uses of their personal data. Such consent is not informed and is therefore invalid, hence the release of the research data in example 3 via a DOI would be illegal.

1.5.4.4 Example 4

Picture a researcher who is participant of a project which is participating in the Open Research Data Pilot. The project focuses on the creditworthiness of people in different Member State areas of the EU. The data generated are anonymised in such a way that direct identifiers, for example names and social security numbers, are removed but descriptive information such as postcode and age of the test persons remain. Based on this information, creditworthiness is assigned to different Member State areas and age groups. To guarantee anonymity, in each area there are at least 10 persons assigned to each age group. The data thus anonymised are uploaded to a research data repository and made openly available to validate the research results presented in an article in a scientific journal.

1.5.4.4.1 Personal data

Personal data comprise any information relating to an identified or identifiable natural person[576]. In example 4 the research data consist of information on the creditworthiness of people in different Member State areas and age groups. In its raw form, i.e. before the data are anonymised, the information is assigned to individual natural persons. Therefore those data are personal data within the meaning of data protection law.

1.5.4.4.2 Processing

Processing of personal data includes any operation or set of operations which is performed on personal data or on sets of personal data[577]. In example 4 personal data are collected, analysed, anonymised and made openly available via a research data repository. Thus the data are processed within the meaning of data protection law.

1.5.4.4.3 Consequences

The researcher, as the individual who collects, analyses, anonymises and makes the data openly available, determines the purposes and means of the processing and acts as the data controller[578]. The research data repository is thus used as a tool. It processes the personal data on behalf of the controller and has no power of disposition concerning the data. The repository therefore acts as a processor[579].

---

[576] Art. 4(1) GDPR; Art. 2(a) Data Protection Directive.
[577] See Art. 4(2) GDPR; Art. 2(b) Data Protection Directive.
[578] See Art. 2(d) Data Protection Directive; Art. 4(7) GDPR.
[579] Art. 2(e) Data Protection Directive; Art. 4(8) GDPR.

Personal data processing is lawful only if and to the extent that a legitimisation applies[580]. A legal basis for the processing in example 4 is not applicable. A scientific research exemption is not relevant since such an exemption does not cover the initial collection of data but just a longer storage period[581] or a further processing for another scientific purpose[582].

That is why the processing (collecting, analysing, anonymising, making available) must be based on consent of the data subjects to avoid illegal processing. To obtain consent for collecting, analysing or anonymising of data, these actions need to be named and described in a declaration of consent so that data subjects can give their free, specific, informed and unambiguous consent[583].

After the anonymisation, the personal data are supposed to be made openly available to the general public for free use. As already mentioned[584], consent to such wide and open use of personal data is not possible under the rules of data protection law. The open access release of personal data would infringe data protection principles.

However, in example 4 it is questionable whether data protection principles are applicable to the data sets that are to be released. The collected and analysed data are anonymised before they are opened up on an open access basis.

Data protection law should not apply to anonymous information. This would mean that anonymised data could be made openly available without consent of data subjects because data protection law is not applicable. Anonymised information is information which does not relate to an identified or identifiable natural person[585]. Provided that the data subject is not or no longer identifiable, data are anonymised.

Data are deemed anonymous when the attribution to an identifiable person is possible but disproportionate (relative anonymity). In this respect the question is not whether data are anonymous but whether they are anonymous enough[586]. Anonymisation can be understood as removing information necessary to identify the data subject without having to invest excessive costs, time or activities. But in fact, effective anonymisation is not a simple task. It has to be made impossible to establish any connection between personal data and the natural person to whom they relate. The removal of directly identifying characteristics, such as the name, does not always offer a sufficient guarantee that the data are not personal data.

---

580 See Art. 6 GDPR; Art. 7 Data Protection Directive; Art. 8(2) EU Charter.

581 See Art. 6(1)(e) Data Protection Directive); Art. 5(1)(e) GDPR.

582 See Art. 6(1)(b) Data Protection Directive; Art. 5(1)(b) GDPR.

583 See Art. 4(11) GDPR; Art. 2(h) Data Protection Directive.

584 See above Section 1.5.3.5.

585 Recital 26 GDPR.

586 Dingledine, *The Free Haven Project*, 2012, text available at: http://www.freehaven.net/doc/freehaven.pdf, p. 13.

Anonymisation requires that the data subject is not identifiable at all, either by the controller or any third party. Especially in the context of sharing data under free licences on an open access basis, the likelihood that any other person will have the means and will use those means to re-identify the data subjects increases very significantly[587].

In every case, it must be evaluated very carefully whether effective anonymisation of personal data in such an open access environment is possible at all.

In example 4 the personal data are anonymised in such a way that direct identifiers, for example names and social security numbers, are removed. But descriptive information such as postcode and age of the test persons remains. Based on this information, creditworthiness is assigned to different Member State areas and age groups. To guarantee anonymity, in each area there are at least 10 persons assigned to each age group.

Based on this already relatively detailed information it is not possible to determine whether the data are effectively anonymised. There are too many variables, for example the size of the areas, the detailed age groups etc. The general rule is the smaller the group, the higher the risk.

In example 4, at least 10 persons are assigned to each age group. This number does not seem very high. It can at least not be ruled out that any third person is able to re-identify single data subjects, for example by re-assigning direct identifiers to other data sets, possibly from other sources as well.

From a legal point of view it is hardly possible to determine whether such anonymisation as described in example 4 is sufficient or not. It depends, for example, on what data are freely available in public registers, what information is held by other institutions, how those data can be combined and at what cost etc. As data that is shared on an open access basis is freely available, potentially for ever, it is necessary to consider what the situation will be in the future. This is no easy task, but absolutely necessary to guarantee effective anonymisation.

1.5.4.5 Conclusion for repository use of personal data

As it turns out, the use of datasets in a research data repository has to be regarded as an individual project. Where personal data are concerned, any operation or set of operations which is performed on the data has to comply with data protection rules. For example the collection, analysis, uploading to a research data repository, making available to individuals or the general public and even the anonymisation of personal data are acts of processing and subject to the data protection rules.

---

587 Article 29 Data Protection Working Party, *Opinion 6/2013 on open data and public sector information ('PSI') reuse*, p. 13.

whether personal data are involved must be evaluated on a case-by-case basis. If a researcher uses a research data repository to perform their tasks on the data, they act as a controller and are primarily responsible for data protection compliance. As long as the repository processes the personal data merely on behalf of the controller and does not have any power of disposition concerning the data, the repository acts as a processor and is not responsible for compliance with data protection rules. However, if the data are retrieved and consulted by other persons, such as colleagues, publishers or reviewers, those persons may become controllers too.

The legitimate basis for the processing of personal data for research purposes is consent of the data subject. The upcoming GDPR even takes account of the specific situation of scientific research and research projects and gives the opportunity to consent to the use of personal data at least to certain areas of research or parts of research projects[588]. However, it must be kept in mind that the purposes of processing have to be specified to some extent as it is not possible for data subjects to consent to open access uses of their personal data, which would mean consenting to further as yet unknown uses of their personal data by unknown third parties.

It may be possible, at least in some circumstances, to legitimise the data collection with Art. 6(1)(f) GDPR, which allows data processing without consent if processing is necessary for the purposes of the legitimate interests pursued by the controller or by a third party, except where such interests are overridden by the interests or fundamental rights and freedoms of the data subject. But such legitimisation is the exception rather than the rule and needs to be carefully determined in the individual case[589]. In any case Art. 6(1)(f) GDPR is not applicable to processing by public authorities (Recital 47 GDPR).

The scientific research exceptions provided for in the law cannot legitimise the initial processing of the personal data since such an exception can only legitimise a longer storage period[590] or a further processing[591] for another scientific purpose. The act of data collection does not fall under the exceptions.

However, Art. 5(1)(b) GDPR provides that further processing of personal data for archiving purposes in the public interest, or scientific and historical research purposes or statistical purposes shall, in accordance with Art. 89(1) GDPR, not be considered incompatible with the initial purposes. This means that subsequent processing operations for scientific research purposes will be considered as compatible with the initial purpose of data collection and thus be legitimised.

---

[588] See Recital 33 GDPR.

[589] See above Section 1.4.4.4.

[590] See Art. 6(1)(e) Data Protection Directive); Art. 5(1)(e) GDPR.

[591] See Art. 6(1)(b) Data Protection Directive; Art. 5(1)(b) GDPR.

But this exception to the general rule of purpose limitation for scientific or historical research purposes is somewhat limited. The processing of personal data for scientific or historical research purposes should be subject to appropriate safeguards of the rights and freedoms of the data subject; those safeguards should ensure that technical and organisational measures are in place in order to ensure, in particular, the principle of data minimisation[592]. Personal data have to be anonymised or at least pseudonymised if the purpose of research can be fulfilled in that manner[593]. This means that anonymisation of personal research data is the standard set by law.

In any case anonymisation is the best way to avoid data protection risks also in the field of data processing for research purposes. Data protection law should not apply to anonymous information. This means that if data are anonymised, they can be processed without any legitimising basis such as consent. Anonymised information is information which does not relate to an identified or identifiable natural person[594]. Whether the data in question are effectively anonymised needs to be evaluated in the individual cases.

---

592 Recital 156 GDPR.

593 See above Section 1.4.4.4.

594 Recital 26 GDPR.

2 Public sector information and university libraries

In Part two of the study the legal barriers to data sharing in the context of the Open Research Data Pilot as regards public sector information (PSI) are analysed. The aim is to provide a better understanding of the extent to which OpenAIRE, and the projects taking part in the Open Research Data Pilot, fall under the obligations imposed on public sector bodies with regard to the access and re-use of information, and what the exact consequences of those obligations are.

2.1 Introduction

This research targets the relationship and impact of the Public Sector Information Directive (PSI Directive)[595] on public libraries, including university and research libraries. The aim is to analyse: (i) whether, and if so how, the PSI Directive applies to public libraries and, as a result, (ii) what it means in practice for these public libraries, with a focus on research libraries. In other words, how are the documents held by libraries affected, in terms of accessibility and further re-use, by the principles set forth in the PSI Directive and to what extent does it require implementation on the part of the libraries?

The PSI Directive, as opposed to freedom of information legislation, addresses the transparency requirements of PSI, not so much as an end in itself, but rather as a means to stimulate economic activity by the private sector on the back of this PSI. As such, the PSI Directive aims to facilitate and encourage the re-use of PSI in the EU by harmonising the basic conditions for re-use. The task involves establishing a series of guiding principles regarding both substantive (e.g. type of institution, type of document subject to re-use) and formal (e.g. recommended type of licence, price and format) aspects of the information. Libraries were only included in the scope of the revised directive in 2013, together with other cultural establishments such as museums and archives.

In line with the subject matter covered by the PSI Directive, which is aimed at the public sector, the present part of the study focuses on those libraries that are also public libraries, for example libraries that are incorporated and funded, in part or in full, by the public sector, as defined by domestic legislation, and which, as a result, undertake a public task in order to fulfil a public interest. National libraries, city libraries, institutional libraries, museum libraries and university libraries are all public libraries and pillars of our information society. The main distinguishing trait among them is their mission and intended users. Bearing in mind the academic

---

595 Directive 2003/98/EC of the European Parliament and of the Council of 17 November 2003 on the re-use of public sector information and Directive 2013/37/EU of the European Parliament and of the Council of 26 June 2013 amending Directive 2003/98/EC on the re-use of public sector information.

and research nature of the partners taking part in the Open Research Data Pilot, the analysis is built around university, academic or research libraries[596]. These are libraries servicing students, professors, researchers and the academic community at large.

Research libraries as a whole are not the actual object of the PSI Directive. The object is not the institution itself but the collections they hold. To be able to implement PSI legislation we need to address and exemplify the actual documents that the law refers to when it asks libraries to open up resources and facilitate re-use. Some of them will be included in the scope of the law but others will not.

In this respect, it is undeniable that, at least intuitively, the type of document that has traditionally been covered by the PSI Directive is of a different type from that held, using the terminology of the directive, by cultural institutions. Nonetheless, it is also clear that the concept of PSI, as defined by the law, is broad and, as Drexl explains, "… brings many different kinds of information within the scope of the PSI Directive, including judicial decisions, geographical or commercial data held by public registers, meteorological data, but also the contents of archives and public libraries as well as objects of art in public museums"[597].

As will be analysed in the following pages, reports commissioned by the European Commission also evidence this much. Indeed, cultural institutions are largely regarded as curators and custodians of works generally produced by third parties, often individuals. That is, whereas traditional PSI is information produced by the public sector in the execution of its public task, the rationale for re-using works that have not been produced by the public sector and that were private at some point, appears to conflict with the public-to-private principle of the PSI Directive. Though generally at the core of their very existence, it would almost seem as if cultural institutions did not already have a public task to make these works accessible to the public at large. In some circumstances, one-sided interpretations of the PSI Directive could risk such capricious conclusions. There are, nevertheless, solid arguments for the inclusion of cultural establishments in the law. Whether in practice this inclusion amounts to a significant change in the way libraries conduct their activity is a different matter, which should be tackled separately.

Further, the analysis of the impact of the PSI Directive on the documents and works held by research libraries, in particular, requires twofold consideration. The first aspect is common to libraries as a whole and is the changing role of public

[596] In the present study we will use the terms university, academic and research to refer to a specific type of library interchangeably.

[597] Drexl, 'The Competition Dimension of the European Regulation of Public Sector Information and the Concept of an Undertaking', in Drexl/Bagnoli, *State-Initiated Restraints of Competition*, Cheltenham, Edward Elgar Publishing, 2015, pp. 70 et seq.

libraries[598]. PSI legislation is largely the result of digitisation[599] and availability and re-use in a digitised environment require not only plain accessibility, but also investments in providing user-friendly search capabilities and linked (meta)data, that is data one can work with. These requirements for increasingly sophisticated information management tools and databases are increasingly taking up resources in libraries. Does this investment, forcing public libraries to become more innovative in their services, lead to the creation (and ownership) of more works in-house? If so, is the PSI Directive legislator targeting these in-house works in the scope of the law? It should be borne in mind that the PSI Directive refers not to public information as a whole, but specifically to that public information which falls under the public task of the public sector body. Thus, the role of (research) libraries today, and where the public interest lies, needs to be addressed and defined if one wants to properly target and make sense of the PSI Directive[600].

A second consideration is the particular role of research libraries as an intrinsic part of university dynamics, as custodians of university works but also as information managers for the universities themselves. As compared to other public libraries, research libraries, as a result of their mission and the type of user, hold a relatively large number of their own documents, produced by university students, professors or researchers[601]. However, the legal relationship between universities and their (research) libraries should also be taken into account, given that the PSI Directive differentiates both very clearly, and universities are expressly excluded from the scope of the law.

In any case, both of the considerations mentioned above make the interpretation of the inclusion of (research) libraries in the scope of the PSI Directive particularly problematic. Further, they also have implications with regard to IPR legislation, which the PSI Directive sets out to leave unaffected, but which is at the core of the activity of libraries and cultural establishments in general.

---

598 It is therefore not only the data as a by-product (of knowledge) but also the data itself as an end, as a source of knowledge. Much has been written about the role of libraries over previous centuries. In the last couple of decades the discussion has focused on the role of libraries in the age of the Internet and to what extent the functions of both remain complementary. Another debate is the prioritisation and the (need for) rationalisation of public funding. In that context it would be interesting to analyse the public interest role of libraries today, and whether it is evolving or remains unchanged (e.g. whether information management has replaced information accessibility).

599 Together with related movements such as Open Access. Though the role of Open Access is not that of PSI legislation, both share the principle of accessibility of publicly funded information.

600 It should be noted that the importance of this increases in a time when the divide between the public and the private sectors is not always clear and business/legal constructs such as outsourcing are increasingly used.

601 Stemming from this characteristic is the debate revolving around access to information (e.g. open access publishing), very relevant in academia, where the producers of knowledge are also the consumers.

To address the aforementioned issues the PSI part of the study is structured in four sections. The analysis begins with an overview of the PSI Directive, as well as the rationale for the inclusion of libraries in its scope after the 2013 revision. Establishing this rationale should help to assess the envisaged, or desired, impact of the law on (research) libraries. Secondly, the study will focus on the terminology used by the legislator in order to see what type of libraries and documents should be included. The intention of the legislator in this respect is key, given the often vague terminology used and the lack of exemplification, in part due to the original focus of the law on traditional administrative PSI as opposed to cultural works, but also as a result of the legislator's decision to minimise intervention.

Once the rationale and the terminology used by the law have been discussed, the ways in which selected EU Member States have interpreted and applied PSI legislation will be outlined. In spite of the July 2015 deadline for domestic implementation, public libraries are still addressing the practical impact of the law in their legal and operational frameworks and considering whether this involves changes to their activity or not. Throughout the analysis national public libraries have been included in order to both understand the domestic interpretation of certain legal criteria and serve as a benchmark against which research libraries can be compared[602].

Ultimately, the study of the rationale for and impact of the inclusion of public (research) libraries under the PSI Directive should allow us to present a series of conclusions and recommendations for research libraries on how they should facilitate re-use on the basis of PSI legislation in an increasingly digitised world, taking into account their unique position as cultural institutions in the context of academia.

2.2 The legislative background

2.2.1 The 2003 PSI Directive

The original PSI Directive was adopted in November 2003 (2003 PSI Directive). It aimed to facilitate the re-use of PSI in the EU by harmonising the basic conditions for re-use and removing the perceived major barriers (legal, commercial, financial or otherwise).

The guiding principle of the 2003 PSI Directive goes somewhat further than freedom of information or open government principles, or at least takes a slightly different turn. The directive is concerned not so much with transparency itself as with commercial activity as a result of this transparency. The main rationale

602 At this stage we have decided to exclude public city libraries due to the lack of sufficient information collected and the relatively lesser relevance to the stakeholders of this study.

behind the legislation on the re-use of PSI is, therefore, an economic one, strengthened by an aim to harmonise the way public data are made re-usable, so that they can be easily accessed, combined and linked.

As with so many other aspects, digitisation and the Internet have changed the public's perception of the worth and usefulness of the information produced and collected by the public administration and public bodies in general. Digitisation not only simplifies access to information by the individual citizen, allowing for multiple and simultaneous access, but it also allows for the creation of value-added commercial propositions by the private sector through the processing of this public information. At the core of this penchant for wide accessibility is the idea that "the public has a right to information which has been gathered on behalf of the public authorities using tax revenue"[603] and, once this information has been digitised, we could argue that there is little justification to prevent re-use of that information to serve other purposes.

The 2003 PSI Directive provides a series of rules and principles on how public bodies should release information to third parties for re-use (e.g. open formats, licensing terms, financial conditions), with the aim of establishing a minimum set of harmonised conditions among the Member States. The principles are, arguably, largely procedural, leaving the Member States the far more relevant issue of deciding if, and when, certain documents should be allowed to be re-used.

Re-use is defined as the use of documents, held by public sector bodies, with either commercial or non-commercial aims, different to the original purpose for which they were produced in the context of the public task. In addition to a certain level of harmonisation, this framework of fair and non-discriminatory access to PSI in the exercise of the public task was meant to set the basis for a level playing field that would stimulate innovation as well as competition among commercial players. Nonetheless, the original 2003 PSI Directive did not actually require the release of any documents to the public. The directive only applied to those documents that already qualified as capable of being accessed by the public under domestic legislation.

---

[603] See Report of 7 December 2012 on the Proposal of the European Parliament and of the Council amending Directive 2003/98/EC on re-use of public sector information (COM (2011) 0877 – C7-0502/2011 – 2011/0430(COD)); Committee on Industry, Research and Energy (Rapporteur: Ivailo Kalfin). Of course, a different matter, is whether this argument suffers from an over-simplification, given that tax-funded services do not necessarily (have to) lead to free availability (in either price or accessibility).

Additionally, the original 2003 PSI Directive excluded cultural, educational and research institutions. The reason for this was not so much the conviction that cultural documentation should not be released for re-use but rather that it was not appropriate to have it under the general rule of the PSI regulation. Different reasons were provided to justify the need for special treatment[604].

2.2.2 The review of the directive

The Digital Agenda for Europe, a growth pillar of the Europe 2020 strategy, is an ambitious set of initiatives that revolve around the creation of a Digital Single Market and which are led by the EU Commission's Directorate-General for Communications Networks, Content and Technology (DG CONNECT).

As the Commission explains, "a connected digital single market requires Europe to overcome barriers related to infrastructure, broadband accessibility, copyright and data protection, by enhancing the use of online services and digital technologies"[605]. Among the various instruments to achieve this, the PSI legislation features prominently, if only because it plays a key role in bridging the (commercial) gap between the public and private sectors.

Actually, the need to revise the PSI Directive had been in the minds of the Commission for quite some time and appeared relatively evident as early as in 2009 when the Commission first looked into reviewing the PSI Directive. Unfortunately, it also considered at the time that, although progress had been made under the 2003 PSI Directive and the market had experienced certain growth, as evidenced by the stakeholders consulted at the time, the barriers that remained were still too high to call the directive a success. Thus, in spite of the interest and growth experienced by some sectors (e.g. geographical, meteorological, administrative), most policymakers agreed that the impact of the 2003 PSI Directive on the actual policies and practices undertaken by the Member States had been relatively minor[606]. In other words, there appeared to be a disconnect, a certain lack of "bite", between law and practice, which dampened the envisaged impact of the legislative instrument on the growth of certain industries. Factors such as public sector bodies' own financial interests, their increasing competition with the private

---

604 A good overview is provided in Bogataj/Jancic/Pusser et al., *The Proposed Inclusion of Cultural and Research Institutions in the Scope of PSI Directive* (LAPSI Policy Recommendation n. 5), Brussels, European Commission, 2012, pp. 6 et seqq.

605 As per the Commission's own description of what the strategy is concerning the creation of the digital single market. The text is available at: https://ec.europa.eu/digital-single-market/en/the-strategy-dsm.

606 See, for example, Janssen, 'Open Data as the Standard for Europe? A Critical Analysis of the European Commission's Proposal to Amend the PSI Directive', European Journal of Law and Technology 2013.

sector and several practical issues[607] meant that further growth and harmonisation remained an uphill battle. As a result, the Commission entrusted the Member States with the task of addressing issues regarding the "full and correct implementation and application of the directive". In its Communication, the Commission postponed any actual reform to 2012, "when more evidence on the impact, effects and application of the directive should be available" said that it would "consider legislative amendments at that stage, taking into consideration the progress made in the meantime in the Member States".

In late 2011 the Commission released its Open Data Strategy, under which the review of the 2003 PSI Directive was a key component in the Digital Agenda for Europe[608]. Around the same time, in December 2011, as a result of extensive public consultation and external reports, the Commission also presented a proposal to amend the directive[609]. Its Questions & Answers describes the revision of the 2003 PSI Directive, already contemplated by its own Art. 13, as one of three pillars on which the Open Data Package is based[610]. Evidence of success stories (mainly in the geo-information sector) and the optimistic forecasts of some studies are provided to back up the proposal. Further, as Drexl notes[611], it is important to bear in mind the growth the open data movement had achieved by that time, and which strengthened the arguments in favour of a revision. Also, the fact that the Commission included digitised books from libraries as an example of open public data gave a good idea of the importance attached by the Commission to re-assessing and extending the scope of the directive.

---

607 See Communication from the Commission - Re-use of Public Sector Information: review of Directive 2003/98/EC – [SEC(2009) 597], COM/2009/0212 final, p. 10: "Big barriers still exist. These include attempts by public sector bodies to maximise cost recovery, as opposed to benefits for the wider economy, competition between the public and the private sector, practical issues hindering re-use, such as the lack of information on available PSI, and the mindset of public sector bodies failing to realise the economic potential."

608 See the official press release by the European Commission, 'Digital Agenda: Turning Government Data into Gold'. In essence, the European Commission devised a strategy expected to deliver a €40 billion boost to the EU's economy each year, text available at: http://europa.eu/rapid/press-release_IP-11-1524_en.htm?locale=en.

609 See the proposal for a directive amending the 2003 PSI Directive and SEC (2001) 1552, Executive Summary of the Impact Assessment.

610 Memo 11/891 of 12 December 2011 (IP/11/1524), Digital Agenda: Commission's Open Data Strategy, Questions & Answers. The other two include the Commission's decision on the re-use of the Commission's own information, and the Commission's Communication entitled 'Open Data – An Engine for Innovation, Growth and Transparent Governance'.

611 Drexl, 'The Competition Dimension of the European Regulation of Public Sector Information and the Concept of an Undertaking', in Drexl/Bagnoli, *State-Initiated Restraints of Competition*, Cheltenham, Edward Elgar Publishing, 2015, p. 65 has pointed out how "… by the time of its revision in 2013, the directive had also become an important element of the EU's open data policies that are designed to make publicly held data widely available to the public".

Indeed, looking back at the proposal's Explanatory Memorandum, the Commission declares that "the regulatory challenge is to provide the market with an optimal legal framework to stimulate the digital content market for PSI-based products and services, including its cross-border dimension, and to prevent distortions of competition on the Union market for the re-use of PSI". Similarly, the directive in its Recitals 6–8 also notes the considerable differences among Member States that the exploitation of PSI has developed in very disparate ways and how minimum harmonisation should be undertaken in such a way that it provides a general framework for the conditions governing re-use of public sector documents in order to ensure fair, proportionate and non-discriminatory conditions for the re-use of such information.

The impact assessment, which supplemented the draft proposal for a new directive, also highlighted the main obstacles that (had) stood in the way of full implementation of the PSI principle: (i) the lack of information on the available data and licensing conditions, (ii) the uncertain data covered in the scope of re-use and (iii) the lengthy and complex processes to gain permission for re-use[612]. Similarly, the Commission also spoke of locked resources such as data, "in particular cultural public domain material, is subject to re-use, albeit under unregulated conditions so the rationale for the exemptions has to be subjected to a new cost/benefit analysis".

As a result, the Commission decided to impose binding rules, "to create a true European information market based on PSI ...". In addition, the Commission acknowledged the good timing of the revision, given "the growth of the open data movement since 2009 provided an opportunity for the Commission to strengthen its PSI policy by linking it to this much more fashionable and popular concept"[613]. Noticeably, the proposal made ample use of open data and open access terminology in justifying the economic rationale and the strengthening measures of the revised directive. Subsequently, the Commission's proposal introduced a general right of re-use of PSI and adopted marginal-cost pricing as the default charging policy. Finally, the Commission proposed to extend the scope of application to cultural institutions.

In the course of 2012 the Commission's proposal, along with the aforementioned issues, were discussed in the Council and the European Parliament. Amendments were proposed by the different Committees and some interesting observations were made, generally aimed at providing more specific and detailed legislation. Some parties emphasised the need to harmonise metadata, others focused on the legislative interplay with copyright or data protection.

---

612 See Explanatory Memorandum, Section 1.1 of the Commission's proposal on insufficient clarity and transparency.

613 Janssen, 'Open Data as the Standard for Europe? A Critical Analysis of the European Commission's Proposal to Amend the PSI Directive', European Journal of Law and Technology 2013.

Despite the many comments and amendments that were made to the original Commission proposal, the final directive still leaves unaddressed some important issues. After a lengthy process in the Parliament, the final text was the result of a trialogue procedure between the institutions. In April 2013 the European Commission announced the agreement of the EU Committee of Member States' Permanent Representatives (COREPER) with the revisions of the directive, and the final text was drafted. The text was approved by a vote of the European Parliament's Committee on Industry, Research and Energy followed by the plenary vote in the Parliament in June 2013, which led to the adoption of the revised Directive 2013/37/EU (2013 PSI Directive). Domestic implementation was to be completed by 18 July 2015, at the latest.

The revised directive is very much the result of the different Member States pushing for a flexible and open instrument that would still allow them, and the public bodies, to adopt their own strategy. Thus, amendments made during the parliamentary process, generally seeking clarification, were deleted from the final text to allow for this flexibility. However, the core proposal of the Commission remained, and the new instrument "tightens" the general principle of re-use and sets out a uniform procedure for dealing with requests for re-use. In fact, as regards accessibility of PSI, the law creates a default mechanism whereby once data are public, or not restricted, under the legislation of the Member States, they are considered to be open to the public at large for all purposes. The guiding principle, a general right of re-use, is described in Art. 3(1), which provides that "Member States shall ensure that documents to which this directive applies … shall be re-usable for commercial and non-commercial purposes". But the article does not create an overriding principle, and substantive matters, especially those applicable to cultural establishments, remain to a large extent the responsibility of the Member States. Further, the new directive adopts the Commission's proposal and addresses the subject of pricing by restricting trigger-happy approaches to charging by public sector bodies. The amended Art. 6 establishes the benchmark of the "marginal cost" and Art. 11 prohibits exclusive agreements whereby re-use by one party is allowed under exclusive rights.

Looking at the impact on cultural establishments specifically, there are some issues that limit the impact of the revised directive. The first is that there is a specific exemption to these conditions which permits libraries (including university libraries), archives and museums to apply charges over and above the marginal costs for the re-use of their information. Exclusive agreements, are allowed up to ten years for cultural establishments. Secondly, there is the issue of pricing. Unfortunately for policymakers, efforts to quantify the economic benefits of PSI and its re-use have not always been successful, given the lack of homogeneous parameters and metrics used in the different studies. In addition, the European Data Protection Supervisor (EDPS) has suggested that the law should also consider allowing costs of pre-processing (such as digitalisation), anonymisation and aggregation to be charged to licence-holders where appropriate. As a result, the directive avoids legislating on financial detail, which means that references in the law to pricing and charging (e.g. return on investment (ROI)) remain largely vague.

Financial considerations are not the only vague concepts in the directive. The definition of "document", "public sector information", "public task" and "public body" also remain broadly sketched and the directive still grants a large degree of autonomy to the Member States. Unfortunately, this could set back the creation of a harmonised internal market of PSI. The Commission, following the suggestion made by stakeholders during the approval phase, did publish a set of guidelines in 2014, thus targeting a harmonised market[614]. The effect of these guidelines, if any, will become evident over the coming years.

A final source of diverging interpretations among the Member States is the legislative instrument itself and how the Member States construe its implications. As Janssen explains, this fact had already been observed during the approval process[615]. Some believe it to be a mere extension under freedom of information legislation and government transparency rather than an economic instrument. This not only has formal implications (e.g. amending freedom of information legislation and having a separate instrument), but also substantive ones, leading to some Member States not prioritising the economic rationale of the law.

2.2.3 The revised scope of the 2013 PSI Directive

As was mentioned in the previous section, the revised directive tackled the scope of the subject matter. As part of the obligation to regularly review the suitability and effectiveness of the directive under the old Art. 13, the Commission was also

---

[614] European Commission, Commission Notice – Guidelines on recommended standard licenses, datasets and charging for the reuse of documents of 24 July 2014, 2014/C 240/01; text available at: https://ec.europa.eu/digital-agenda/en/news/commission-notice-guidelines-recommended-standard-licences-datasets-and-charging-re-use.

[615] Janssen, 'The Influence of the PSI Directive on Open Government Data: An Overview of Recent Developments', Government Information Quarterly 2011, 446: "... For some types of re-use, particularly commercial re-use, the difference with access to information is easy to see, for example for information products and services such as dedicated weather services, satellite navigation systems, or credit ratings. However, the broad definition of re-use that was discussed earlier, i.e. any use for commercial or non-commercial purposes outside of the public task, also includes many other forms of use, including re-use by citizens creating user generated content based on public sector data, for example on blogs, online communities or forums. This type of re-use is much more difficult to distinguish from access to government information than true commercial use" and "This difficulty in distinguishing between access or freedom of information on the one hand and reuse of PSI on the other hand already came up during the preparatory process of the PSI Directive".

responsible for reviewing the subject matter and, specifically, for considering "whether cultural, educational and research organisations and public broadcasters, which are currently excluded from the scope, should be covered"[616].

The Commission had already settled upon the matter back in 2011, when it included several cultural establishments in the revised scope of its proposal to the Parliament. The scope remained unchanged in the course of the legislative process and hence, in 2013, the revised directive brought libraries (including university libraries), museums and archives within its subject matter and scope (Art. 1). Recital 14 already anticipates that much: "the scope of Directive 2003/98/EC should be extended to libraries, including university libraries, museums and archives". Cultural sector public bodies are therefore expected, in principle, to make information available to other users for re-use. Specifically, Art. 3.2 of the 2013 PSI Directive notes that "for documents for which libraries (including university libraries), museums and archives have *intellectual property rights*, Member States shall ensure that, where the re-use of such documents is allowed, these documents shall be re-usable for commercial or non-commercial purposes in accordance with the conditions set out in Chapters III and Chapter IV". That is, under this article, the information should be made available in the context of the institution's public task and as long as it has previously already been made available for re-use.

However, not all cultural establishments are included. Information held by institutions such as orchestras, operas, ballets and theatres has not been included in the scope of the amended directive. Recital 18 attempts to explain the reason for including some cultural establishments while leaving others out. It explains that:

> *... other types of cultural establishments (such as orchestras, operas, ballets and theatres), including the archives that are part of those establishments, should remain outside the scope because of their performing arts specificity. Since almost all of their material is covered by third party intellectual property rights and would therefore remain outside the scope of that directive, including them within the scope would have little effect.*

Also excluded are public broadcasting organisations, probably the outcome of their hybrid nature, significant third-party intellectual property and successful campaigning.

Unfortunately, the directive does not explain how, to what extent and for what reason other educational, research and cultural institutions remain exempted from the application of the PSI Directive. Consequently, it will become difficult in some circumstances to separate university libraries from the universities themselves for the purpose of the directive.

---

616 See Communication from the Commission - Re-use of Public Sector Information: review of Directive 2003/98/EC – [SEC(2009) 597], COM/2009/0212 final, p. 6.

2.2.4 Rationale for extension of the subject matter to libraries

In principle, the rationale for the inclusion of certain cultural establishments in the scope of the 2013 PSI Directive does not vary much from the original PSI re-use principle: the documents held by these cultural establishments are considered to be sources of potential socio-economic added value[617]. It therefore follows that (i) re-use should be encouraged, and (ii) the principles and processes under which PSI is accessed are as harmonised as possible across the EU, contributing, in turn, to the realisation of the Digital Single Market. That is, the same criteria apply to the extension of the scope as to the revision of the directive in general.

Art. 3(2) of the 2013 PSI Directive explains that the general principle allowing re-use does not apply to documents held by libraries, museums and archives, which remain subject to the prior 2003 principle whereby Member States decide where re-use should be allowed. The inclusion of these cultural establishments represents a carefully drafted compromise, especially as concerns the university library, arguably the institution that stands out the most from the rest[618]. In addition to the peculiarities of university libraries, it is fair to say that, in general, evidence presented by the different commissioned studies on cultural establishments was not able to offer unequivocal conclusions regarding the potential extension in the scope of the directive. In addition, the documents held by cultural establishments have unique characteristics when compared to traditional PSI, as was pointed out by the socio-economic studies conducted in 2009, when the Commission first attempted to identify potential amendments to the 2003 PSI Directive. The 2009 Rightscom Report, *Economic and Social Impact of the Public Domain: Cultural Institutions and the PSI Directive* had concluded that "whilst there is little doubt that PSI held by the cultural sector has a significant potential value for re-uses, the advantages of including cultural heritage institutions within the scope of the directive are currently difficult to assess and require further investigation over time"[619]. Though PSI re-use did appear to be on the increase at the time, feedback was quite divided on the question of the inclusion of cultural institutions.

---

617 Keller/Margoni/Rybicka/Tarkowski, 'Re-use of Public Sector Information in Cultural Heritage Institutions', International Free and Open Source Software Law Review 2014, 1 (2).

618 This is an aspect confirmed by parties participating in the negotiation phase at the time. Further, to give an idea on the difficult balance, the Committee of the Regions when consulted in 2012 on the draft proposal for a revised directive, pointed out, in Recital 18 of its document, that inclusion of cultural establishments should "minimise the possible financial effects and not impose a major administrative burden and significant additional expenditure on such bodies; underlines that, while cultural institutions should not be forced into digitalisation, the proposed method of setting charges over and above the marginal costs, should not undermine digitalisation and long-term archiving efforts of the aforementioned bodies due to high digitalisation and data storage costs and more limited money-earning options".

619 Davies et al., *Economic and Social Impact of the Public Domain: Cultural Institutions and the PSI Directive*, London, Rightscom, 2009, p. 5.

Cultural institutions were, and probably still are, perceived as a hybrid sector where the level of available PSI is modest and difficult to justify as a sort of by-product easily re-used by a third party. Similarly, PSI held by cultural establishments (public sector content) has typically been distinguished from information generated in a dynamic and ongoing manner by the public sector (e.g., meteorological data, geo-spatial data, business statistics). Rather, it is perceived to have little connection with the day-to-day job of the public sector, it is not produced by the public sector and is therefore static (i.e. an established record), held by the public sector rather than being generated by it (e.g. cultural archives, artistic works where third-party rights may be important)[620]. Similarly, in the report *Digital Broadband Content: Public Sector Information and Content*, produced by the OECD in early 2006[621], cultural establishments are generally considered to be curators of third-party content. Furthermore, other barriers needed to be taken into account. Financial concerns, especially in light of the expensive digitisation projects, called for caution in any legislative measure that could lead to a loss of income. All in all, the decision to include cultural institutions in the scope of the revised directive also required the inclusion of several caveats[622].

In terms of business dynamics it is difficult to find a unifying thread. A study carried out to inform the Commission's second attempt at a justified revision of the directive in early 2011[623] found, that "very few institutions are dependent on the income they receive from re-use in order to undertake their public task. However, the income that they receive from re-use is in many cases essential to enable future re-use and development of re-use services". In the analysis conducted, the range of income generated from re-use varied between 0% and 3.2% of total gross income[624]. What became apparent was the vast differences among cultural institutions themselves, including the materials they held, the regulatory framework and the cultural environment. For example, as the report explains, "two national libraries charge for re-use of their bibliographic metadata, whereas another two do not" (and in fact, needed to be prompted to consider

---

620 Vickery, *Review of Recent Studies on PSI Re-use and Related Market Developments*, Paris, Information Economics, 2011.

621 OECD Working Party on the Information Economy, *Digital Broadband Content: Public Sector Information and Content*, DSTI/ICCP/IE(2005)2/FINAL, Paris, OECD, 2006, p. 16.

622 During the review phase, the Commission noted concerns about the inclusion. Some Member States considered "that at this stage the scope should not be widened, since the administrative burden and associated costs would not be outweighed by the potential benefits. They point out that a large part of the material held by these institutions is also covered by third party intellectual property rights, and would therefore not in any case fall within the scope of the directive"; Communication from the Commission - Re-use of Public Sector Information: review of Directive 2003/98/EC – [SEC(2009) 597], COM/2009/0212 final, pp. 6 et seq.

623 Clapton/Hammond/Poole, *PSI Re-use in the Cultural Sector: Final Report*, CC462D011-1.1, Surrey, Curtis+Cartwright Consulting Ltd, May 2011, text available at: http://www.umic.pt/images/stories/publicacoes6/cc462d011_1_1final_report.pdf, p. 19.

624 Ibid., p. 2.

sharing their metadata as re-use – both viewed sharing their metadata as an obvious activity). As one put it, "There are not so many requests for use of our metadata, but we do contribute [it] for example to Europeana – free of charge, of course)"[625]. In other words, the report "found very limited evidence of the active re-use of public sector information provided by museums, archives and libraries"[626]. According to the study, where cultural institutions reported revenues on the commercial licensing of re-use, the returns appeared to be marginal. Further, in a significant number of cases, the cultural institutions did not account for the full economic cost of production, distribution and preservation in the calculated return on licensing activity.

Indeed, the extension of the scope of application rested on the significant amount of digital public domain content that can be exploited by commercial added-value services[627]. The amended directive notes in its Recital 19 that:

> *digitisation is an important means of ensuring greater access to and re-use of cultural material for education, work or leisure. It also offers considerable economic opportunities, allowing for an easier integration of cultural material into digital services and products, thus supporting job creation and growth. These aspects were underlined in, amongst others, the European Parliament's resolution of 5 May 2010 on "Europeana – the next steps"....*

Further, the directive notes in its Recital 18 that:

> *the extension of the scope of Directive 2003/98/EC should be limited to three types of cultural establishments – libraries, including university libraries, museums and archives, because their collections are and will increasingly become a valuable material for re-use in many products such as mobile applications. Other types of cultural establishments (such as orchestras, operas, ballets and theatres), including the archives that are part of those establishments, should remain outside the scope because of their "performing arts" specificity. Since almost all of their material is covered by third-party intellectual property rights and would therefore remain outside the scope of that directive, including them within the scope would have little effect.*

---

625 Ibid., p. 27.

626 Poole, *Briefing Paper on the Proposed Amendments to the PSI Directive & Museums, Archives & Libraries*, Collections Trust, January 2012, available at: http://www.museumsassociation.org/download?id=661788, p. 3.

627 See Drexl, 'The Competition Dimension of the European Regulation of Public Sector Information and the Concept of an Undertaking', in Drexl/Bagnoli, *State-Initiated Restraints of Competition*, Cheltenham, Edward Elgar Publishing, 2015, p. 72.

In parallel, the ePSI Platform, a European Commission (DG CONNECT) initiative with the objective of promoting a PSI and open data re-use market across the EU, notes the significance of homogeneous metadata, to which the 2013 PSI Directive could contribute[628]. This would mean that:

> *cultural heritage institutions can connect their databases with each other, sharing knowledge and giving users access to the metadata and digitised objects from a single authoritative source; in order to ensure that this metadata can be shared broadly and easily, it needs to be shared using a common machine-readable language and free from legal, organisational or policy restriction.*

The Europeana Foundation is cited as an example since it established in 2012 "a common standard for the Cultural Heritage dataset under the Creative Commons Zero Public Domain dedication (only made possible by providing institutions with a compatible machine-readable language with Europeana Data) ...".

So, on the one hand, Recital 15 of the 2013 PSI Directive[629] states that libraries, museums and archives "hold a significant amount of valuable public sector information resources, in particular since digitisation projects have multiplied the amount of digital public domain material". On the other hand, the "re-usable by default" rule introduced by the 2013 PSI Directive[630] is not applicable to them. This means that cultural heritage institutions can choose whether or not to make documents available for re-use (unless they have already been made available). That is, the old general rule of the 2003 PSI Directive continues to apply. According to Art. 1, the directive is not applicable to:

- non-public sector bodies;
- activities outside the public task of these public sector bodies;
- documents for which third parties hold IPR;
- documents held by educational and research establishments except university libraries.

---

628 Pekel/Fallon/Kamenov, *Public Sector Information in Cultural Heritage Institutions*, Brussels, ePSIplatform, Topic Report 2014.06, 2014.

629 The full Recital 15 reads as follows: "One of the principal aims of the establishment of the internal market is the creation of conditions conducive to the development of Union-wide services. Libraries, museums and archives hold a significant amount of valuable public sector information resources, in particular since digitisation projects have multiplied the amount of digital public domain material. These cultural heritage collections and related metadata are a potential base for digital content products and services and have a huge potential for innovative re-use in sectors such as learning and tourism. Wider possibilities for re-using public cultural material should, inter alia, allow Union companies to exploit its potential and contribute to economic growth and job creation.".

630 See Keller/Margoni/Rybicka/Tarkowski, 'Re-use of Public Sector Information in Cultural Heritage Institutions', International Free and Open Source Software Law Review 2014, 1 (2), for a definition of the "re-usable by default" rule.

Further, the re-use of works held by these cultural establishments is allowed to be (i) at a price that is not capped by law[631], and (ii) under exclusive terms (for up to 10 years) with third parties, as long as it is done in the public interest or for digitising a cultural resource. Indeed, traditionally, many cultural establishments have teamed up with commercial parties to undertake some of the more costly projects, which, in turn, require some form of exclusivity to guarantee a certain return on investment. This argument is well explained in the proposed amendment 15 of the proposal for a new directive of the 2012 Committee on Industry, Research and Energy report, which had proposed to include Art. 10(b) as an explanation for the extended scope. The amendment, which disappeared in the final version together with many other explanatory texts, reads as follows:

> *(10b) As regards the description, digitisation and presentation of cultural collections, there are numerous cooperation arrangements between libraries (including university libraries), museums, archives and private partners which involve public sector bodies granting exclusive rights of access and commercial exploitation to cooperation partners. Practice has shown that such public-private partnerships can facilitate worthwhile use of cultural collections and at the same time that they accelerate access to the cultural heritage for members of the public. Directive 2003/98/EC should therefore not preclude the conclusion of agreements granting exclusive rights. Moreover, cultural institutions should be free to choose for themselves the partners with which they wish to cooperate, subject to compliance with the principles of transparency and non-discrimination.*

All in all, the careful wording used to include cultural establishments, and the narrow scope of the documents that are likely to fall in the category, essentially amount to the desire to have institutions proactively share the documents they hold, that is, a kind of best efforts, or best practices, guidance. In other words, the extension appears not so much as an imperative but rather as a first step in the creation of an EU-wide cultural works portal for re-use, on the back of commercial partnerships and following the example set by the Europeana Foundation. As such, given the number of exceptions, the financial position of these institutions is not likely to be endangered as a result of the 2013 PSI Directive.

---

631 Art. 6.1 of the PSI Directive states that "where charges are made for the re-use of documents, those charges shall be limited to the marginal costs incurred for their reproduction, provision and dissemination".

2.2.5.1 Libraries as public bodies

The PSI Directive takes the definitions of "public sector body" and "body governed by public law" from the public procurement directives[632]. Public undertakings are not covered by these definitions. A public sector body is "the State, regional or local authorities, bodies governed by public law" and a body governed by public law is one that has legal personality. Finally, a university, which should allow us in turn to define the university library, is described as "any public sector body that provides post-secondary higher education leading to academic degrees".

Directive 2004/18/EC[633], which repeals the original Directive 92/50/EEC mentioned by the PSI Directive, contains non-exhaustive lists of what are considered public law bodies under national legislation. The definition is identical to that of the repealed directive except where it refers to the Annex, which contains a list of bodies and categories of bodies. The current Procurement Directive is careful to highlight that the list is non-exhaustive[634]. It first defines a body governed by public law, Art. 1(9), as any body:

(a) *Established for the specific purpose of meeting needs in the general interest, not having an industrial or commercial character;*

(b) *Having legal personality; and*

(c) *Financed, for the most part, by the State, regional or local authorities, or other bodies governed by public law; or subject to management supervision by those bodies; or having an administrative, managerial or supervisory board, more than half of whose members are appointed by the State, regional or local authorities, or by other bodies governed by public law.*

---

632 See Council Directive 92/50/EEC of 18 June 1992 relating to the coordination of procedures for the award of public service contracts; Council Directive 93/36/EEC of 14 June 1993 coordinating procedures for the award of public supply contracts; Council Directive 93/37/EEC of 14 June 1993 concerning the coordination of procedures for the award of public works contracts 93/37/EEC and Directive 98/4/EC of the European Parliament and of the Council of 16 February 1998 amending Directive 93/38/EEC coordinating the procurement procedures of entities operating in the water, energy, transport and telecommunications sectors.

633 Directive 2004/18/EC of the European Parliament and of the Council of 31 March 2004 on the coordination of procedures for the award of public works contracts, public supply contracts and public service contracts, OJ L 134, 30.4.2004, pp. 114–240.

634 The former directive, Council Directive 92/50/EEC of 18 June 1992 relating to the coordination of procedures for the award of public service contracts, simply stated in its Art. 1(b) *in fine* that "these lists shall be as exhaustive as possible and may be reviewed in accordance with the procedure laid down in Art. 30b of that directive".

Non-exhaustive lists of bodies and categories of bodies governed by public law, which fulfil the criteria referred to in (a), (b) and (c) of the second subparagraph, are set out in Annex III. Member States shall periodically notify the Commission of any changes to their lists of bodies and categories of bodies.

Within Annex III of the 2004 Procurement Directive, one can find the list of bodies and categories of bodies governed by public law by country. Given that they are not specified by name, one can at least see that cultural establishments could be included under the loosely formulated heading of "Contracting Authorities", which refers to "the State, regional or local authorities, bodies governed by public law, associations formed by one or several of such authorities or one or several of such bodies governed by public law". The 2004 Procurement Directive also notes that "Member States shall periodically notify the Commission of any changes to their lists of bodies and categories of bodies".

In the case of university libraries, the main challenge to a distinct interpretation is that posed by requiring the public body to have legal personality. In fact, the university library is generally legally owned by the university itself. As a result, the distinction made by the PSI Directive between one (the university library) and the other (the university itself) is far from evident when it comes to examining the works they each, or both, hold, especially as the directive provides little guidance on how one should interpret this perceived dichotomy.

In the course of the approval process of the revised PSI Directive, the Committee on Industry, Research and Energy[635] drafted amendment 28 for its 2012 report. The proposed amendment represented a new paragraph in Art. 1.1.1(a) of the Commission's proposal for a directive and reads:

> *(1a) In paragraph 2, point (b) is replaced by the following:*
>
> *(b) documents in which third parties hold intellectual property rights, including documents held by a university library in which the university holds intellectual property rights.*
>
> *Justification: this amendment is intended to clarify that the directive does not apply to documents held by a library which forms part of the university which holds the intellectual property right (IPR) in the document. A university and its libraries may constitute a single legal entity. Without amendment, the exclusion of documents subject to third-party IPR would not apply where a library holds the document but the IPR is held by the university because the university would not be a separate (i.e., third) party.*

This explanatory text, along with others suggested in the consultation phase, was eliminated in the final text, thus acceding to the demands of some Member States to retain maximum flexibility to legislate and decide domestically. As a result, uncertainty remains as to whether (i) public university libraries that are legally a

[635] A7-0404/001-055, Amendments 001-055 by the Committee on Industry, Research and Energy, 6 June 2013.

part of the university are also fully fledged actors under the PSI Directive, (ii) the text is drafted in very broad terms to intentionally give the freedom to the universities and their libraries to decide, or (iii) if the directive simply went a step too far in its pursuit of loosely defined terms.

The cultural establishments included within the scope of the 2013 PSI Directive are different from each other. In particular, the inclusion of libraries, especially university libraries, is difficult to grasp: libraries rarely own the copyright in the documents or books or documentation they hold. And university libraries, as we noted earlier, are rarely separate legal entities from the educational and research centres that produce original content and are excluded from the scope of the 2013 PSI Directive. Unfortunately, the directive does not define either. The UK National Archives (NA) has provided some useful guidelines as to how the directive should be interpreted. The NA defines "university library" as a library attached to a higher education body. The NA notes that:

> *it is not merely a physical building as many are now also digital repositories. Therefore, university library refers not only to the library itself, but can also refer to the parts of a university with library collections management functions, and to the information service that controls and disseminates information from within the higher education parent body*[636].

In addition, the NA warns of how this definition might bring about overlaps with, for instance, archives or museums[637]. In these cases, the NA recommends that guidance for other cultural sector bodies is followed.

2.2.5.2 The activities of libraries as public task

The 2013 PSI Directive applies to documents whose production or availability responds to the public task of the public sector bodies concerned, as defined by relevant laws. Art. 1(2)(a) of the directive explains that it shall not apply to

> *documents the supply of which is an activity falling outside the scope of the public task of the public sector bodies concerned as defined by law or by other binding rules in the Member State, or in the absence of such rules, as defined in line with common administrative practice in the Member State in question, provided that the scope of the public tasks is transparent and subject to review.*

---

636 NA, *Guidance on the Implementation of the Re-use of Public Sector Information Regulations 2015 – for the cultural sector*, July 2015, available at: http://www.nationalarchives.gov.uk/documents/information-management/psi-implementation-guidance-cultural-sector.pdf, p. 11.

637 There will be overlaps for many university libraries with archival and museum information, for example where archives and museums are part of a library, special collections in a library hold archives, or archives and museums hold rare books.

Recital 10 of the 2013 PSI Directive recognises that:

> *in the absence of such rules, the public tasks should be defined in accordance with common administrative practice in the Member States, provided that the scope of the public tasks is transparent and subject to review. The public tasks could be defined generally or on a case-by-case basis for individual public sector bodies.*

In other words, whereas the existence of a public task by the institutions of the 2013 PSI Directive is, by definition, necessary and should be transparent and generally available, the actual description of that public task is left to the discretion of each Member State or institution, under their own laws, statutes or administrative practice. The one criterion that the directive highlights is the need to carve out public tasks from private tasks, given that re-use would not apply to works outside the public task (Art. 1(2)(a) PSI Directive: documents the supply of which is an activity falling outside the scope of the public task of the public sector bodies concerned).

As the ePSI platform explains, the concept of public task is a crucial element of the PSI Directive[638]. The description of tasks is what establishes the boundaries for PSI re-use. In the particular case of cultural establishments, the description of their public task is as important, if not more so, as that of other entities because potentially profitable activities, such as the sale of image libraries, are also likely to be problematic borderline activities. As the Rightscom report already reported in its conclusions, it is decisive that it is examined "whether image libraries or other services provided by cultural institutions fall within or outside the public task"[639]. The PSI Directive does not take sides in this respect.

Perhaps one of the most interesting lines of thought on the subject of the public task is the one that examines the extent to which the development of the public sector is, in some ways, blurring the traditional boundaries of the public and the private spheres. For example, the role of libraries today is different to what it was a couple of decades ago, if only because digitisation allows low-cost copying. In many ways, the sophistication of today's marketplace renders obsolete the traditional dichotomy of public versus private. For instance, public entities often outsource specific services that fall under the public task. These outsourced or commissioned services have their own arrangements in terms of intellectual property, exclusivity etc. Further, copyright contract rules of each Member State allow for differences in the treatment of intellectual property in these commissioned or outsourced works. Finally, tying in with the definition of public task, the traditional distinction between public and private also raises the strategic question of whether privatised entities formerly in public hands, or some public undertakings

---

638 Pekel/Fallon/Kamenov, *Public Sector Information in Cultural Heritage Institutions*, Brussels, ePSIplatform, Topic Report 2014.06, 2014, p. 14.

639 Davies et al., *Economic and Social Impact of the Public Domain: Cultural Institutions and the PSI Directive*, London, Rightscom, 2009, p. 48.

under domestic legislation, might hold PSI worth regulating by the directive. Similarly, the role of competition law has to be taken into account. Recital 29 of the 2013 PSI Directive establishes that "competition rules should be respected … avoiding as far as possible exclusive agreements between public sector bodies and private partners". However, the recital continues, "in order to provide a service in the public interest, an exclusive right to re-use specific public sector documents may sometimes be necessary. This may be, inter alia, the case if no commercial publisher would publish the information without such an exclusive right". That is, carving out the public task also requires a careful assessment of profitable business models and the financial structure of each cultural institution. All in all, these considerations would merit a separate examination but are worth noting to give an idea of the level of granularity the subject can lead to.

2.2.5.3 Intellectual Property Rights & Cultural Establishments, in particular Libraries

The PSI Directive applies to documents that are held by cultural establishments. Both terms are purposely vague. The generic reference to "document" leads to a broad concept, which includes not only traditional tangible copies. As Drexl explains,

> *while the term document seems to indicate a tangible manifestation, this is not confirmed by Art. 2(3) of the PSI Directive, which defines a document as any content whatever its medium (written on paper or stored in electronic form or as a sound, visual or audiovisual recording) and any part of such content*[640].

That is, again the legislator opts for a broad definition, which cuts across the different categories of documents and ultimately calls for the educated appraisal of the respective cultural establishments.

Furthermore, the legislator is also vague on the status of these documents as regards any applicable IPR. PSI legislation does not interfere with IPR. It does not deal with the copyright status of PSI (usually handled by national copyright laws) and it does not alter the IPR status of documents that fall under PSI legislation. The 2013 PSI Directive, through its recitals, clearly reverts to applicable legislation in IPR or to the Orphan Works Directive[641]. In other words, no causal relationship of any kind should be established between PSI policy and copyright legislation as such.

This does not mean that the 2013 PSI Directive is always unambiguous in its references to IPR. As such, the actual type of works, or documents, covered by the directive is not clear either. If we focus on the actual material held by libraries,

---

640 Drexl, 'The Competition Dimension of the European Regulation of Public Sector Information and the Concept of an Undertaking', in Drexl/Bagnoli, *State-Initiated Restraints of Competition*, Cheltenham, Edward Elgar Publishing, 2015, p. 70.

641 Directive 2012/28/EU of the European Parliament and of the Council of 25 October 2012 on certain permitted uses of orphan works (Orphan Works Directive).

we have to assume that a key reason that the legislator chose to include documents held by certain cultural establishments in the scope of the directive is because there are sufficient documents with their own IPR or with no (or expired) copyright to justify said inclusion. In fact, this is the rationale followed *a contrario* from the statement of Recital 18[642]. However, the question arises whether material the copyright protection of which has expired should automatically become accessible pursuant to the PSI Directive[643]. Moreover, what material is actually covered in the case of, in particular, university libraries? As was briefly mentioned earlier, the type of material held by cultural establishments is, to a large extent, very different from the traditional notion of PSI. For instance, the Open Public Data Memo 11/981 of the Commission, published on the occasion of the Commission's proposal of 2011, explains that open public data include not only statistical, meteorological or geographical data, but also digitised books. That is, the Commission, in the case of cultural and educational works, establishes a distinction between the physical object (e.g. a physical book held by a library, the IPR in which are probably owned by a third party) and the digital object (e.g. a digitised book). This distinction corresponds to the different nature of the information, which is not always produced, collected or held in the same way. Recital 9 of the 2013 PSI Directive states that:

> *documents on which third parties hold intellectual property rights should be excluded from the scope of Directive 2003/98/EC. If a third party was the initial owner of a document held by libraries (including university libraries), museums and archives that is still protected by intellectual property rights, that document should, for the purpose of this directive, be considered as a document for which third parties hold intellectual property rights.*

---

642 Recital 18 of the 2013 PSI Directive ends with the following statement: "... Since almost all of their material (of orchestras, operas, ballets and theatres) is covered by third party intellectual property rights and would therefore remain outside the scope of that directive including them within the scope would have little effect".

643 In a similar fashion, Bogataj/Jancic/Pusser et al., *The Proposed Inclusion of Cultural and Research Institutions in the Scope of PSI Directive* (LAPSI Policy Recommendation n. 5), Brussels, European Commission, 2012, p. 3 already warned of the potential counterproductive effects of the PSI Directive. They specifically mentioned the case where "cultural establishments would purposefully seek for the third parties to retain rights on the content they acquire, thus sparing themselves a hassle of making it accessible."; Even the Commission noted the fact. In its Communication COM (2009) 212 final, p. 7, it declared the importance of "keeping public domain works accessible after a format shift. In other words, works in the public domain should stay there once digitised and be made accessible through the internet. There is, however, a tendency among cultural institutions to charge for accessing or re-using digitised public domain material. This may lead to the privatisation of public domain material in the digital age, instead of allowing the widest possible accessibility and use for the benefit of citizens and companies".

The vast majority of the documents cultural institutions hold fall under this exemption. Most works are bought or commissioned, and thus first owned by others. Donated works also have a first owner. One could therefore wonder what type of works are left to fall under the scope of this provision. Does the extension in the scope of the directive only impact internally generated documents?

The wording of this provision gives rise to some ambivalence. In a more literal sense, the exception would also apply to situations in which public sector bodies, as licensees, are able to grant sub-licences for the use of such documents[644]. This reading seems to be confirmed by Recital 9 of the 2013 PSI Directive, which states that documents held by libraries, museums and archives should be considered documents for which third parties hold IPR as long as the term of protection of those rights has not expired. However, as *Drexl* explains[645], the directive refrains from clarifying the cases of re-use arising from the sub-licensing of IPR. Recital 9 explains how intellectual property legislation is not affected by the directive and that

> *if a third party was the initial owner of the intellectual property rights for a document held by libraries, including university libraries, museums and archives, and the term of protection of those rights has not expired, that document should, for the purpose of this directive, be considered as a document for which third parties hold intellectual property rights.*

This rather cryptic reasoning would lead us to exclude orphan works from the scope of re-use (Directive 2012/28/EU – the Orphan Works Directive). As Keller et al. explain, the key here, attending to the underlying rationale of the directive, would be to distinguish between the holding of a physical copy and ownership of copyright. As they conclude:

> *Recital 9 of the 2013 PSI Directive should be interpreted as simply meaning that documents are outside the scope of the directive when the cultural heritage institution holds a document for which it does not simultaneously hold the intellectual property rights, including the situation where the right holder is unknown*[646].

All in all, documents held by cultural heritage institutions would fall under the scope of the directive if: (i) they are in the public domain, either because they were never protected by copyright or because copyright has expired; or (ii) the cultural heritage institution is the original right holder or assignee of the IPR. In the first case, Art. 3(1) PSI Directive would be applicable. That is, documents shall be

---

644 In turn, this would follow the spirit of Recital 22, which explains that public sector bodies "should exercise their copyright in a way that facilitates re-use".

645 See Drexl, 'The Competition Dimension of the European Regulation of Public Sector Information and the Concept of an Undertaking', in Drexl/Bagnoli, *State-Initiated Restraints of Competition*, Cheltenham, Edward Elgar Publishing, 2015, p. 72.

646 Keller/Margoni/Rybicka/Tarkowski, 'Re-use of Public Sector Information in Cultural Heritage Institutions', International Free and Open Source Software Law Review 2014, 1 (5).

reusable if they are already generally accessible. In the second case, where IPR exist (because the library owns or has acquired the IPR), the special rule of Art. 3(2) applies: the cultural institutions can decide on allowing re-use or not.

Once more, as was mentioned earlier in the context of digitisation, it is important to clarify the exact status of digitised material. Again, one of the amendments (for a new Art. 7a) proposed by the Committee on Industry, Research and Energy[647], explained that:

> *documents in which the intellectual property rights have expired and which consequently enter the public domain constitute a very important part of the collections of libraries, archives and museums and should be given priority in digitisation campaigns; it is therefore desirable to ensure that such digitisation does not alter their legal status. Access to, and re-use of, those data must be guaranteed in order to respect the fundamental right of access to culture, information and education.*

2.2.6 Licensing and charging

Even before libraries were included in the scope of the PSI Directive, the 2009 Rightscom report for the Commission noted that, though committed to providing free access to end users, cultural institutions "are inclined to regard commercial re-use as a separate matter for which they should be reimbursed and in some cases as a potential significant income generating source". At that time, as noted by the report, "32% of the respondents charge for licences to re-use content, showing a tendency among some cultural bodies to distinguish between access and (commercial) re-use in the charging policies"[648].

The 2009 Rightscom report also confirmed that "reported balances of income over cost from enabling re-use are mainly small or negative"[649]. Similarly, image libraries, probably the most widespread commercial activity undertaken by libraries, cannot be described as a large profitable business for libraries. Nonetheless, the potential loss of these revenues by libraries and the probable absence of budgetary compensation remains a fear for many large cultural institutions.

The issue of licensing documents held by libraries, including university libraries, is not completely trivial. As a matter of fact, the European Commission was asked during the parliamentary process to assist the Member States in this respect by providing a set of guidelines. As a result, the Commission has published an additional document with guidelines on, among other things, licensing[650]. On the

---

647 A7-0404/001-055, Amendments 001-055 by the Committee on Industry, Research and Energy, 6 June 2013.

648 Davies et al., *Economic and Social Impact of the Public Domain: Cultural Institutions and the PSI Directive*, London, Rightscom, 2009, p. 6.

649 Ibid.

650 The document (2014 Commission guidelines), which provides non-binding guidance on best practices on standard licences, datasets and charging for the re-use of information, is, to a large extent, the result of the EU Parliament's demands in this respect.

other hand, as regards (university) libraries, many of the documents expected to fall under the scope of the 2013 PSI Directive are those already in the public domain. In that sense, the very idea of licensing might cause some controversy. A (copyright) licence modulates the terms and uses where copyright is concerned and thus, in the absence of copyright, licensing of IPR becomes a misrepresentation with no practical effect.

However, in practice, the scenarios are not always unequivocal. We must also look at the copyright regimes of the different Member States. For instance, in the UK, where Crown copyright resides in many public documents, the influential NA has developed the Open Government Licence (OGL), instead of the arguably more commonplace Creative Commons licensing scheme. Though we will not go into licensing proper, the key item among the different licensing schemes remains compatibility and that covers copyright and database rights, should they be of application[651].

In the course of the EU parliamentary procedure, we have seen how some raised the need for licensing to be harmonised across Europe, especially regarding metadata. In that context, the Europeana Licensing Framework, through the Europeana Data Exchange Agreement, imposes the use of the Creative Commons Zero (CC0) licensing scheme for the exchange of metadata between participating institutions and Europeana. It is put forward as a best practice example[652]. In any case, the PSI Directive contains no explicit recognition of open licences[653] as the way forward, though talk of standardisation is indeed mentioned in those instances where licensing can take place[654].

---

651 The OGL is interoperable with Creative Commons. In addition the UK has developed charged licences, as opposed to the free OGL, where necessary.

652 Pekel/Fallon/Kamenov, *Public Sector Information in Cultural Heritage Institutions*, Brussels, ePSIplatform, Topic Report 2014.06, 2014, p. 5: "… To make a real difference you need a few things. You need prices for the data to be reasonable if not free – given that the marginal cost of your using the data is pretty low. You need to be able to not just use the data: but re-use it, without dealing with complex conditions ... We are giving you new rights for how you can access their public data for re-use, but also extending rules to include museums and galleries. That could open up whole new areas of over 25 million cultural items digitised and available for all to see – with metadata under an open, CC0 licence.".

653 For a description of some open access licences see Guibault/Wiebe (eds.), *Safe to be open*, Göttingen, Göttingen University Press, 2013, pp. 148 et seqq.

654 The 2014 Commission guidelines provide more insight into the matter.

Finally, it is also worth noting the competitive dynamics given that, in some cases, as Drexl explains, "the ability to charge also acts as an incentive to the ability to produce" and thus some public bodies are exempted from the marginal cost standard, in particular those that "have to rely on their own revenue to finance the collection, production, reproduction and dissemination of PSI"[655].

2.2.7 The issue of digitisation

To date, digitisation projects at cultural institutions have mostly involved out-of-copyright works in partnership with the private sector. Best practices in this respect have therefore been those followed by those institutions which allow unrestricted re-use of the images, in line with the public domain status of the underlying subject matter. The PSI Directive, as far as cultural institutions are concerned, does not (intend to) change the status quo[656].

The Communia Association noted in 2015 that Member States are struggling with many challenges in the implementation of the directive into domestic law. Further, the association underlines that the correct choice of licensing, charging and redress mechanisms is an especially difficult one. As other parties have also pointed out, they note that the implementation of the changes required by the new directive could do more harm than good when it comes to access to digitised cultural heritage in Europe[657]. What Communia refers to in the latter statement is indeed a pending legal question in the legal treatment of cultural heritage material, namely, what the state of the resulting acts of digitisation of public domain material under intellectual property legislation is, and whether this can lead to

---

655 See Drexl, 'The Competition Dimension of the European Regulation of Public Sector Information and the Concept of an Undertaking', in Drexl/Bagnoli, *State-Initiated Restraints of Competition*, Cheltenham, Edward Elgar Publishing, 2015, pp. 80 et seq. His reasoning is, nevertheless, more extensive. He also argues that, in the context of the marginal cost rationale (arising from the consideration of PSI as by-products) "it is overlooked that, under the marginal-cost standard, prices do not reflect the full costs of the production and provision of the information and that, accordingly, private commercial re-use is at least cross-subsidised by tax payers' money. In many instances, as has already been pointed out, individual citizens and companies are charged fees although the specific activity falls within the scope of the performance of public tasks. For instance, if the marginal-cost standard were to be applied to the publication of court decisions, the parties to the underlying proceedings, who finance these proceedings through their fees, would cross-subsidise the businesses of private publishers. Hence, in this regard, it is welcomed that Art. 6(2)(a) of the revised directive provides for an exception of the marginal-cost standard for public sector bodies that are required to generate revenue to cover a substantial part of their costs relating to the performance of their public tasks beyond the cases in which the marginal-cost standard would negatively impact the production of information. This provision allows Member States to prevent cross-subsidisation of private re-use of PSI through other private parties under the marginal cost standard".

656 Gallica, the image database of the French National Library, notably charges for commercial uses of ist digitised public domain works. See https://espacepersonnel.bnf.fr/views/vel/mon_panier.jsf#tooltip3 and http://gallica.bnf.fr/html/und/conditions-use-gallicas-contents.

657 See http://www.communia-association.org/tag/psi-directive.

additional rights. Again, an obstacle here appears to be the territoriality of copyright legislation and the different cultural establishments' own policies and funding mechanisms.

Whether or not the material concerned should be charged for, or if digitisation creates new copyright, remains outside the scope of this study. Nevertheless, a conclusion can be drawn and that is, once more, the lack of legal and commercial certainty as regards this matter, which creates an obstacle to re-use both domestically and cross-border. Regardless of the existence of IPR in digitised images, the lack of certainty does not help (i) the implementation of the PSI Directive, as long as the institutions involved do not clarify whether particular documents, the number of which could be quite significant, are covered, or should be covered, by the directive on the basis of their intellectual property status. In addition, it does not help (ii) the potential re-user when libraries do not clearly state on what basis private users are charged. In other words, does one have to pay for the re-use because a particular document has IPR owned by the library that need to be cleared or is it rather on the basis of an administrative expense?

2.3 Country overview: Implementation of the 2013 PSI Directive

There are obvious differences regarding the implementation of the PSI Directive by the Member States, even from a purely formal point of view. Some Member States have chosen to implement the European directive under their freedom of information legislation (e.g. France), interpreting the PSI Directive as an extension of the principle of transparency of the public bodies. Others, however, have chosen to adopt specific regulations on re-use (e.g. the UK).

What the domestic implementation of the PSI Directive has meant in practical terms for national libraries is still rather unclear. There are various reasons for this. First, the implementation of the directive is still recent and libraries themselves are still in the process of agreeing policy in this respect. Second, the PSI Directive leaves plenty of leeway according to jurisdiction. Third, the definitions underlying the PSI Directive are largely domestic, which means that interpretation can be quite different until the ECJ renders a decision on a related matter. Finally, we are aware that many libraries have already been working on the basis of the PSI Directive and the overall implications of digitisation of their works for some years now. In that sense, the changes, if any, brought about by the PSI Directive specifically are far from evident. Capgemini provided some figures for 2016. According to their analysis, the direct market size of open data is expected to reach €55.3 bn for the EU 28+ Member States. In addition, between 2016 and 2020, the market size is expected to increase by 36.9% to a value of €75.7 bn in 2020 (corrected for inflation). For the period 2016-2020, the cumulative direct market size is estimated at €325 bn[658]. The study is based on earlier pioneering studies in the field. In determining the direct overall EU open data market size, the value of the open data market size for each EU28+ country is calculated and aggregated.

However, it is difficult to estimate how much of the growth is directly related to the implementation of the PSI Directive. In particular, it is difficult to establish a link between this growth and the inclusion of cultural establishments. In general terms, as seen clearly in the Capgemini study, the weight of the cultural and educational sector in the total sectorial breakdown of open data impact is small, especially when compared with the public administration or professional services, or real estate.

Attempts were made, through a questionnaire sent to selected OpenAire2020 partners, to obtain country-by-country insight into the implementation of the revised PSI Directive and, in particular, how libraries have been impacted by the new legislation. More specifically, input was requested on the formal implementation of the rules of the directive in the UK, Spain, Germany, Poland and the Netherlands, as well as on the qualification of university libraries under the law, the definition of their public tasks and the content of their collections. Unfortunately, the outcome of this quest for information remains modest and lacks homogeneity. The absence of relevant information can indeed be explained by the very recent character of the new rules on the re-use of PSI as applied to libraries, archives and museums.

2.3.1 The United Kingdom

In the UK the Re-use of Public Sector Information Regulations 2015 (SI 2015 No. 1415) (the 2015 Regulations) have been in force since 18 July 2015. They implement the revised 2013 PSI Directive.

The UK has been one of the pioneers in establishing open data portals for the government. The NA has played a central role in its guidance to cultural bodies on the necessary steps to comply with the PSI Directive. It has published reports on both the PSI itself as well as guidance for UK institutions on how it should be implemented[659]. However, it also notes that “many cultural sector bodies are already complying with the 2015 Regulations through their best-practice approach to the information they produce, hold or disseminate. Essentially this means

---

658 See the European Data Portal, Creating Value Through Open Data, A study on the Impact of Re-use of Public Data Resources (November 2015).

659 The changes being introduced are set out in the NA’s introductory guide. The NA is working with universities in the UK and the British Library to produce advice and guidance for public sector libraries on the changes in the amended directive and the forthcoming UK legislation; information is available at: http://www.cilip.org.uk/blog/what-do-changes-psi-regulations-mean-libraries.

making their information re-usable[660]. In addition, the existence of the Office for Public Sector Information (OPSI), now under the scope of the NA[661], which acts as a one-stop-shop for the licensing of (government) information, has fuelled the development of economic activity in this respect[662].

The 2015 Regulations specify in reg. 3 a list of institutions and departments that should be considered as public sector bodies; they contain no specific definition of cultural institutions, which could be included under the rather generic associations or corporations. Perhaps the most characteristic UK body is the trading fund, which, though a state entity, functions with a relatively high level of autonomy and funding. Only public undertakings are expressly excluded from the directive (see Recital 10 of the 2013 PSI Directive).

In addition to the lack of express inclusion of cultural institutions, a challenging aspect in the interpretation of the law is the definition of public task. Reg. 5(1) of the 2015 Regulations explains that the requirements applicable to PSI do not apply where "the activity of supplying the document is one which falls outside the public task of the public sector body, provided that the scope of the public task of that body is transparent and subject to review …". As a result, the British Library and many university libraries have drafted and published statements of the public task, a fundamental document to understand what documents fall under the scope of the PSI Directive and the principles that guide the institution itself. It certainly is advisable for libraries to publish a statement of public task in order to clarify which of their works and documents actually fall under the scope of the directive. Subsequently, libraries also need to establish and publish their formal procedures to address requests for information and, if necessary, redress.

A key aspect with respect to the public task and one which evidences the importance of releasing it to the public is to ascertain whether certain commercial initiatives fall under this category. The RLUK, the association of UK research libraries, captures this fine line between financial self-sustainability and PSI legislation commitments:

> *public-private partnerships have become one option for funding large-scale digitisation efforts … Libraries are claiming exclusive rights in digitised versions of public domain works and are entering into exclusive relationships with commercial partners that hinder free access. The PSI Directive will challenge the position of libraries that generate income directly from digitisation of historic materials. In principle, RLUK has adopted a strong*

---

660 NA, *Guidance on the implementation of the Re-use of Public Sector Information Regulations 2015 – for public sector bodies*, July 2015, available at: http://www.nationalarchives.gov.uk/documents/information-management/psi-implementation-guidance-public-sector-bodies.pdf, p. 8.

661 See http://www.opsi.gov.uk/psi.

662 Wretham, *PSI Implementation in the UK - Successes and Challenges*, 2009, text available at: http://www.nap.edu/read/12687/chapter/4.

and respected position on open access but may need to ask difficult questions of itself when faced with balancing an instinct for freely available content and the desire to raise funds from that same content[663].

All in all, the flexibility afforded by the law to the Member States and cultural institutions themselves makes it difficult to paint a homogeneous picture of the implementation of the 2013 PSI Directive. In any case, most university libraries certainly refer on their websites to the directive and how its scope has been extended to cover libraries. In practical terms, the library of the University of Birmingham, for instance, provides a clear list of information assets, which gives the user a good idea of the categorisation of documents held by the university library and, thus, those that are potentially included under the scope of the 2013 PSI Directive[664]. In this particular case, the assets fall under (i) publication scheme, (ii) information relating to the governance and management of library services, (iii) library collections, (iv) digital collections and (v) catalogue and information data. Among these, the category that is likely to pose greater challenges, and arguably more interest for potential re-users, is that comprising digital collections. Within these digital collections, the library itself notes the following:

> *the ePapers repository contains some material that is included within the scope of the PSI regulations. This is where the copyright is held by the University*[665]. *However, copyright in a significant number of deposits within ePapers is retained by third parties and such items are excluded from release under the PSI regulations. Such items may, however, be freely viewed for reference purposes.*

Further, a final disclaimer applicable to the list of information assets as a whole declares that:

> … *there are some limitations that may restrict the release of information for re-use. These include where the copyright is not held by the University, where personal data is involved or where release would not be agreed if a similar application had been made under existing access legislation, such as the Freedom of Information Act 2000*[666].

---

663 As per the RLUK's National Digitisation Review of December 2014, available at http://www.rluk.ac.uk/wp-content/uploads/2014/12/RLUK-National-Digitisation-Review-CPressler.pdf.

664 See http://www.birmingham.ac.uk/libraries/public-sector-information-regulations/the-re-use-of-public-sector-information-regulations-2015.aspx.

665 The library further explains that its ePapers repository is for research material produced by members of the university, and includes working papers, conference papers and technical reports. It is an Open Access repository, aiming to make the material available to the widest possible audience. This ePapers repository contains material that has not been through a formal peer-review process and is a companion to the ePrints repository of refereed publications.

666 See the List of information assets, available at: http://www.birmingham.ac.uk/libraries/public-sector-information-regulations/list-of-information-assets.aspx.

What is noteworthy in this example is that documents held by the University of Birmingham, as opposed to those only owned by the university library, appear to be included in the scope of the 2013 PSI Directive. One possible reason for this is that the university library and the university are part of the same public body and thus, third-party IPR refer to ownership outside the single legal entity formed by the university and its library. This interpretation is legally sound as it follows the requirements set out in the PSI Directive. However, as was pointed out earlier, that same reasoning conflicts with the same 2013 PSI Directive, given that universities and research centres in general are expressly excluded from the scope of the directive. In any case, in practical terms, the principle of releasing PSI under re-use provisions should be considered as good practice, regardless of which the university/library will always have the ultimate decision on individual documents.

Together with the list of information assets, the university library provides the required statement of public task and states that "all information linked to the performance of the Public Task falls within the scope of the PSI regulations". Unfortunately, the description of public tasks is broad (e.g. to develop the library collections and associated work-study environments in line with changing user needs). So, ultimately, the library can decide on the re-use of individual documents. Again, the relatively high level of discretion set out by the law remains an obstacle for a clear assessment of re-use.

Other UK university libraries do not mention the implementation of PSI regulations (e.g. University of Exeter, University of Sussex). Among those that do (e.g. University of Cambridge, Nottingham Trent University , University of Edinburgh) the common characteristic is their description of the PSI regulations together with a statement of public task and explanation of the procedure to follow in order to request re-use. Again, the description of public task is rather a broad mission statement. All universities generally explain the process of requesting authorisation for re-use, the existence of limitations to the right of re-use and the fact that the statement of public task is subject to review after a period of time. The period itself may vary per institution.

The University of Edinburgh library, though potentially restricting what could have otherwise been a broader scope, defines more clearly its (public) task in the context of the PSI regulations. It explains that its public task under the re-use of PSI covers "… permission to use digital copies of manuscripts, documents, and objects in our collections for re-use in publications or through other media". However, it explains that "The University's museum and archival collections are not covered by the PSI Regulations. For administrative convenience, Edinburgh University Library has decided to apply the same terms and conditions to both library materials and the archival and museum collections it holds for the University."[667] In other words, the University of Edinburgh has decided to impose the

---

[667] See http://www.ed.ac.uk/information-services/library-museum-gallery/crc/services/copying-and-digitisation/image-licensing/statement-of-public-task.

same licensing conditions on all of its works, whether these are held by the library, or any other entity acting on behalf of the university. That is, the university is providing transparency and much-needed clarity to the somewhat artificial distinction established by the PSI Directive between works held by university libraries and the universities themselves. Further, the University of Edinburgh, in common with other cultural establishments, acknowledges the existence of different pricing and licensing schemes for the reproduction of digitised images[668], reminding any interested party that:

> *the rights of copyright holders are quite separate to our ownership rights. If you want to reproduce images which are still within copyright protection and where the copyright is not owned by the University, you must produce written evidence that you have obtained permission to reproduce the images from the copyright holder*[669].

As mentioned earlier it could be somewhat confusing for interested (re)-users to understand for what reasons and under what regulation they are being charged (regardless of whether this makes a difference in practical terms). For example, is it copyright law or is it PSI regulations? Is the university exercising IPR over some digitised images or is it a fee to cover certain costs? The rights of the University of Edinburgh, as opposed to those of the library, might imply that the licensing is irrespective of the PSI legislation; in other words, the guidelines on licensing have not been affected by the extension of the scope under the PSI Directive.

Finally, the library of the University of Cambridge notes that indeed some rights are asserted over digitised content though, at this stage, their main objective is to be transparent as to the rationale, as well as the terms and conditions applicable in each case. For example, these are now dependant on the type of usage (commercial, teaching and research etc.) rather than on the type of user, which favoured university members, for example. In any case, the library is still working on the adoption of the PSI Directive and it is likely that adjustments will be made in the future. For this purpose, the advice provided by the NA is key[670].

2.3.2 Spain

In Spain the 2013 PSI Directive has been transposed by Ley 18/2015[671], which, in the words of the legislator, extends its scope to, inter alia, libraries due to the wealth of documents they hold and the digitisation projects they have undertaken.

---

[668] See http://www.ed.ac.uk/information-services/library-museum-gallery/crc/services/copying-and digitisation/permission-to-reproduce-images.

[669] Please note that the University of Edinburgh changed its policy and is now licensing content under the licence CC-BY, free of charge, see http://www.ed.ac.uk/information-services/library-museum-gallery/crc/services/copying-and-digitisation/image-licensing.

[670] See http://www.nationalarchives.gov.uk/documents/information-management/psi-implementation-guidance-public-sector-bodies.pdf.

[671] Ley 18/2015, de 9 de julio, por la que se modifica la ley 37/2007, de 16 de noviembre, sobre reutilización de la información del sector público.

On the subject of the revision of the directive, the Spanish legislator notes that the inclusion of cultural establishments responds to the significant amount of information resources held by these establishments and the digitisation projects that are taking place[672].

The Spanish National Library (BNE) has drafted a plan to encourage re-use of information, published in March 2016. It contains the main action points to comply with Real Decreto 1495/2011 (RD 1495/2011), which develops the Spanish Act on re-use (Ley 37/2007), which implemented the old 2003 PSI Directive[673]. Indeed, the Spanish public administration has been actively developing guidelines for access and re-use of PSI since 2008, when it launched the *Proyecto Aporta* (aimed at educating and encouraging stakeholders). Together with the UK and Slovenia, Spain has been a pioneering EU Member State on the subject of public sector open data portals. The project, among other things, included the launch of a one-stop-shop online portal bringing together PSI from the different public administrations[674]. Another spin-off was the launch of datos.gob.es, the online government data portal, in line with RD 1495/2011. For that purpose, the Secretary of State responsible for Telecommunications and the Information Society decided to incorporate a public corporate entity (*entidad pública empresarial*) Red.es. Red.es falls under the responsibility of the Ministry of Trade and Industry, in cooperation with the Ministry of Finance and Public Administration.

The Spanish implementation of the PSI Directive does not change the general definition of public sector body as per the 2013 PSI Directive. It adds, however, that the PSI regulation should also be applicable to those public bodies not strictly mentioned by Art. 2 but still governed by administrative law[675]. The Spanish law, as per its fifth additional provision on the re-use of documents, archives and collections of private origin, dictates that the re-use of these works should comply with the conditions established in the legal instrument that led to their being held by the respective cultural institutions. This would, thus, appear to justify a broad interpretation of the IPR ownership whereby licensing of certain IPR, as opposed to a full assignment, would suffice to allow re-use. This would also be consistent with the statement in Art. 3, which provides that the exercise of IPR of the public sector should be done in such a way that facilitates re-use.

---

672 See http://administracionelectronica.gob.es/pae_Home/pae_Actualidad/pae_Noticias/Anio2015/Julio/Noticia-2015-07-13-Ley-RISP.html#.VvPI24UrLcs.

673 Ley 37/2007 sobre reutilización de la información del sector público.

674 See http://www.aporta.es, accessible by the public since March 2010, when a first version of the online catalogue of public information (*catálogo de información pública en internet*) was released.

675 As per its Second Additional Provision on applicability to other bodies, which extends applicability to those bodies subject to public law, in particular those under public law (Ley 30/1992, de 26 de noviembre, de Régimen Jurídico de las Administraciones Públicas y del Procedimiento Administrativo Común).

Further Art. 4 breaks down re-use into four different categories: (i) re-use free of conditions, (ii) re-use under standard licensing (*licencias tipo*), (iii) re-use under prior request, as per Art. 10 and (iv) re-use under Art. 6. These articles refer to the re-use request procedure and to exclusive rights (under commercial agreements) respectively.

If we focus on public libraries, the Plan RISP of the BNE generally follows very closely the guidelines of RD 1495/2011, and, among other things, adopts the four different categories mentioned above. The guidelines of RD 1495/2011 also deal with recommendations on licensing. They recommend clear terms of use, which include the requirement of attribution and non-modification. Otherwise, standard licences (*licencias tipo*) are used, they recommend that they are as non-restrictive as possible.

The BNE is actively working on the impact of the digitisation of their collections in general and on the implementation of the PSI Directive guidelines in particular. For now the data released for re-use by the BNE is available under datos.gob.es, the government's open data portal[676]. The BNE's own Plan RISP aims to extend availability to other groups of (non-bibliographic) data as of 2017.

The BNE acknowledges the importance of the PSI Directive in how it puts museums, archives and libraries in the spotlight as regards re-use initiatives. In practice, the BNE has already undertaken a large part of the job by incorporating 10 datasets, mostly bibliographical, in the datos.gob.es portal. According to the BNE, the 2013 PSI Directive does expand its prior strategy, also as regards the documents themselves, given that they now have the task of identifying other non-bibliographical datasets that might be of interest for the potential re-user. Work towards the identification of these datasets has already been carried out by means of a so-called Process Map (*Mapa de Procesos*). Currently, before making data available for re-use, there is an internal approval process (internal stakeholders such as management and RISP Committee). A similar approach is being taken as regards IT software and databases whenever they have been developed in-house. The BNE is currently exploring the opening up of these resources.

Given the ultimate goal of the 2013 PSI Directive to allow cultural establishments to determine themselves what documents, and under what conditions, should fall under the scope of the PSI legislation, the main item that needs consideration is the actual external and, mostly, internal processes that need to occur before a document is made accessible.

Finally, it is worth noting that the BNE has also signed another agreement with Red.es, the public corporate entity part of the Spanish Ministry of Trade and Industry, in the context of the PSI Directive[677]. The aim of the agreement is to "encourage the transfer and re-use of content, promoting innovation and the creation of new products and services". For instance, the activities should facilitate

---

[676] See http://datos.gob.es.

[677] See http://www.bne.es/webdocs/Prensa/Noticias/2016/0310-Red-es.pdf.

new forms of access and data visualisation together with tools (such as geo-reference), books in e-pub format, own collections, virtual communities for students, teachers or developers, interactive publications etc.

Regarding university libraries, specific policies on re-use are still being devised. The XXIII General Assembly of the REBIUN, the Spanish Association of University Libraries[678], held in November 2015, concluded that one of the most relevant action points was to support open access by achieving a twofold objective: (i) having a coordinated licensing policy regarding metadata of registry and digital resources among the institutions and (ii) encouraging education and publicity of open access publishing (as per Art. 8 of the Spanish law of 2015).

2.3.3 Germany

Germany implemented the revised 2013 PSI Directive by Art. 1G of the Act of 8 July 2015. The Act amended the Federal Act on the Re-use of Public Sector Information (IWG). It entered into force on 17 July 2015. The Act contains a few sections relating to cultural establishments. Specifically, Art. 1(2) no. 6 IWG implements Art. 1(e) of the directive. It states that "the act is not applicable to information held by educational and research establishments including organisations established for the transfer of research results, except university libraries". Art. 1(2) no. 7 IWG implements Art. 1(e) of the directive and includes libraries, including university libraries within the scope of German PSI legislation. Accordingly, the Act is not applicable to information held by cultural establishments other than public libraries, museums and archives. Art. 2a IWG implements the general principle laid down in Art. 3 of the directive. According to Art. 2a IWG, information to which the Act applies is re-usable in accordance with the conditions set out in the IWG. For information in which libraries, including university libraries, museums and archives, hold copyright, related rights or industrial property rights, this is only to the extent that re-use is legitimate according to the named rights or the establishment has allowed re-use; the conditions of re-use have to comply with the conditions set out in the IWG. According to Art. 2 no. 3 IWG, re-use is the use of information for commercial or non-commercial purposes.

As regards definitions and terminology it might be worth noting that the IWG uses the term "information" instead of the term "documents" used in the directive. But this does not appear to make any difference. The term "IP rights" is not used in Art. 2a IWG because it is not clearly defined in Germany which rights fall under the term "IP" (*Geistiges Eigentum*). Thus it is more accurate to name the potentially relevant types of rights. Art. 1(2) no. 4 clarifies that the Act is not applicable to information that is covered by copyrights or related rights or industrial property rights of third parties.

---

[678] Note that REBIUN also has private university libraries among its members.

Further, the IWG does not define the terms university, university library or public task. It does explain, however, that "public sector body" includes (Art. 2 no. 1 IWG) (a) the regional authorities including their separate funds under public law, (b) other legal entities established for the specific purpose of meeting needs in the general interest, not having commercial character and dominated by the state (materially identical with Art. 2 no. 2 PSI Directive), (c) associations which fall under lit. (a) or (b).

2.3.4 Poland

In Poland the President signed the Act implementing the amended PSI Directive on 12 March 2016. The Act entered into force in three months after publication (publication 15 March 2016; entry into force 16 June 2016) apart from certain provisions which became effective on 1 January 2017.

The Act applies to public finance sector entities and other state entities, as well as semi-private entities with majority public ownership or financing. However, the following are explicitly excluded:

a) public radio and television as well as the Polish Press Agency (Polska Agencja Prasowa S.A.);

b) cultural institutions as defined in the Act of 25 October 1991 on cultural activity, except for museums, public libraries and archives (as defined in separate, respective Acts);

c) universities, the Polish Academy of Science and scientific institutions as defined in a separate Act of 30 April 2010 on financing of science, except for scientific libraries, the Institute of Meteorology and Water Management, and the State Institute of Geology;

d) scientific libraries not organised by public sector entities;

e) entities enumerated in Art. 2 of the Act of 7 September 1991 on education.

The excluded entities, however, are still obliged to make available public information as defined in the Act on access to public information (in Polish law, public information and public sector information are two different sets of information). It follows that university libraries are covered by the Polish Act. However, scientific libraries organised by entities that are outside the public sector are explicitly excluded. Of course, there may also be some libraries that will not fall within the scope of the public finance sector.

The actual implementation of the law and the ongoing discussion on how best to achieve it are not different from those elsewhere. According to Barbara Szczepańska (Polish eIFL coordinator) and Anna Pełka (Warsaw University Library deputy director) it appears that most libraries are still waiting until the Act enters into force in 2017 and analysing the law's possible impact on their activities. Warsaw University Library already makes publicly available many catalogues as well as various public domain documents, but it is still discussing internally how to approach re-use issues such as charging, application for re-use procedure and forms, as well as terms of re-use.

Documents (such as books, etc.) held by the libraries may be subject to third-party copyright. There is no exact data available, but it should be expected that the majority of works held by libraries are copyrighted, although some of those copyrights might already have expired.

2.3.5 The Netherlands

The 2013 PSI Directive was implemented in the Netherlands by the Act of 24 June 2015 on the re-use of public sector information[679]. For the purposes of the application of the Act, Art. 1 defines library as

> *a universally accessible library facility which is funded largely by one or more municipalities or maintained, the Royal Library, referred to in Art. 1.5 of the Act on Higher Education and Scientific Research or the library facility of a university mentioned in the appendix to the Law on Higher Education and Research.*

Art. 1.5 of the Act on Higher Education and Scientific Research (AHESR) is aimed at the Royal Netherlands Academy of Arts and Sciences (KNAW) as well as the Royal Library (KB) of the Netherlands. From the Annex to the same Act, it follows that basically all public universities of the country fall within the scope of the Act on the re-use of public sector information (namely Leiden, Groningen, Amsterdam, Utrecht, Delft, Wageningen, Eindhoven, Enschede, Rotterdam and Maastricht), as well as the special universities (namely the Vrije Universiteit Amsterdam, the Catholic University of Nijmegen and the Catholic University of Tilburg), all technical universities, philosophical universities, academic hospitals and the Open University. However, it is unclear whether the libraries of all these higher educational institutions possess a separate legal personality from that of the university itself. Pursuant to the AHESR, the public universities, the KNAW and the KB qualify as institutions based on public law, while the special universities are legal persons with full capacity.

The public tasks of all institutions mentioned above are also laid down in the AHESR. University libraries such as the library of the University of Amsterdam publish their mission statements on their websites but make no mention of the application of the Act on the re-use of public sector information.

---

[679] Wet hergebruik van overheidsinformatie, Staatsblad 2015, 271.

The Act on the re-use of public sector information applies to documents defined as a document or other material containing data written by an institution entrusted with a public task. With respect to documents held by university libraries in which copyright or other IPR may vest, Art. 3(6) and (8) of the Act on the re-use of public sector information provides the following:

> (6) *Without prejudice to the stipulations in the fifth paragraph, a museum or library may reject an application for re-use if the museum or the library is the owner of the rights on the information within the meaning of the Copyright Act, the Act on neighbouring rights or the Database Act.*
>
> (8) *If a museum or library refuses a request for re-use as the request concerns information as defined in Art. 2, paragraph b, the identity of the beneficiary or the licensor of the requested information does not need to be disclosed.*

These provisions essentially permit libraries to refuse applications for re-use of information in respect of which they own IPR, arguably to enable them to exercise their rights in relation to the information. Further information on how universities and other higher educational institutions have implemented the provisions of the Act on the re-use of public sector information in their daily practice and workflow is unavailable.

2.4 Conclusion

The focus of the PSI Directive is to encourage commercial activity in the hope that this leads to new business models and economic growth. Further, activities undertaken in different forums (e.g. LAPSI, Communia, OpenAire2020), under the EU's Open Data Strategy, have raised much-needed awareness with respect to open data, that is, data that is freely accessible and embodied in machine-readable formats. Ultimately, the ambition of the EU institutions is to create a harmonised (public) information market across the EU, both in terms of the type of underlying works and in terms of compatibility of processes, licensing and formats.

So, does the extension of the 2013 PSI Directive to cover (university) libraries contribute to the objectives of the Commission?

Unfortunately, despite the above well-intended and logical process, a harmonised Digital Single Market of PSI is still far from being reality. This is particularly the case with (university) libraries included in the scope of the 2013 PSI Directive given their unique position with respect to other public bodies. (University) libraries (i) are carved out from the guiding "open by default" principle, which means that the responsibility reverts to the Member States and institutions themselves, (ii) hold a large amount of third-party intellectual property, (iii) have on occasion already developed successful business models as a means to make additional income and (iv) hold a delicate position between public libraries, on the one hand,

and on the other the universities that house them, also legally, and which are excluded from the scope of the PSI Directive. In other words, the significant caveats applicable to university libraries would lead us to believe that the inclusion of these libraries in the PSI Directive does not respond to a well-thought-out plan for university libraries but rather as an afterthought on the inclusion of public libraries.

Nevertheless, the fact that significant obligations under the PSI Directive are waived does not necessarily mean that the 2013 PSI Directive is of no use where (university) libraries are concerned. On the contrary, the 2013 PSI Directive plays a much-needed role in balancing the different interests of our modern information society: privacy and data protection, IPR, freedom of information, transparency and the public task in the public sector etc.

In our view, the 2013 PSI Directive prompts libraries, and the public bodies in general, to define their role in the age of mass-digitisation, especially at a time when the roles of the public and private sectors are more intertwined than ever. Secondly, it encourages libraries to digitise and open up the material they hold in a consistent and transparent manner to encourage re-use at EU level. Needless to say, many libraries have already been aware of the impact of digitisation on their public mission for a while and most of them had already entered public-private digitisation partnerships long before the 2013 PSI Directive. Finally, the PSI Directive offers guidelines which, in combination with the open data principles and licensing guidelines, should serve to draw a line between the public and private sectors.

In the end, the flexibility afforded by the law is mostly one where cultural establishments can choose what to include in their definition of public task. The PSI Directive encourages libraries to publish their own policies so that potentially interested parties can have a clear idea of the permissions and business models required. Libraries should afford clarity as to what documents fall under the PSI Directive. Once this has been established, the library should afford a comprehensive yet (technically) user-friendly overview of the documents over which it holds IP or which are outside copyright protection and are considered to fall under the public task[680]. In other words, libraries should be transparent and clarify the exact scope of their public task and also the rationale for their pricing schemes. Certainly, the definition of public task is likely to change over time to a larger or lesser extent, and so the directive provides for, and there are borderline scenarios where,

---

[680] See the very accurate description of the UK National Museum Directors' Council: "the PSI Directive is not intended to disrupt operating models where a museum, archive or library earns income from the licensing of material in which it owns the intellectual property rights (IPR) or where the creation of those documents has required substantial investment. Similarly, it is not intended to disrupt the museum's pursuit of their public task. However, it is intended to require museums to be transparent about what information can be re-used, the pricing of it, and the terms and conditions on which that re-use can take place"; available at: http://www.nationalmuseums.org.uk/media/documents/nmdc_eu_psi_directive_guidance_for_museums.pdf.

in the case of cultural institutions, the directive leaves room for, the Member States and the institutions themselves to decide. These are those cases where the definition of ownership is blurred (e.g. where copyright contracts/licences exist with express or implied provisions on intellectual property, on where the work is commissioned and/or outsourced and what that implies). In an increasingly accountable world, libraries cannot take a passive stance or, even worse, use the PSI Directive as an excuse to close information as regards the user. They must rather take the initiative to draft clear lines of action in a coherent and transparent way. Such a stance would address the criticisms voiced in the past with respect to the 2003 PSI Directive, concerning the lack of transparency and complex processes.

As a result, the following best practices for OpenAire2020 partners and Open Research Data Pilot participating institutions are put forward:

- Disclose to the public the nature of their relationship with the university to which they are affiliated, so as to bring certainty to the application of the PSI Directive with respect to public sector bodies.
- Define their strategy, together with the universities that house them, regarding legal ownership of works they hold, and the respective metadata, and these legal relationships tie to the provisions of the PSI Directive. This applies to both third-party works, own works and university personnel works.
- Inform the public of the works that are in the public domain and the PSI/licensing policy that applies, if any, and why.
- Publish to what extent their public task falls within the scope of the PSI Directive and what procedure interested parties have to follow to request specific material for re-use.
- Strive for compatibility in terms of licensing and formatting, in line with the Commission's non-binding Guidelines. Thus, by stressing the need to avoid unnecessarily restricting re-use and supporting the adoption of common practice across the Union, the directive urges Member States to deliver openness and interoperability in the licensing policies. Moreover, the PSI Directive noted the importance of clarity in this respect and the revised directive includes in Art. 2(6)-(8) the definitions of machine-readable format, open format and formal open standard, which highlight the importance of interoperability.

As can be observed from the above, this study attempts to stay away from adopting a stance on the subject matter itself, that is on what works should be included under the PSI Directive and on what basis. Cultural institutions, including (university) libraries, need to establish a matrix-like chart, clearly explaining to potential users the basis on which a particular document is available and whether the (re-)use needs to be licensed and/or charged for[681].

In practice, the implementation of the PSI Directive in some Member States contains provisions allowing charges, as long as done under transparent conditions etc. The Spanish implementation even notes, in its Art. 7.5, that different tariffs can be applied depending on whether the use is for commercial or non-commercial purposes. This line of thought is not uncommon in the literature. Further, it is not uncommon in the literature to find a justification for different pricing schemes depending on the (final) use[682]. The validity of this argument becomes more problematic when public domain material is at stake. As a matter of principle, the public domain should not distinguish between commercial and non-commercial uses[683]. Perhaps the institution itself does, but this fact should be clearly pointed out. Of course, these are matters for Member States, and particularly for the institutions, to decide on and there are institutions that are required to generate revenue in order to cover public task activities. More importantly, we believe the rationale for this price differentiation should be determined, given that it is not one that lies in copyright law itself. Our concern is that the (re-)user knows if they are to be made to pay under one or another concept. Are they paying under IPR conditions or are they subsidising the free re-use of PSI by private individuals?

Implementation of these measures by cultural institutions, including (university) libraries, should enhance overall transparency and help us understand and assess the effectiveness of notions such as marginal pricing, ROI or the interplay with costs in general, whether material or immaterial (IPR/non-IPR related). It might be advisable to examine first in detail the cost structures of these public bodies before determining how works held by these institutions should be made available to the public.

Ultimately, best practices will hopefully be shared among cultural establishments, leading to (harmonised) pan-European re-use portals that encourage private initiatives to develop products and services destined for a single

---

681 See also Reaction of the Communia association to the proposal to amend Directive 2003/98/EC on re-use of public sector information, Brussels, 22 January 2012.

682 In this respect Pekel, *Democratising the Rijksmuseum*, The Hague, Europeana Foundation, 2014, makes an interesting read. The author provides a good overview of the policies and business models of the Rijksmuseum regarding its image bank and public domain material. It also makes recommendations on what could be viable business models for similar cultural institutions. One of the options contemplated is to discriminate between commercial and non-commercial uses, which arguably extend to public domain material.

683 See Keller/Margoni/Rybicka/Tarkowski, 'Re-use of Public Sector Information in Cultural Heritage Institutions', International Free and Open Source Software Law Review 2014, 1 (6): "the current best practice with regard to digitization of public domain materials by cultural heritage institutions is to make these materials available for free and without restrictions on re-use".

European Market. In that respect, Europeana and the like should represent a stepping stone on the path to expanding the re-use potential of cultural heritage works. Until that time, we would expect commercial players, in cooperation with the cultural institutions, to stimulate the demand for these works through feasible working models that will take over from somewhat cautious political and legislative bodies and take re-use to the next level.

3 (Policy) Recommendations

3.1 Open Research Data and data protection

The Open Research Data Pilot within Horizon2020 seeks to improve and maximise access to and re-use of research data generated by projects, comparable to open access strategies for research results. Thus, anyone who is interested should be able to use free of charge the generated data in order to enhance the information society and knowledge. However, as analysed above, apart from intellectual property issues[684] data protection laws, in particular the GDPR, would be applicable if the data shared had to be qualified as personal data. As demonstrated, it is sufficient that the research data of a project could be related to an identified or identifiable natural person[685].

Hence, any sharing and opening up of data on an open access basis would be treated as processing the data[686], thus requiring consent (in the case of sensitive data even an explicit consent) or a specific legal permission:

- As shown, consent would hardly work as a solution as *ex post* sharing (and processing) would in most cases not be in line with the original purpose(s) of data collection and processing as the new purposes of processing would likely differ from the original ones. The data subject must be informed *ex ante* about the use of their data and about the recipients – which is clearly not the case if data are shared afterwards for purposes other than originally envisaged[687].
- Regarding legal permissions the GDPR provides for some specific research exemptions but also requires intensive efforts to safeguard data protection, in particular by means of anonymisation (see Art. 89(1) GDPR)[688]. Moreover, the Open Research Data Pilot does not limit the sharing of data to scientific purposes. That is why the use of personal data in the Pilot cannot be legitimised by a research exception.

To achieve any kind of sharing of research data it is essential to avoid any relationship between data and individuals, in other words to effectively anonymise the data that are to be opened up[689]. However, the GDPR unfortunately does not specify which conditions have to be met in order to anonymise personal data

---

684 See Guibault/Wiebe (eds.), *Safe to be open*, Göttingen, Göttingen University Press, 2013, *passim* with more references.

685 Art. 4(1) GDPR; Art. 2(a) Data Protection Directive.

686 See above Section 1.5.3.2.

687 See above Section 1.5.3.5.

688 See above Section 1.5.3.4.

689 See above Section 1.5.3.6.

effectively and to dismiss any personal character of data. Even though the ECJ shed some light on the notion of personal data in the decision on IP addresses[690], it is still unclear whether any (legal) effort by anyone in the world has to be taken into account to assess whether data can be related to a data subject – or if only reasonable efforts by the data controller are taken into account (relative approach). In parallel to discussions about so-called "big data", research data which are shared in a free manner are prone to be identified by third parties – legal barriers for these third parties do not play any role here as data should by definition be shared freely. Thus, third parties could combine research data with any other kind of data available; the bigger the data sets gets the easier it probably is to re-identify data subjects.

Thus, different core issues have to be considered:

- requirements for anonymisation (and harmonisation);
- reduction of requirements for consent;
- extension of specific research privileges;
- definition of research purposes.

In the context of policy recommendations we first have to clarify the different options for policymakers, according to the level of changes, be they

- at the level of the GDPR;
- at a lower level such as guidelines etc.; or
- by self-regulation as offered by Arts 39 et seq. GDPR.

Each of these options must be discussed for every core issue. However, beforehand we must stress the different restrictions for every optional instrument/approach:

- Whereas in theory the GDPR could be modified it seems from a political perspective very unlikely that the "package" of the GDPR would be opened again soon, given the intense discussions before a final compromise was reached. Moreover, we have to bear in mind that the ECJ has laid more and more stress on constitutional guarantees for data protection, such as in the decisions concerning Safe Harbour agreements as well as data retention. Hence, even a change in the GDPR has to meet the constitutional tests established by the ECJ. Even though, due to the constraints of the project, we cannot analyse in depth the limits of changes, in particular relaxation of data protection in order to enhance research and sharing of data, it is very likely that constitutional guarantees of data protection would not allow for a wide extension of research privileges or for some sort of weak require-

[690] ECJ Case C-582/14 (19.10.2016), *Breyer v Germany*.

ment for consent. Thus, for practical as well as constitutional reasons we will discard the option of modifying the GDPR in the short or even mid term.

- In contrast, actions at a lower level than the GDPR itself could be taken more easily. Of course, these actions have to respect the existing framework of the GDPR (as well as constitutional constraints) – however, the GDPR offers some leeway for European institutions as well as for self-regulation so that the focus will lie upon these opportunities.
- Finally, we also have to take into account changes to the existing Open Data Research Policy of the Commission, which could be adopted at a policy level, probably combined with contractual obligations for researchers.

3.1.1 Anonymisation

As set out, anonymisation is one of the key parameters for the application of data protection law concerning research data but it is not defined. Thus, common Europe-wide standards for anonymisation of (research) data are needed. Whereas it seems that any specification at the level of the GDPR cannot be recommended as laws and Acts on a general level should stick to abstract notions, more precise criteria could be developed by institutions at a lower level than the Regulation itself.

In particular, the successor to the Article 29 Working Party, the European Data Protection Board, could issue guidelines on requirements for anonymisation in order to specify cases where re-identification of data subjects is unlikely and where not, and to specify reasonable efforts by controllers which render any re-identification improbable. Such guidelines would have a stronger impact than before on a harmonised enforcement of the GDPR regarding the assessing of personal data.

Moreover, the instrument of codes of conduct offered by Arts 39 et seq. GDPR should be used, in particular, for research data to draw the borderlines between anonymised data and data that are still personal due to re-identification risks; in other words, to identify the reasonable efforts which could be undertaken by a third party in order to re-identify anonymised data. As data supervisory authorities have to acknowledge these codes of conduct they may serve as a means to respect the specific needs of different sectors, such as research institutions and sharing data. Thus, for instance, LIBER, the Association of European Research Libraries, could probably act as an issuer of codes of conduct. Moreover, supervisory authorities have to take into account and respect those codes of conduct when assessing a certain processing action. However, many legal issues still remain unclear, in particular how these codes of conduct could bind outsiders, i.e.

parties which are not part of a certain association[691]. Given the fact that codes of an association may in principle only bind those who are members of the association, the sharing of data should then be restricted to those who agreed to be bound by the codes of conduct or who are members of the association.

3.1.2 Consent

As shown, under the existing legal framework of the GDPR, consent of the data subject cannot really be used as a means to allow data processing (and sharing) in an open access environment. However the GDPR at least includes some provisions on consent to processing for scientific research purposes. Recital 33 of the GDPR acknowledges that:

> *It is often not possible to fully identify the purpose of data processing for scientific research purposes at the time of data collection. Therefore data subjects should be allowed to give their consent to certain areas of scientific research when in keeping with recognised ethical standards for scientific research. Data subjects should have the opportunity to give their consent only to certain areas of research or parts of research projects to the extent allowed by the intended purpose.*

The GDPR therefore takes account of the specific situation of scientific research and research projects and provides the opportunity to consent to the use of personal data, at least to certain areas of research or parts of research projects. Nevertheless, this extension for research purposes does not allow general consent to open access or research use of personal data.

Thus, one could think about further lowering the requirements for consent for specific research purposes, such as allowing for a general consent of the data subject to all kinds of research-related purposes, thus creating an exception to the strong purpose principle. Hence, a data subject would no longer have to be informed about all potential subsequent purposes of data processing. A blueprint for this more general concept of consent could follow the copyright example of Open Source or Open Access Licences such as the Creative Commons Licences or the General Public License (GPL) – given the fact that copyright is also (from a continental European perspective) closely connected to personality rights. Such a relaxation could distinguish between general data (Art. 6 GDPR) and sensitive data (Art. 9 GDPR) as the GDPR itself already does.

However, such a relaxation could only be realised at the level of a modification of the GDPR. The requirements for consent are quite specific and do not leave very much leeway for a relaxation at the level below the GDPR, be it by the European Data Protection Board or by a code of conduct. The GDPR clearly stresses the conditions for informed consent *ex ante* and the principle of purpose.

---

691 See Spindler, 'Die Selbstregulierung nach der EU-Datenschutz-GrundVO', ZD 2016, 407.

Hence, any attempt to rely upon a broader concept of consent would entail modification of the GDPR – which is (as set out) unlikely to happen, even if we disregard any constitutional constraints here.

3.1.3 Extension of research privileges

If consent may not be used in order to permit sharing of research (personal) data, it is evident that the other pillar of permissions for data processing comes into play, the legal permissions. Here, one might argue in favour of extending the research privileges provided by the GDPR as analysed above[692].

The GDPR already extends permission for the processing of personal data for research purposes. Subsequent processing operations for scientific research purposes shall be considered as compatible with the initial purpose of data collection (Art. 5(1)(b) GDPR) and personal data may be stored for longer periods as the data will be processed solely for scientific or historical research purposes (Art. 5(1)(e) GDPR). Nevertheless, Art. 89(1) GDPR requires the implementation of appropriate safeguards of the rights and freedoms of data subjects. In particular it requires that personal data be anonymised to the greatest extent possible[693].

This means that the research privileges are somewhat limited and not all-encompassing in scope. An extension of the research privileges would, once again, entail a modification of the GDPR. Given the fact that Art. 89 GDPR already provides for obligations for research institutions to anonymise data as much as possible in order to safeguard data protection, it is not very likely that the GDPR would be changed. Moreover, these provisions probably reflect the level of constitutionally required data protection – even though this issue cannot be dealt with in depth here.

Thus, similarly to the preconditions for consent to justify data processing, institutions and/or normative guidelines below the level of the GDPR may not alter the provisions of the GDPR. Hence, neither the European Data Protection Board nor any code of conduct could really improve the existing legal framework.

3.1.4 Definition of research purposes

As outlined above, under the regime of the Data Protection Directive there is a great deal of uncertainty as to what is meant by the term “research purposes”[694]. None of the countries analysed in this study provides a satisfactory definition.

The GDPR gives some further guidance and Recital 159 GDPR states that the term “scientific research” should be interpreted in a broad manner, including, for example, technological development and demonstration, fundamental research, applied research and privately funded research. This definition is meant to provide

---

692 See above Sections 1.4.4.4 and 1.4.4.6.

693 See above Section 1.4.4.4.

694 See above Section 1.3.7.5.

more clarity on what is to be understood as scientific research. Nevertheless, this definition is still vague. It is, for example, still unclear whether processing such as the big data analyses carried out by many commercial and non-commercial actors already qualifies as scientific research. With good reason, such analyses could already be classified as research purposes. Otherwise, such an understanding would be extremely broad and privilege actions with no scientific background.

Here, the European Data Protection Board may serve the needs of harmonisation by establishing common criteria for the notion of "research purposes". Also codes of conduct may give guidance concerning the interpretation of "research purposes". However, it is still unclear how these codes might bind supervisory authorities in interpreting such abstract notions.

3.1.5 Changes to the Commission's Open Data Research Policy

In sum, the need for a change in the Open Data Research Policy seems to be indicated: a reduction of the risk of re-identifying previously anonymised data is crucial in order to avoid any legal risk. Thus, in contrast to the existing policy approach, a narrowing of users having access to research data, including personal data, may reduce the risk of re-identification, thus making a sharing of data among a circle of researchers more legitimate. Unfortunately, in contrast to the existing policy of sharing all data with everybody, it must be pointed out that such a policy would entail the risk of re-identification even if data had previously been anonymised. Hence, a compromise would lie in narrowing the circles of those who can have access to data, even if data are anonymised.

Thus, a procedure might be introduced by which data controllers (research institutions, platforms) can check the research purpose of the third party applying to have access to research data. Even though from a strict legal perspective such a procedure would not alter the legal responsibility of the data controller, it might in fact considerably reduce the risk for the platform and/or data controller of being held responsible for unjustified transmission of personal data.

Moreover, even though data would then be qualified as personal data, an additional instrument would be a contractual binding obligation to comply with data protection principles, such as that used in cases of order processing. However, it must be noted that sharing of data is not equivalent to order processing as third parties will process data on their own behalf – in contrast to the situation of order processing. Nevertheless, such a contractual obligation would make it easier for data controllers to prove that they had adopted safeguards to control data protection. Even though such contracts would not waive the responsibility of data controllers (platforms that operate data sharing and those who have uploaded the data), contracts might enable controllers to have recourse against third parties that have abused the data.

Another benefit of such a system could be better usability of the existing data protection exceptions for scientific research. As the system is now, legally collected data could in theory be further used and/or stored for individual scientific purposes as long as the conditions of Art. 89 GDPR are met. However, it is not legally possible to upload such data to an open research data repository[695]. In fact this means that even if the data could be used for further research, the researcher would not be able to access the data because they are not freely available.

Here a repository or at least a register of available research data could help. Such a register could include information on which data are stored, where, and for what (research) purposes, and on any other conditions that apply. Interested research institutions and potential data controllers (research institutions, platforms) could create an account and access the registry, check the research purposes and conditions for having access to the individual research datasets, and directly contact, and download the data from, the initial controller if this could be legitimised by the research exceptions.

From the data subject's perspective, it might be an option to implement a new form of consent that goes beyond the simple binary model. The individual who has their data stored in a repository could give consent or not to different uses of their data throughout their relationship with the service provider, rather than having a simple binary choice at the start. This can be linked to "just in time" notifications. For example, at the point when a new controller wants to use personal data from the repository for an analysis, the user can immediately be asked to give their consent, for example via a mobile app[696].

3.2 Open Research Data and public sector information

As outlined above, the inclusion of university libraries in the new PSI Directive causes many problems as regards how to align them with public libraries, on the one hand, and (excluded) universities on the other. Hence, the next review of the PSI Directive should clarify the stance of the EU concerning university libraries.

However, given the flexibility which the new PSI Directive accords to university libraries, we should wait to see what the future holds. As libraries may define their own role concerning digitisation with regard to public-private partnerships and to making available digitised documents, we should carefully assess how libraries interpret their role and even how competition between different institutions may enhance free access to documents, including licensing guidelines.

---

695 See above Section 1.5.3.4.

696 See on the issue of big data: ICO, 'Big data, artificial intelligence, machine learning and data protection', Version 2.0, 1 March 2017, p. 30, available at: https://ico.org.uk/media/for-organisations/documents/2013559/big-data-ai-ml-and-data-protection.pdf.

In this framework, transparency plays a prominent role, for instance in relation to what documents should fall under the PSI Directive and what documents are covered by third-party licences and/or are protected by IPR, or which documents fall within the public task. As stated above, university libraries should disclose and clarify their relationship with the universities to which they are affiliated, including their general strategy towards making documents accessible. In particular, they should provide information as to what extent their public task falls within the scope of the PSI Directive and what procedure interested parties have to follow to request specific material for re-use[697].

On a more general level, even though the PSI Directive grants liberty to university libraries concerning the use of licences (and which type), issues of compatibility in line with the Commission's non-binding Guidelines should not be omitted. In particular, machine-readable format, open format and formal open standards should be fostered in order to facilitate interoperability.

Another issue concerns the charging of fees for making documents available under the regime of the PSI Directive. As argued already, whereas in principle there should be no distinction between commercial and non-commercial use[698], it should be left to the institutions and to Member States to decide how to cope with price differentiation, as long as the reasons for different pricing and the goals are made transparent to users. As long as empirical data and economic analysis of different pricing and its impact on libraries policies are not available, a review of the PSI Directive should refrain from regulating more in-depth issues of charging fees etc., given also the different policies of financing public institutions in the Member States.

---

697 See above Section 2.4.

698 Ibid.

www.ingramcontent.com/pod-product-compliance
Lightning Source LLC
LaVergne TN
LVHW080041210926
848481LV00011B/3250